WAYS IN
Analyzing and
Responding
to Literature

Dust of Snow

The way a crow
Shook down on me
The dust of snow
From a hemlock tree

Has given my heart
A change of mood
And saved some part
Of a day I had rued

— x —

1985

WAYS IN
Analyzing and Responding to Literature

Leo Rockas
University of Hartford

BOYNTON/COOK PUBLISHERS, INC.
UPPER MONTCLAIR, NEW JERSEY 07043

ACKNOWLEDGMENTS

CHATTO AND WINDUS LTD. "An Upheaval" and extracts from "The Kiss," from *The Tales of Tchehov*, translated by Constance Garnett. Reprinted by permission of the translator's Literary Estate and the publisher.

J.M. DENT & SONS LTD. Excerpts from *A Doll's House* by Henrik Ibsen, translated by R. Farquharson Sharp. Everyman's Library Series. Reprinted by permission of the publisher.

DOUBLEDAY & COMPANY, INC. Excerpt from *An Introduction to Haiku* by Harold G. Henderson. Reprinted by permission of the publisher.

HARCOURT BRACE JOVANOVICH, INC. Excerpt from *Theory of Literature*, Third Edition by René Wellek and Austin Warren. Reprinted by permission of the publisher.

HARPER & ROW, PUBLISHERS, INC. "Lady Lazarus" from pages 244–47 of *The Collected Poems of Sylvia Plath*, edited by Ted Hughes. Copyright © 1963 by Ted Hughes. Excerpts from pages 116, 117 and 118 of "Poetry [November 1939]" in *One Man's Meat* by E.B. White. Copyright, 1940, by E.B. White. Both reprinted by permission of the publisher.

HARVARD UNIVERSITY PRESS. Emily Dickinson poems on pages 9, 10, 16, 18, 19, 84, 95, 96. Reprinted by permission of the publisher and the Trustees of Amherst College from *The Poems of Emily Dickinson*, edited by Thomas H. Johnson, Cambridge, MA: The Belknap Press of Harvard University Press. Copyright © 1951, © 1955, 1979 by the President and Fellows of Harvard College. 'Dear March—Come in—' © 1983 by the President and Fellows of Harvard College.

HOLT, RINEHART AND WINSTON, PUBLISHERS. Robert Frost poems on pages 1, 14, 22, 23, 28, 33, 38, 45, 51, 55, 182, 183, 188 from *The Poetry of Robert Frost* edited by Edward Connery Lathem. Copyright 1916, 1923, 1928, 1930, 1939, 1947, © 1969 by Holt, Rinehart and Winston. Copyright 1936, 1944, 1951, © 1958, 1962 by Robert Frost. Copyright © 1964, 1967, 1975 by Lesley Frost Ballantine. Reprinted by permission of the publisher.

ALFRED A. KNOPF, INC. "A & P" from *Pigeon Feathers and Other Stories* by John Updike. Copyright © 1962 by John Updike. Originally appeared in *The New Yorker*. Reprinted by permission of the publisher.

LITTLE, BROWN AND COMPANY. Poem #1333 from *The Complete Poems of Emily Dickinson*, edited by Thomas H. Johnson. Copyright 1914, 1942 by Martha Dickinson Bianchi. Reprinted by permission of the publisher.

MACMILLAN PUBLISHING COMPANY, INC. "An Upheaval" from *The Lady with the Dog and Other Stories* by Anton Chekhov and excerpts from "The Kiss" from *The Party and Other Stories* by Anton Chekhov, both translated by Constance Garnett. Both copyright 1917 by Macmillan Publishing Co., Inc., renewed 1945 by Constance Garnett. Reprinted by permission of the publisher.

RANDOM HOUSE, INC. Excerpt from Act I of "Beyond the Horizon" by Eugene O'Neill. Copyright 1920 and renewed 1948 by Eugene O'Neill. Reprinted from *The Plays of Eugene O'Neill* by permission of the publisher.

SCHOCKEN BOOKS INC. Excerpts and sketches from *The Diaries of Franz Kafka, 1910–1913*, copyright © 1948 by Schocken Books Inc. and from *The Diaries of Franz Kafka, 1914–1923*, copyright © 1949 by Schocken Books Inc., copyright renewed © 1976 by Schocken Books Inc. Reprinted by permission of the publisher.

CHARLES SCRIBNER'S SONS. Excerpts from *The Sun Also Rises* by Ernest Hemingway. Copyright 1926 by Charles Scribner's Sons; copyright renewed 1954 by Ernest Hemingway. Reprinted by permission of the publisher.

Library of Congress Cataloging in Publication Data

Rockas, Leo.
  Ways in.

  Summary: A brief introduction for college students
to literary analysis and criticism explaining in simple
terms and examples three different approaches to analysis
and the basic elements of criticism.
  Includes a glossary of literary terms.
  1. Criticism—Problems, exercises, etc.   2. Literature—
Study and teaching.   [1. Criticism—Problems, exercises,
etc.   2. Literature—History and criticism]   I. Title.
PN83.R59   1983   801'.95   83-15749
ISBN 0-86709-075-8

For information address Boynton/Cook Publishers, Inc.
52 Upper Montclair Plaza, P.O. Box 860, Upper Montclair, N.J. 07043
ISBN: 0-86709-075-8

84 85 86 87 88 5 4 3 2 1

Preface

When Cinderella's fairy godmother turned the mice into horses and the pumpkin into a coach, everyone was astonished. Could such wonders be? As the golden coach drove by with its noble horses, smart footmen, and its beautiful rider, it was profusely admired—a stunning, gorgeous phenomenon. The fairy godmother was a creative artist and had shown the populace what it was to create a work of art.

But the fairy godmother had another power which is not so often admired. After midnight she could reduce the coach and horses to pumpkin and mice again. If she could magnify, she could diminish too. If she could tie the magic knot, she could untie it too. The coach really did exist for a while, but now she could just as easily show what it had come from. To see the possibility of, the wish to become, the glorious coach in the mere pumpkin; and to look the other way, to see, deep in its past, the seed of the pumpkin in the coach and the mice in the footmen—these are the abilities needed, I believe, by readers and writers of literature.

The backward process, the loosening of the completed whole to its humble origins, is called analysis. The forward process, the magical transformation, is called creation—or, more technically, perhaps—synthesis. Both processes are somewhat mysterious and awe-inspiring. The American philosopher and essayist Ralph Waldo Emerson (1803–82) said: "Is not the sublime felt in an analysis as well as in a creation?" Though no one, not even a very great creator or critic, understands exactly how either process happens, both processes, I believe, can be grasped to a surprising degree of excitement, even by someone who is, as you may think you are, a complete beginner.

You may have decided to study literature on your own or you may be sitting in a required course. You may be expecting to be entertained and delighted by literature—good, then we begin by agreeing on the main function of literature. But still you may be wondering, what's the point of it all? Why bother with literature? Isn't it a leisure-time activity—on a par with bowling or tennis or dancing, for those so inclined—but not really necessary to people who want mainly to accomplish something practical in life?

This question presupposes that literature can be, like those other activities, avoided. But if you think of the whole scope of literature, you will see at once that it can't be. All of us engage in what might be called live literature—gossiping, telling what happened during the day at the dinner table, trying to get people to like us and seeing how we like them, reviewing the day to see how it has gone. Think—all of this, if captured on a tape recorder, by a camera, or on a piece of paper, becomes bits of literature—stories and conversations and meditations.

Nor can we avoid literature in finished form. We don't have to read lots of books, of course, but we can hardly avoid advertisements, political slogans, lyrics of popular songs, television programs and movies—which are all, at least in part, literary scripts or performances of them. When we encounter a large story in the news, such as the death or marriage of an important public figure, our whole reception of it and response to it becomes our contemplation of, our recollection of, a literary form, a tragedy or a comedy.

So literature is inescapably in all our lives and the question is only whether we are to receive passively the literary bits and wholes others have programed for us, or to gain a larger view of all its possibilities, which the more careful study of literature provides.

Another way of approaching the question of the use of literature is to ask, What is most important to you? What do you spend your spare hours thinking and hoping about? Naturally, getting the job that you want to get, but also, I trust, understanding how you fit into the pattern of your family and friends, winning the friendships or the loves you desire, and having reason to think well of yourself. These are just the issues literature addresses. It takes you outside yourself—into the lives of other people known or imagined by the author—and brings you back to yourself with new visions that may indirectly inspire your own life more significantly than any amount of direct worry about your problems would have accomplished. We are, each of us, limited to one life, one set of possibilities, but literature tells us of the many possibilities open to others and permits us to live those other lives in our imaginations. You are not exactly a hero or a villain, a queen or a clown, a judge or a convict; but literature can tell you what it feels like to be those and more than those.

But even if literature, as written down or performed, were completely avoidable—let us say, in the life of a hermit or nun removed as far as possible from human communication—one form of literary experience is deeply and inescapably there for all of us: our dream lives, during our hours of sleep and in our daydreams. Dreams are the stories we tell ourselves, the literary scripts composed by the psyche, those we somehow need to fascinate or frighten ourselves with. Experiments have shown that sleepers denied dreams—awakened as they are about to begin dreaming—become jumpy and frustrated, just as societies denied the outward expression of dreams in the arts become repressed and neurotic and inhumane. It appears that individually and collectively we need our dreams and the embodiment of those dreams in the arts.

The stories and poems we read, the movies and plays we see, are like dreams we add to the store of our own dreams, which enlarge our dream-making powers and possibilities for whatever use we can make of them. I can't promise that your dreams will be getting better and better night by night if only you read more poems and stories; but I know you will have more images and situations and characters available to think and dream about, awake or asleep.

Let's assume you have agreed by now that literature is necessary as well as pleasurable to most people and that you are willing to give it a real chance to bring about the greatest result in your life and your imagination that it is capable of. What is the point of studying it, as if it were a course in mathematics—or analyzing it, as if it were a combination of secret chemical ingredients you have to take apart? What will you have gained by a close study and a careful discrimination between the different kinds of things it is capable of doing to you?

Your taste in literature so far may run to jokes and jingles, and maybe soap operas or westerns; these are all literary forms suitable for entertainment and deserving of study. But they are not all there is. Only by experiencing at least a little of all its possibilities can you become an active, instead of just a passive—a critical, instead of just a dumfounded—receiver of the literature your life will be full of.

Analysis, plus a bit of practice in creativity, will make you a better judge of all the movies you see, stories you're told, songs you hear. You will learn what the different emphases in various works of literature are, and not expect something a given work has no intention of fulfilling. A great many airy judgments of literature are based on false expectations. Mystery-story fans derive their pleasure primarily from complications in the story-line; what will they make of a movie or play without much of a story-line? Some readers and critics want literature to be heavy with message (and often with a given message) and have no use for works that don't much care to promote any message. Readers sometimes proclaim a book dull because it didn't do what they wanted it to do; but the critical question is how well it did what it was trying to do. You don't want to be in the position of a vegetarian at a barbecue or a non-drinker at a wine-tasting.

Shouldn't literary artists have as much choice among all the possibilities of literature as they have an earlier choice of whether to paint or sculpt or write, or, if to write, whether to write poems or plays, or certain kinds of poems or plays? Can't the artist decide what kind of artist to be? The analytic reader learns to read (or perhaps to reconsider and contemplate) in a state of suspended judgment and will let the work tell what it's trying to accomplish. Analysis does not prohibit judgment; it simply puts the reader's judgment more in line with the given author's creation. You will learn to be ready for all the tastes and pleasures literature has to offer. Eventually you will discover, I trust, the truth of this idea: the more understanding, the more pleasure.

Each reader brings something special to every literary work, and you may be wondering why any response to a literary work isn't a right response. If you feel this way, I agree with you in large part. Every good teacher wants to encourage diversity in students' responses to literature. Identical responses may be appropriate in math and other classes, but not in literature classes. But every teacher, good and bad, also fears that students may go "really off the track." A student may have misunderstood a crucial word or expression, or failed to relate two related scenes or characters, and so have gone off on a tangent. Of the two problems—responses so diverse some may really be "wrong" versus responses as close to the teacher's own as possible—I think I prefer the diversity, on the grounds that criticism itself, at the highest levels, is always rediscovering the track it should be on. Students are always trying to see the point in what teachers say; it seems to me teachers should be trying to return the favor.

On the other hand, teachers have an obligation to tell students honestly how they respond to the students' responses. If a teacher sincerely and sympathetically feels the response is off, there's nothing like a frank statement with an explanation of what else may be involved. The fascination of teaching a course in literature is—something like the fascination of taking one—that each reader responds to the text a little differently and that the teacher can teach the same works over and over with continuing profit to both herself and her classes.

So literature inspires various interpretations and responses and analyses. It also inspires new creativity in the sympathetic and alert reader. I hope to arouse that creativity too. Most of our study of literature has to be after the fact. We find it finished, published, produced. It seems almost to have been composed by the printing press or made up by the actors playing the parts. We too often forget the author quietly at work, not sure anyone else will ever see, much less appreciate, the effort. This book aims at least partly to remedy this defect, to put you in the author's study, contemplating something begun but not finished, puzzling over different versions of the same passage, and trying your hand at continuing or completing a fascinating beginning or rewriting it from scratch. You will in small measure become the producer as well as the receiver of literature. Many people, and I am one of them, believe that the best way to appreciate literature is to try your own hand at it.

You will find scattered through the book copies of manuscripts that were the origins of some of the brief works included. I hope that seeing the scratchings on the paper of famous authors will help you realize that all writing begins in scratches much like your own. In the sketches from Kafka, you'll see an imagination similar to the imagination he displays in his writing, but these sketches were not illustrations of the Kafka passages I have selected.

The first half of this book is devoted largely to theory, the second half largely to practice. But theory and practice need to be so continuously combined that you will find lots of practice in the first part and lots of suggested theory in the second part. I have preceded each of the twelve theoretical sections with exercises intended to arouse your curiosity and creativity, to prepare and put you in the mood for, the discussion that follows. The literary passages in these exercises are sometimes unfinished and so leave you free to speculate on what should be done to them. The questions following are as open as I can make them. At least I do not always know the answers to them or am unsure between two or more possible answers. When you finish each exercise you will already have asked and partly answered the questions the discussion following is devoted to. These exercises are based on the workbooks of two authors, Emily Dickinson and Franz Kafka. The discussions themselves are based mostly on the poems of Robert Frost, who is our most approachable recent poet.

In the second part of the book you will find three pairs of interestingly contrasted works, all based on a similar subject, "ways of saying goodbye." You will also find there my attempts at analyzing these works, further practice exercises in analyzing on your own, and suggestions on doing analyses of fiction, drama, and poetry.

If your teacher gives you a choice on how to go about reading this book, I suggest you begin at the beginning, with Part I, and try out some of the exercises and discussions that follow them. If these discussions begin to seem difficult and you are hankering to work more directly on short but slightly longer works, I suggest you turn to Part II of the book and try the stories by Chekhov and Updike with the commentary on them, and then the exercise that follows, which allows you to put in practice what you have learned so far. Then, you may wish to go on to the two dramatic selections in Part II, or you may feel ready to return to the first part. Another approach altogether would be to work directly, and almost entirely at first, on the second half of the book, using the glossary when stumped by a hard word or idea. Eventually you will return to the first half of the book which gives the theoretical basis for the practice in the second half.

Your teacher may wish to assign sections of the book as I sometimes do in the "introduction to literature" course, which is usually in three divisions—fiction, drama, poetry. In the fiction part of the course, I assign the sections on formal and rhetorical analysis, together with the section on fiction; in the drama part of the course, I assign the sections on plot, character, and theme, together with the section on drama; in the poetry part of the course, I assign the sections on sound, diction, and setting, together with the section on poetry. This approach provides a mixture of theory and practice which may be helpful to you and your teacher. The book as a whole aims to give you a coherent, if rudimentary, guide to the study of literature. After you read the book and take the course that accompanies it, you should be ready for more specialized courses in literature and more difficult courses in criticism, if you care to carry your study that far. If not, if this is to be your last course in studying literature, I, and I assume your teacher, wish you increased understanding of, and pleasure in, the literary experiences you will inevitably encounter, and those you choose for yourself, later in life.

Some students or teachers may wish to pursue the three types of literary analysis in this book to their first and leading proponents. Analysis of form begins, as I see it, in the first literary treatise, the *Poetics,* by the Greek philosopher Aristotle (384–322 B.C.)—formal design in ch. 12 and formal development in chs. 7 and 18. The German novelist and playwright Gustav Freytag (1816–95) formulated the pyramid of dramatic development in his *Technique of the Drama* (1863). A vivid modern treatment of formal development can be found in the essay "Psychology and Form" by Kenneth Burke (born 1897) in his book *Counter-Statement* (1931). Rhetorical analysis begins, as I see it, in a striking passage of the *Republic,* Book III, pages 392c–394c by the Greek philosopher who was Aristotle's teacher, Plato (427?–347 B.C.). My own work, *Modes of Rhetoric,* was an attempt to make sense of Plato and such nineteenth-century rhetoricians as E. S. Dallas, Alexander Bain, and J. F. Genung; I have adapted and simplified some of my former work here. Analysis of elements begins in Aristotle's *Poetics,* ch. 6. Among many modern elaborations of this kind of analysis, I have been most influenced by that of Northrop Frye (born 1912) in the Fourth Essay of *Anatomy of Criticism* (1957). I am also indebted to *Theory of Literature* (1949) by René Wellek and my teacher Austin Warren, for my general approach toward literature.

I wish to thank the following friends and colleagues, who have read the manuscript in pieces and offered helpful suggestions: Elaine Bender, William Bottorff, Gilbert Davis, Larry Dennis, Donald Edge, the late Hans Gottschalk, Glen Howerton, Barbara Hull, Emanuel Mussman, Thornton Parsons, Arline Prendergast, William Slavick, Gerald Smith, Eric Smithner, and my wife Virginia. I wish to thank Gerald Else and John Hagan for helping me to understand Aristotle and Chekhov, respectively. I have also profited from careful and complete readings of the manuscript by my friends Leonard and Rosemary Deen, Clayton Hudnall, and William Stull. I have also learned a great deal about analyzing literature from George Michael Evica. To Robert Logan and James Vinson I am indebted for the release time which enabled me to revise and finish the book.

This book is for Virginia

Contents

First

Suppose a group of people have just read a literary work—a story, a play, or a poem: there are several ways they might talk about it. First, they might try to explain it to each other: maybe they understood some of the action differently; maybe there was an especially difficult passage only one of them can explain; maybe some sort of key needs to be supplied to unlock the secret of the whole work. This activity is called explanation or explication. Second, they might want to comment on the work: maybe one is a historian, one a biologist, one a psychologist, and so on; each will seize on a different part or emphasis in the work as relevant to his or her own interests. This activity is called commentary, or interpretation. All of them, of course, will be interested in deciding how good the work is, in judgment or evaluation. Let them postpone that activity for a while, because so far they have not discussed it primarily as a literary work. The sort of conversations they have had up to now might have been stimulated by an experience no one would call literary: an automobile accident, a news report, a walk in the park. After all, any experience can be explained, interpreted, and judged. Sooner or later, if they want to talk about it as a literary work of art they will have to take it apart, which is an activity not of destruction, but of analysis. You may sometimes feel analysis "ruins" the work, but after numerous analyses you may find that your appreciation of all literature has been immeasurably increased. If you agree in the end that you admire a work, you will realize that no analysis will be as interesting or enjoyable as a new reading of the work. But if you want to talk about it as literature at all you will have to analyze it according to its uniquely literary qualities.

Here is the first of many poems in this book by Robert Frost (1874–1963). In it he tells of a certain type of bird heard mostly in mid-summer, and he speculates on the significance of its song to those who hear it.

The Oven Bird

There is a singer everyone has heard,
Loud, a mid-summer and a mid-wood bird

1

Who makes the solid tree trunks sound again.
He says that leaves are old and that for flowers
Mid-summer is to spring as one to ten.   5
He says the early petal-fall is past
When pear and cherry bloom went down in showers
On sunny days a moment overcast;
And comes that other fall we name the fall.
He says the highway dust is over all.   10
The bird would cease and be as other birds
But that he knows in singing not to sing.
The question that he frames in all but words
Is what to make of a diminished thing.

This poem might raise various problems of explication or commentary, and various judgments. A botanist or ornithologist might estimate the accuracy of Frost's account and question the things he has the bird say or ask. A religious person might point to "that other fall we name the fall" and observe that the reference is not only to autumn, but to the fall of Adam and Eve, and that the bird is a symbol of man's "diminished" life on earth, after the "spring" of paradise. Some readers might think the poet's pretense that the bird can talk coy and offensive, and judge the poem weak; others might think its talk a legitimate device for conveying the mid-summer mood of the poem. But analytic readers would set aside all these comments and judgments until they have seen what in fact the poem is like.

First they might note that in design the poem is and is not a sonnet: like most sonnets, it is a pentameter poem in fourteen lines, but unlike most sonnets it has no recognizable rhyme-scheme. In the poem's development, analytic readers would note the doomsday tone of line 9, which is climactic. They would see the rhetorical sequence of the poem as beginning with a kind of definition-description of the bird, proceeding to a kind of mock-drama in reporting what the bird says. But the bird's conversation is actually the poet's thoughts and feelings in listening to the bird, and the dominant mode of the poem is reverie rather than drama. Finally analytic readers would note that the plot and "characters" (of the bird, of the poet—both observers and commentators on the "diminished") are slight in contrast to the setting and theme, which are strong. Setting is especially emphasized in the first three lines and line 10, which describe a present setting, and in lines 6–8, which describe a past setting; theme is especially emphasized in the last four lines. Analysts would keep refining such observations and would all the time be learning more and more about the poem as a literary work of art. They might very well have to combine explication with analysis, but they would not venture on commentary or judgment until they were fairly confident of their analysis.

Literature is sometimes thought to occupy a central position between the arts of the eye and the arts of the ear, or those of space and of time—that is, between the plastic arts, including painting and sculpture, and music. (Northrop Frye, *Anatomy of Criticism,* pp. 243–44). Writers cannot capture your eye as well as a sculptor, or your ear as well as a composer, but they can partially engage both senses, which may in the end seem a more impressive achievement. Though they cannot present sights in space, they can describe sights, as a musician cannot; though they cannot play sounds, they can give a sequence in time, as a painter cannot. Because the art of literature is more like the other arts than it is like anything else (history, psychology, ethics, or other disciplines), what is special about literature can best be seen by comparing it with the other arts. This book is based on three completely different analyses of literature. In order to show why these three are necessary, and how each analysis makes a separate appeal to the eye and the ear, consider literature as pottery and as music. If you're interested in what goes into pots or songs it would help to visit a potter's or composer's studio; so too it would help to be in a writer's studio, in order to find out how the writer works. Some students may wish to study the various drafts that have sometimes been preserved of certain literary works, for a glimpse of how writers work. Unfortunately, it isn't always possible to do this, and even if it were, craftsmen, of whatever sort, may be mostly unconscious of their artistry. For purposes of analysis, it's best to begin with finished works of art, poems and pots and songs, all different kinds.

Look at the pot; it has clearly different parts, the inside, outside, the bottom or foot, the top or lip. The literary work also has obvious parts, divisions and subdivisions, chapters, stanzas, or sections. These can be separately laid out in space for study. A song may also be in separate parts that might be regarded in space, but if you're studying a song, you might be more interested in how one note leads to another, how one passage develops into the next. Now you're studying not just a design that can be seen all at once, but a development that happens in a passage of time. Literature also happens in time, and can be studied like music. All this is formal analysis.

Pottery takes certain conventional shapes, which determine the function of pots. These are usually but not always distinct from each other. When does a dish become a bowl, a bowl a vase, or a vase a bottle? Similarly, literature takes certain conventional shapes or genres, which are more like spatial designs than temporal developments. The definition of a tragedy or a sonnet aims to picture it as far as possible all at once. But in order to determine the basis of literary genres it's necessary to consider the modes of literature—description, narration, drama, and reverie—which are progressions in time. In a given literary work you can usually tell exactly what modes or combinations of them have been used. The chief mode used will usually determine the genre of the work. All this is rhetorical analysis.

The finished pot is hard and fused, and the original elements are no longer visible in it, but they are known to have been earth, air, fire, and water, in different proportions. How can you tell which pots were fired longer, or were made with heavier or moister or airier clay? You can tell only by trying to specify as far as possible such vague distinctions as dense, vitreous, porous. A chemist might be able to give an analysis of a pot according to its chemical elements, but not even a chemist can analyze the four ancient elements of a pot. So, too, in the finished literary work the elements are fused, and the proportion of its elements is hard to discern. The elements of literature, here slightly adapted from Aristotle's *Poetics,* are plot, character, theme, sound, diction, and setting. By carefully comparing and contrasting many literary works, you can come as close as possible to figuring out what the emphasis of elements in the whole work is. But the emphasis of elements may vary in different parts of the work. As in music, one passage may be more rhythmic, another more melodic, so in literature one passage may emphasize plot, another character, and so on. All this is analysis of elements.

The elements of literature are discussed in the section below on analysis of elements. I offer no further definitions of them here, because they are widely used in criticism, and in teaching at all levels. The modes of literature are discussed below in the section on rhetorical analysis. But because they underlie much of the discussion in this book, I offer brief, simple definitions of them here, with brief, distinctive examples of each, from *The Sun Also Rises,* by Ernest Hemingway (1899–1961), the first and second examples from chapter XI, and the third and fourth examples from chapter XIII.

Description is a report of appearances, of how places or persons or objects strike the senses of an observer.

1. There was a low, dark room with saddles and harness, and hay-forks made of white wood, and clusters of canvas rope-soled shoes and hams and slabs of bacon and white garlic and long sausages hanging from the roof. It was cool and dusky, and we stood in front of a long wooden counter with two women behind it serving drinks. Behind them were shelves stacked with supplies and goods.

Narration is a report of actions, of what people did separately or to each other on a given occasion.

2. Two of our Basques came in and insisted on buying a drink. So they bought a drink and then we bought a drink, and then they slapped us on the back and bought another drink. Then we bought, and then we all went out into the sunlight and the heat, and climbed back on top of the bus.

Drama (also called dialogue) is a report of conversation, of people talking back and forth.

3. "How'd you like the bulls?"
   "Grand. It's grand the way they bring them out."
   "To-morrow come the Miuras."
   "When does the fiesta start?"
   "Day after to-morrow."

"We've got to keep Mike from getting so tight. That kind of stuff is terrible."
"We'd better get cleaned up for supper."
"Yes. That will be a pleasant meal."
"Won't it?"

Reverie (also called "reflection" or "stream of consciousness") is a report of thoughts and feelings, of what goes on in a particular person's mind.

4. It was like certain dinners I remember from the war. There was wine, an ignored tension, and a feeling of things coming that you could not prevent happening. Under the wine I lost the disgusted feeling and was happy. It seemed they were all such nice people.

You may now be thinking, "This talk of parts and modes and elements seems highly technical. What I want from reading a book or seeing a play is a reflection of my life, a comment on what happens between people, as a great novelist or movie scriptwriter envisages it. If I'm going to study something I want first to see its importance to my life."

If you feel this way, you're right, but you will, I hope, by the end of the book, have found out a great deal about how the writer works up the magic that makes that electric connection between the life in the movie, on the stage, or in the book—and the life of the expectant viewer or reader.

Part One

1

Formal Analysis

Design

Below are two short poems by Emily Dickinson (1830–86), who lived all her life quietly in Amherst, Massachusetts. Only a handful of her poems were published during her lifetime; the complete 1775 poems were not published in full until 1955.

In the first of these poems she tells of something she has seen, a snake; and in the second of a couple of things she hasn't seen, a moor (open land on which heather grows) and the sea. Read these poems over carefully, taking note of what they do to you. The expression "a transport/Of cordiality" can be restated as "a rush of friendliness."

(The numbers of the poems come from the complete edition of her poems by Thomas H. Johnson.)

(986)

A narrow Fellow in the Grass
Occasionally rides—
You may have met Him—did you not
His notice sudden is—

The Grass divides as with a Comb   5
A spotted shaft is seen—
And then it closes at your feet
And opens further on—

He likes a Boggy Acre
A Floor too cool for Corn—   10
Yet when a Boy, and Barefoot—
I more than once at Noon

Have passed, I thought, a Whip lash
Unbraiding in the Sun

When stooping to secure it   15
It wrinkled, and was gone—

Several of Nature's People
I know, and they know me—
I feel for them a transport
Of cordiality—   20

But never met this Fellow
Attended, or alone
Without a tighter breathing
And Zero at the Bone—

(1052)

I never saw a Moor—
I never saw the Sea—
Yet know I how the Heather looks
And what a Billow be.

I never spoke with God   5
Nor visited in Heaven—
Yet certain am I of the spot
As if the Checks were given—

On a blank sheet of paper, put down any questions you have and any observations you wish to make about these poems. Begin with what is most obvious—don't be worried that any question or observation is too obvious. Then go on to other observations, guided—but not limited to—such questions as these:

1. Why does the first poem have six stanzas—bundles of four lines—and the second only two? Could either have more, or fewer?
2. Without being too fussy about it for now, try to tap out the rhythm of the poems. Is every line of the same length, or are some longer? (Clue: the first and third lines of the first two stanzas of the snake poem and the third lines of each stanza of the moor poem are a little longer.) Can you see any reason for the longer lines, or do you think she just thought of more words there?
3. Do you see any pattern of rhymes? In the snake poem, start from the last stanza—whch has an obvious rhyme—and work back to the first. Do you see any almost-rhymes? In the moor poem, start with the first stanza and note that the second one almost matches. In fact, all the stanzas of both poems similarly rhyme or almost rhyme. What can you conclude about the poet's tendency to rhyme? Do rhymes have to be perfect to figure in the shape of the stanzas?
4. Note the poet's casual habits of punctuation. She liked dashes, as many

students do. Do you have trouble following her meaning because she uses dashes where you might expect periods or question marks? How would you go about regularizing her punctuation? That's what early editors of her poetry did. Nowadays we let her poems appear with the punctuation she herself preferred.

5. Note the things and persons of the poems, as indicated by nouns and pronouns. In the snake poem, why is the snake male ("Fellow," "him," "His," "He.") Why is the speaker of the poem (the "I") also male ("Boy")? Is it acceptable to pretend to be a sex you aren't in a poem? In the moor poem why has she chosen a moor and the sea? What would she have to do to see them in reality instead of in her imagination?

6. Note comparisons in the poems. For instance, "rides." Does a snake ride? Or "as with a Comb," "Whip lash." What does the word "Unbraiding" do for you? What about "Zero at the bone"? What if she had used a much more familiar expression there, such as "Chills up my spine"? In the moor poem, what's the relationship between heather and moor, between billow and sea? Between moor and God, between sea and heaven? The word "Checks" was altered by an editor to "chart." Her modern editor (Thomas H. Johnson) suggests she was thinking of checks as railroad tickets. How does the implication of tickets for a trip to heaven affect your response to the poem?

For a creative response, try writing a stanza or two, coming as close to the pattern she has used as possible. Note that the second stanza of the moor poem is something like a "moral" to the first and that the snake poem has no such moral. Try adding a "moral" stanza to the snake poem, for instance one beginning, "Though this fellow scares me—" In the moor poem, you might pick up the idea of the railroad trip, for instance beginning, "I've started on a trip—" Or choose an entirely new subject, of something you've seen or haven't seen, and try an entire short poem of a few stanzas.

☐   ☐   ☐

Literature is sometimes divided into form and content. Content—what literature contains—is partitioned into the six elements, which I will take up on page 50. Rhetoric studies the surface of literature—its flesh or dress, if you like—and so rhetorical analysis is more substantial than formal analysis but more superficial than analysis of content; I will take up rhetorical analysis on page 25. Now I will take up the form of literature, its design and its development. Naturally these three kinds of analysis are interdependent, not mutually exclusive. But they can be profitably studied in isolation.

Though closely related to content, form can often be seen as somewhat external. You could tell something about the form of a work even if it was in a language you didn't understand. If I handed you a Spanish poem, for example, even if you didn't know Spanish, you could tell how long the poem is, what

parts it falls into, and something about the size and shape of its stanzas or sections. You could tell, that is, something about the poem's design. Now, if
you heard a Spanish poem recited, or saw a Spanish play performed, you could
tell something about how the work was developing by the expressions and in-
tonations of the actors or interpreters, and by how the audience was responding to them. If you heard the work, that is, you could tell something of its
development. Keeping the work in a language you don't know, in fact, is a
way of insuring that you can't be responding to its content and must be responding to its form alone. But since form and content are subtly interrelated,
a thorough analysis of form calls for a full understanding of the language; then
you can keep your formal analysis as separate from content, or as joined, as you
want to make it.

The parts of a literary work may be considered in space or time as pieces
or phases, pattern or rhythm, design or development. First consider the work
as a finished whole in space, whose shape can be seen all at once, like a pot or a
painting. A very short work can be seen almost at once; and even a long work,
as soon as you have finished it, can be reviewed or over-seen all at once. Part of
the pleasure of finishing a long work like a novel is that the beginning and
middle are still clear enough in the memory that by the ending you can see the
work as a whole; during the reading only a partial, though gradually greater,
view of the whole was possible. One function of a table of contents in a long
work is to let you see the design of the whole work before you begin and as you
are reading it.

All literary works are, or may be considered to be, in separate parts, and
it's a good idea to be on the lookout for these early. Usually divisions of some
kind are provided by the author or editor in the way the work has been set up
in print. These may or may not be the only or best possible divisions of the
work, for the actual divisions may have been dictated by considerations external to the form. Novels have been sometimes divided by the length of the
original serial parts—that is, by how much of the novel a magazine editor
wanted to print at a time. Playwrights have often been expected to turn out
plays in five or three acts, no matter how the work actually shaped up in itself.
Modern stories and articles are often divided into sections and paragraphs according to an editor's preference for certain spacings on the page. Poems, such
as sonnets, can be printed in quite a number of different ways, as the editor
prefers. The printing of modern poems usually follows the poet's preference
rather than the editor's or printer's, but there still may be different opinions
on how the poem might or should have been printed.

The first distinction to note in printed literary works is between those in
prose and those in verse. Prose is continuous and can be broken into lines anywhere; verse is divided into separate lines, which the printing must always
respect. Different editions of novels will have entirely different paginations
and divisions of lines; different editions of poems will always have the same
divisions of lines, even if there are different numbers of lines to a page. Dra-

matic works are also divided into "lines," but here the line or speech is how much one actor says before another one speaks.

The longest divisions in prose works are usually called sections, parts, or books; smaller divisions are called chapters, which are themselves sometimes divided by skipped spaces in the course of the chapter; and the smallest divisions are paragraphs and sentences. The longest divisions in verse works are usually called cantos or sections or books; smaller divisions are usually called stanzas, if they are of the same size and shape, or verse-paragraphs, if they vary in size and shape; and the smallest divisions are lines. Divisions of a play are usually called acts and scenes, but the form of a play does not inherently demand these divisions. The ancient Greek philosopher Aristotle (384–22 B.C.) in his *Poetics* gives the divisions of Greek tragedy as prologue and exodus, episode and choric song (ch. 12), for which there are no exact equivalents in modern drama.

One unit exists whether the work is in prose or verse, or whether the work is read aloud or to yourself: the sentence. There's no way of writing or talking except in sentences—that is, if anyone is to understand anything of what is said. The punctuation of English and other languages is almost completely conventional and somewhat arbitrary. Furthermore, the use of different marks of punctuation has changed from Renaissance to modern times. And even in modern times, different writers and editors have preferences among the marks of punctuation. Some modern writers, such as James Joyce or e. e. cummings, may omit all punctuation and capitalization—but that doesn't mean they don't write in sentences.

A safe rule to follow in analyzing form is to try to read the work as if no divisions were supplied at all, in order to see what the real or best divisions are. Those supplied will always be of interest, and are usually the appropriate ones, but a careful analysis may confirm or deny them. In the process you will have understood the basis of formal divisions better than if you had merely accepted those given. A teacher may test students' perception of different units, such as sentences and paragraphs of prose, speeches and scenes of drama, or lines and stanzas of verse, by retyping passages with no divisions at all. In such exercises, if the students are keen, the author (or the editor of the author) is on trial as much as the students. And this process is exactly the one skillful critics and editors of literature follow in analyzing the works they criticize or edit. The practice is not remarkably different from the practice called outlining, though it is more concerned with determining the divisions than with writing summary sentences for the divisions somebody else has supplied. The outliner permits no divisions, unless parts of about equal size or weight remain on either side of the division; and no two divisions of the same depth unless they represent roughly equal pauses in the design of the work.

In the little poem below, Frost reports on a small experience between himself, a bird, and a tree, and gives his feelings about the experience. The word "rued" means "felt sad about."

Dust of Snow

The way a crow
Shook down on me
The dust of snow
From a hemlock tree

Has given my heart   5
A change of mood
And saved some part
Of a day I had rued.

What is the justification for the main division in the middle of the poem, leaving two four-line stanzas, or quatrains? If you consider the meaning of the poem, you see that the first stanza presents something outside the poet, and the second presents the poet's response to it. If you consider grammar, you see that the whole poem is a sentence, the first stanza subject, the second predicate. But the divisions of poems rarely show as much attention to meaning and grammar as this; they usually pay most attention to meter and rhyme— more specifically poetic considerations. In this poem, if you count syllables you see that all but three lines have only four syllables, and that all the lines have only two loud or stressed syllables. Following the practice of marking unstressed syllables with a hook and stressed ones with a stress or slash mark, you would note the pattern for each line as ˘ ´ ˘ ´, or iambic dimeter. This is a very short line and an editor of the poem might consider doubling it, and changing the eight-line poem with four syllables per line to a four-line poem with eight syllables per line—in iambic tetrameter, and perhaps with no division in the middle of the poem. The poem could actually have been so divided. The division given calls more attention to the rapidly recurring rhymes, those between *crow* and *snow* as well as *me* and *tree,* and between *heart* and *part* as well as *mood* and *rued.* Note that the "ow—ee" rhymes bind the first four lines together, and the "art—ood" rhymes bind the last four in a separate bundle from the first four. If the second stanza continued the "ow—ee" rhymes, the design of the poem would not necessarily call for a division in the middle of the poem. In any case, this is a very neatly symmetrical poem; the divisions in other poems may not be so clear-cut.

The following poem by Frost is longer and more difficult and based on a more complex emotion. The poet tells of the fears of a husband when a storm in the night seems to call him outdoors to its fury; he wonders whether he and his family will be able to face the outdoors the next day.

Storm Fear

When the wind works against us in the dark,
And pelts with snow

The lower chamber window on the east,
And whispers with a sort of stifled bark,
The beast,   5
"Come out! Come out!"—
It costs no inward struggle not to go,
Ah, no!
I count our strength,
Two and a child,   10
Those of us not asleep subdued to mark
How the cold creeps as the fire dies at length,—
How drifts are piled,
Dooryard and road ungraded,
Till even the comforting barn grows far away,   15
And my heart owns a doubt
Whether 'tis in us to arise with day
And save ourselves unaided.

In this poem, though every line rhymes with at least one other, the rhymes are
irregularly placed and are obscured by the considerable difference in length of
lines. If this poem were retyped as prose, the lines of verse as printed might
easily be missed even by very astute readers. The only convenient division in
the poem is supplied by grammar and meaning with the sentence-stop in line
8, "Ah, no!" Some readers might also consider the last three lines a separate
afterthought, as they might be considered a separate sentence. The poem then
would be in three parts, with divisions after lines 8 and 15. In this analysis,
since the design of the poem is not very regular, some account has already been
taken of development. The exclamation point of line 8 marks something of a
climax and lines 9 through 15 decline after it; the last three lines may have a
slight rise of their own.

    Most literary works are in two, three, four, or five parts. Works in six or
more parts will usually fall again into larger units of two, three, or four. In
short works, the design is fairly easy to see, but the technique of formal analysis is the same no matter how long the literary work is. The longest poem in
English, *The Faerie Queene,* by Edmund Spenser (1552–99) is divided into
books, cantos, and stanzas, according to the same formal considerations raised
here, though the issues there are much more involved. A long prose work,
such as *War and Peace* by Leo Tolstoy (1828–1910) or *David Copperfield* by
Charles Dickens (1812–70), has no meter and rhyme, but it too is subject to
the same technique of analysis. Any literary work of art has some design which
can be discovered by analysis.

    Of what use is analysis of design? Once you see the parts of the work,
you have some overall grasp over it and can begin to appreciate the parts in
themselves and in relationship with each other. Spectators leaving a play or a

movie, or readers putting down a poem or a story, are often confused just because they have not yet assembled the parts of the work in their minds. Once
they have done so, they are prepared for more elaborate analysis.

Development

Here are two more poems by Emily Dickinson. Both begin with an im-
probability: the first addresses a month of the year as if it were a caller at a
house; the other is a report from someone who is dying and, at the end, dies—
but how then could that person be left to write or speak the report?

(1320)

Dear March—Come in—
How glad I am—
I hoped for you before—
Put down your Hat—
You must have walked—   5
How out of Breath you are—
Dear March, how are you, and the Rest—
Did you leave Nature well—
Oh March, Come right up stairs with me—
I have so much to tell—   10

I got your Letter, and the Birds—
The Maples never knew that you were coming—
Till I called—how Red their Faces grew—
And March, forgive me—
All those Hills you left for me to Hue—   15
There was no Purple suitable—
You took it all with you—

Who knocks? That April.
Lock the Door—
I will not be pursued—   20
He stayed away a Year to call

When I am occupied—
But trifles look so trivial
As soon as you have come

That Blame is just as dear as Praise   25
And Praise as mere as Blame—

(465)

I heard a Fly buzz—when I died—
The Stillness in the Room
Was like the Stillness in the Air—
Between the Heaves of Storm—

The Eyes around—had wrung them dry—   5
And Breaths were gathering firm
For that last Onset—when the King
Be witnessed—in the Room—

I willed my Keepsakes—Signed away
What portion of me be   10
Assignable—and then it was
There interposed a Fly—

With Blue—uncertain stumbling Buzz—
Between the light—and me—
And then the Windows failed—and then   15
I could not see to see—

Jot down any questions or observations you have on these poems. Do it before looking at the following questions that may bring up additional concerns. Remember that no observation is silly or too obvious.

1. One poem is set up with regular stanzas—which is it? What signs of patterning do you see in the other poem? Clue: though not so set up, it's in the same pattern of stanzas. The rhyming words turn out to be mostly partial rhymes as in the second poem: "before—are," "well—tell," "knew—grew," "Hue—you" (four rhyming words), "occupied—pursued" (this one distant), "come—Blame." Note also the mid-line rhyme between "dear" and "mere" at the ending.

2. Instead of "Till I called" (line 13) would you prefer "I declare"? Instead of "And March" (line 14) would you prefer "But March"? She left both versions of each on her manuscript, according to R. W. Franklin, *The Editing of Emily Dickinson* (Madison, Wis., 1967, pp. 104–06, 163–64). Johnson's version reproduces all of both, which makes for intrusive syllables in the rhythm.

3. Note the persons and tenses of the poems. The first poem is very much a "you" poem—a poem of direct address, though it also has an "I." The tense is mostly present; note the exceptions. The "you" is March, and April becomes "He." Who are "the Rest" (line 7)? The second poem is almost entirely an "I" poem and in past tense—a story poem, all the more striking since "I" tells of her or his death. Is the "I" of either poem clearly male or female? The second poem also has people, onlookers at the deathbed, with their eyes and breaths. Who is the "King" of line 7?

4. Consider the first line of each poem. Does "March" set up an expectation of "April"? What would you call the section of the poem in which April appears, a section that fulfills the major expectation the poem is building to? How does the striking first line of the second poem set up an expectation of when the fly will actually appear in the poem? What would you call the section of the poem (lines 11–14) in which the fly

163 Dear March. Come in -
How glad I am -
I hoped for you before -
looked
Put down your Hat -
You must have walked -
How out of Breath you
are -
Dear march, how are
you, and the Rest -
Did you leave Nature
well -
Oh March, Come right
up stairs with me -
I have so much to tell -

I got your Letter, and
the Birds.
The maples never knew
that you were coming -
I declare - how Red their
till I called
faces grew -
But march, forgive me -
and
All those Hills you left
for me to Hue -
there was no Purple
suitable -
You took it all with you

163a

Who knocks? that April -
Lock the Door -
I will not be pursued -
He stayed away a Year
to call
When I am occupied -
But trifles like so trivial
As soon as you have come
the ~~instant that~~

that Blame is just as
dear as Praise
And Praise as mere
as Blame -

appears? What is happening to you, the reader, during the section before April and the fly appear, while you are expecting them?

5. Neither poem has many direct comparisons. The second poem does have
   one in lines 3 and 4, "like the Stillness . . . Between the Heaves of
   Storm." What does that comparison do for the poem? In the first, we are
   to take March as a caller, perhaps a gentleman caller—which might be
   called a personification. Why should March be "out of Breath"? Why
   does the "I" have the job of coloring the hills? Why does April seem to
   be criticized for staying away a year, when March isn't? Why should
   March be welcome and April not? Why does March seem to be associated with "Praise," and April with "Blame"? In the second poem, what is
   that fly there for? Does it seem to catch a certain mood of a certain kind
   of death, or of all deaths? Why should it be the last thing the dying person seems to see?

For a creative response, note that the first poem seems to suggest a moral
about praise and blame when something marvelous comes, whereas the second
poem has no moral. See if you can add a stanza to the second poem suggestive
of a moral, perhaps one beginning, "Why should that fly just then appear—"
Or do a complete rewrite of the first poem, using two other months, for instance, "September dear, how nice of you—"

Though a literary work can be considered all at once, as a design, there's
no doubt that it happens in time, as a development. Aristotle says a work is
composed of beginning, middle, and end, and offers these definitions of
them: "The beginning is . . . what is naturally followed by something else;
the ending is what naturally follows something else. . . ; the middle is what
naturally both follows and is followed by something else" (ch. 7). These definitions may seem so obvious they could hardly be of much use, but they are
hard to improve on, at the times when a reader or critic has a sense that the
parts of a poem or play are not in their best sequence, or that something more
or different is needed somewhere in the work. The German playwright and
critic Gustav Freytag (1816–95) saw the sequence of beginning, middle, and
end in the shape of a triangle, rising to a climax, which he placed at the peak
of the triangle. Freytag saw this development in drama, but it is often applied
by extension to the development of any literary work. The triangle or pyramid
is really a graph of what happens to your emotions as you are reading, in the
form of an isosceles triangle whose horizontal, x-axis is time, and whose vertical, y-axis is something like emotional intensity. As your excitement in-
creases, the action rises to the next climax, after which it falls, till the next
excitement lifts it again. The development of a whole literary work, or of any
major part of it, presumably follows this pyramid. Some literary works might
not follow it exactly, of course. Some may seem to end at their climax, with no

falling action. Some may seem to have so many risings and fallings that no single climax can be identified. But most works can be profitably approached with this pyramid in mind. A longer literary work is probably composed of numerous risings and fallings—"curves of emotion," as Kenneth Burke calls them—each rise higher than the last, to the climax, or highest rise, after which the fallings are longer than the risings. Design and development work together, so that every dip in the graph, or bottom of the pyramid, marks the end of one unit of the work's design.

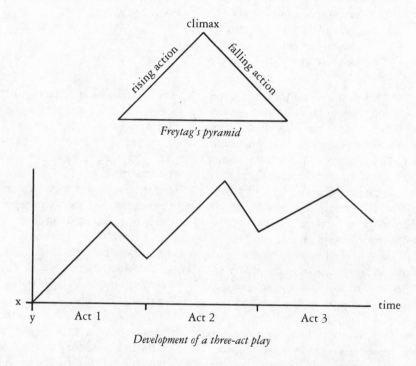

Freytag's pyramid

Development of a three-act play

The basis of Freytag's pyramid, of rise, climax, and fall, in literature and music, can be found in many short natural processes, the development of a storm, or of sunlight in a day; and its natural and clearest basis is in the sexual experience. Longer experiences, such as the duration of a season or a war, of a single human life or a society, are also roughly in the same pattern. Apparently the form taken by temporal works of art follows the form of all temporal experiences—especially the most desirable ones. But whereas the natural experience may prove haphazard and imperfect, the artistic experience can be by comparison ideal or perfect.

The following little poem by Frost may seem almost too short to have much of a development in time; but it begins, develops, and ends like other literary works. The poet tells of how his privacy as a gardener, singing quietly to himself—in "sotto voce" or an undertone—seems to be invaded by a group of schoolboys; and he tells of his feelings as a result of their stopping to look at him.

A Mood Apart

Once down on my knees to growing plants
I prodded the earth with a lazy tool
In time with a medley of sotto chants;
But becoming aware of some boys from school
Who had stopped outside the fence to spy   5
I stopped my song and almost heart,
For any eye is an evil eye
That looks in on to a mood apart.

This poem actually has the same design as "Dust of Snow," except that each line is about twice as long, or has four loud syllables instead of two. The rhyme-scheme is also exactly the same, so that there is the same reason for dividing the poem into two equal stanzas; the meter and rhyme certainly show it to be a poem of two quatrains. Since no division appears, however, you are encouraged to read through the poem as a continuous development, apparently because of the grammar and meaning. There is no convenient pause after the word "school," but stanzas do not need to end together with sentences. According to the punctuation this poem too is only one sentence long, but the stops after "chants" and "heart" are really full grammatical stops, though not full stops in the meaning, and might have been marked by periods; there are three independent subjects and predicates, or three complete clauses. The three clauses also show the development or sweep of the poem, in three rises or "curves of emotion"; the first sets the scene and rises to a slight peak on lines two and three; the second rises to the climax of the poem in line six; and the third, explanatory, brings the poem to rest. The quiet opening, the privacy of the scene, creates a desire or "appetite," to use Burke's term for a conflict of some sort, possibly an intrusion on the scene, which is fulfilled by the arrival of the boys and the poet's response to them—the climax—which is resolved by the general explanation in the last two lines. The rhythm of the poem supports this analysis, for along the way there are quite a number of stray, soft syllables added to the four loud syllables in each line, but from the word "outside" to the first "eye" the rhythm is strictly and starkly iambic (soft-loud, soft-loud), calling attention to this section as climactic. A climax will normally be louder, or more urgent in tone, if read aloud by someone with a feeling for the development.

The next poem by Frost is considerably more complicated in development and in meaning. The poet tells that an old woman who comes as a washerwoman was once a Hollywood star; and then he goes on to offer advice to the reader, advice which will prevent such a humiliating come-down in life. The last words and the title of the poem urge the reader to provide against future misfortune.

Provide, Provide

The witch that came (the withered hag)
To wash the steps with pail and rag,
Was once the beauty Abishag,

The picture pride of Hollywood.
Too many fall from great and good   5
For you to doubt the likelihood.

Die early and avoid the fate.
Or if predestined to die late,
Make up your mind to die in state.

Make the whole stock exchange your own!   10
If need be occupy a throne,
Where nobody can call *you* crone.

Some have relied on what they knew;
Others on being simply true.
What worked for them might work for you.   15

No memory of having starred
Atones for later disregard,
Or keeps the end from being hard.

Better to go down dignified
With boughten friendship at your side   20
Than none at all. Provide, provide!

In this longer poem, sentences and stanzas partly work together. The design of the poem is in stanzas of tetrameter rhyming triplets (gatherings of three lines), no matter how the sentences run. All but the first stanza end with a period, but some sentences end within stanzas too. The design of the poem as printed suggests it is in seven equal parts, but a closer look at the meaning suggests a different possible breakdown in keeping with the development of the poem. The first four lines form a quiet picture; lines 5 through 12 make a unit in which the poet gives direct suggestions or commands to the reader, and rises to a climax in the fourth stanza, as shown by the exclamation point and the italicized or stressed word. The next two stanzas are quieter again and rise to a slighter climax in the last stanza, where the command of stanza four is reaffirmed.

The creation and fulfillment of desire or "appetite" here are harder to designate. The "story" is all over by line 4 and acts as a stimulus for the rest of the poem, which is entirely argumentative moralizing. The story arouses the question, "How can I avoid such a fall?" The answer first assures you of the "likelihood" of its happening to many, and offers two solutions, temporary resolutions in the development: "Die early" or "die in state." As if the point now has been too much stressed, the fifth stanza, in a quieter turn, concedes a few desirable exceptions to the rule; but the sixth stanza insists on the misery of "later disregard," if "being simply true" doesn't work. And so a slightly quieter repetition of the climactic command seems called for, and provides a resolution. The development of expectation and its fulfillment here is not narrative, but argumentative, almost in the form of a syllogism: since many end unhappily, if you wish to avoid an unhappy ending yourself, you'd better make provisions against the future.

The two aspects of form—design and development—clearly work together, and formal analysis must usually include both. In fact, it is unlikely that the form of a work can be analyzed separately from the rest of the work, the content or matter or meaning. If you talk about form at all, you imply that you can consider it by itself and find the same abstract patterns in it as in musical or even in nonartistic experiences; but you cannot fully describe the form of the work unless you take into account its whole meaning. It appears, then, that form both is and is not separable from content—is temporarily separable but must be later unified with content. Formal analysis can operate only briefly apart from the rest of criticism; often formal analysis is so tied up with rhetorical analysis and the analysis of elements that all three must function together. Indeed, the study of formal development leads very naturally to the study of rhetorical progression, for both are based on time.

2

Rhetorical Analysis

Description

Below is the first of several passages from the diaries of Franz Kafka (1883–1924), a Bohemian Jew who wrote in German. During his lifetime he published only a few stories, and at his death he left his unfinished writings to his friend Max Brod with orders that they be burned. But Brod's good judgment prevailed, and he preserved and published them.

In this passage, the speaker (very likely Kafka himself) lies in his room and tells in great detail just what he sees. Read this passage carefully and try as far as possible to see all his visual sensations. (The word "wraithlike" means "like a ghost.")

(October 4, 1911)

Toward evening, in the dark of my room on the sofa. Why does one take a rather long time to recognize a color, but then, after the understanding has reached the decisive turning point, quickly become all the more convinced of the color. If the light from the anteroom and the kitchen shines on the glass door simultaneously from the outside, then greenish—or rather, not to detract from the definiteness of the impression—green light pours down almost the length of the panes. If the light in the anteroom is turned off and only the kitchen light remains, then the pane nearer the kitchen becomes deep blue, the other whitish blue, so whitish that all the drawings on the frosted glass (stylized poppies, tendrils, various rectangles and leaves) dissolve.

The lights and shadows thrown on the walls and the ceiling by the electric lights in the street and the bridge down below are distorted, partly spoiled, overlapping and hard to follow. When they installed the electric arc lamps down below and when they furnished this room, there was simply no housewifely consideration given to how my room would look from the sofa at this hour without any lights of its own.

The glare thrown on the ceiling by the trolley passing down below moves whitely, wraithlike and with mechanical pauses along the one wall and ceiling, broken in the corner. The globe stands on the linen chest in the first, fresh, full reflection of the street lights, a greenishly clean light on top, has a highlight on its roundness and gives the impression that the glare is really too strong for it, although the light passes over its smoothness and goes off leaving it rather brownish like a leather apple. The light from the anteroom throws a large patch of glare on the wall over the bed. This patch is bounded by a curved line beginning at the head of the bed, gives the illusion that the bed is pressed down, widens the dark bedposts, raises the ceiling over the bed.

Put down on a blank sheet of paper any questions or responses you have to this passage. Here are a few things to think about.

1. Note the details and the questioning of his own perceptions, how he corrects "greenish" to "green." He says "at this hour"—what hour do you think it is?

2. Note that there are no persons in this passage other than the perceiver, the "I." What are the things he sees? What are the different sources of light? What objects in the room and outside the room does he mention? What is the tense of the verbs in this passage? How would the flavor of it change if it were put into the past tense instead?

3. Most of the sentences describe what he sees, but there are two exceptions, the second sentence of the first paragraph and the second sentence of the second paragraph. What do these do, if not describe? Note that the first is something like a scientific observation on the human perception, and the second a humorous reflection on how somebody might have exercised more care in arranging for the play of light in his room.

4. Note the changes in vision he records—the window changes from green to blue and white, the globe from greenish to brownish "like a leather apple." The drawings on the glass appear and disappear. What causes these changes?

5. What can you imagine resulting from this scene—a story? a mood? a moral? In what kind of literary work might this passage be included? How would you characterize the state of mind of the perceiver?

For a creative response to this passage, try describing the play of light in your room at an odd hour and include your thoughts on the scene, as Kafka does. Or imagine a small addition to the scene Kafka describes—someone knocks and comes in, perhaps. Then what? Note that if the passage were in the past tense, you would be much more likely to expect something else to happen.

□   □   □

Rhetoric has been defined as the part of persuasion or of decoration— perhaps as the decorative means of winning an audience or reader. I spoke of it earlier as the flesh or dress of literature, to suggest you are no longer studying mere formal design or development, which you could plot or outline in a table or graph apart from the work itself. You are now touching the work itself, but as yet only its outer covering. Analysis of elements, coming up next, is more like trying to tell what is happening inside a live body. Rhetorical analysis, like formal analysis, is external, and your results will always be more superficial than an analysis of content. But then there is an advantage of external over internal analysis: you can be much surer of being right.

In order to make a rhetorical analysis you need to know the language the work is written in, but you need not know it very well, or you need not understand the work altogether. You might read a difficult modern work and be a little uncertain about its meaning, but you would be in little doubt about which parts were descriptive or dramatic, about how much narration and reverie there were along the way and where they came. And if you had a fair idea of literary genres, and how they were rhetorically determined, you could probably decide whether to call the work a story or play or poem, or some variety of one of them, or a borderline case.

All works of art fall into certain classes. A painting may be a portrait, still life, landscape, or some other recognizable kind. A piece of music may be an opera, symphony, string quartet or some other recognizable kind. So works of literature fall into certain classes, known as genres. Even when you find a work apparently of its own kind, or *sui generis,* it will resemble or partake of some other class of works, or at most be the first of a new genre of its own. These genres may be differentiated by their form, especially by their design or shape in space; but they are customarily classed by modes, which have to do, not with space, but time. You can look at a work as a whole, in space, or in passing, in time; both involve rhetorical analysis—one resulting in genre, the other in mode. In this section you will find discussions of the four principal modes of literature—description, narration, drama, and reverie—and at the end of each discussion a brief classification of the best known genres associated with each mode. Four additional modes, parallel to these, will be taken up below under "Theme."

Modes are typical procedures for making single sentences and for getting from one sentence to the next. The modes are differentiated, then, largely by the subjects and predicates of single sentences, and by the connective words between sentences. If you have only one sentence, you can't tell its mode as well as you can the mode of two or more consecutive sentences; then you can look at the separate sentences, and at the connections between them. This process is close to how musicians study the construction and connection of phrases in music; but literature not only happens in a passage of time; it also, unlike music, tells about a passage of time. There is your time as you are reading, and the time of the characters as they are acting. Modes can be differentiated according to how much of the characters' time is covered in equal lengths of the reader's time.

Description is the simplest of the modes of literature and covers none of the characters' time—or you might call it static. What a character in the story sees all at once takes you a while to read: during a description, none or almost none of the time of the story passes. Another way you might put it is to say that description covers the whole time of the story, plus more: here is how the house, or the town, or the garden looked throughout the period covered by the story. Since a description temporarily freezes the action of the story, it's one way of showing an author's special attention to something: he or she stops the motion picture projector to let you focus on a still.

Ernest Hemingway describes a room like this:

There was a low, dark room with saddles and harness, and hay-forks made of white wood, and clusters of canvas rope-soled shoes and hams and slabs of bacon and white garlic and long sausages hanging from the roof. It was cool and dusky, and we stood in front of a long wooden counter with two women behind it serving drinks. Behind them were shelves stacked with supplies and goods.

The usual subject of description is a thing, a nonhuman noun, or the pronoun *it:* in the example above the room and all the things in it. The subject may also be a person if the person is treated as a thing—that is, statically: in the example above, the two women serving drinks. If the person moves, and the writer records the movement, the description has become narration. The usual predicate of description is some form of *to be* or some other verb equally inactive or static: in the example above, the words "was" and "were." Often the verb is altogether missing, and there is just a catalogue of details like the ones in the first sentence of the example above.

That is how separate sentences in description are constructed. The connection between consecutive sentences is the simplest, that of addition, signified by *and* or by nothing—pauses marked by commas, dashes, or semicolons. A typical formula for description then would be two static equations: "The house is white, and the shutters are black."

The poem by Frost below is a sonnet, composed of an eight-line unit (or octave) and a six-line unit (or sestet). The first eight lines are almost purely descriptive. Frost tells of coming on a tiny scene that frightens him, composed of a flower, a spider, and a moth. He sees behind the scene some awful power possibly designed to appall or frighten humankind.

Design

I found a dimpled spider, fat and white,
On a white heal-all, holding up a moth
Like a white piece of rigid satin cloth—
Assorted characters of death and blight
Mixed ready to begin the morning right,   5

Like the ingredients of a witches' broth—
A snow-drop spider, a flower like a froth,
And dead wings carried like a paper kite.

What had that flower to do with being white,
The wayside blue and innocent heal-all?
What brought the kindred spider to that height,
Then steered the white moth thither in the night?
What but design of darkness to appall?—
If design govern in a thing so small.

10

The first two words of the poem might be considered narrative; if they had been "There was" the octave would be purely descriptive. The rest of the octave has no finite verbs, only the verbals "holding," "mixed," "carried," "to begin"—which remain inactive. The rest is an assemblage of descriptive details, separated from each other by commas and dashes. You might note that there are four comparisons, marked by the four "like's." The formula for description—the sequence of static equations—applies also to another literary phenomenon, the comparison, the metaphor or simile. In this poem the comparisons would be called similes since they use the word "like" or "as": a moth like a piece of satin. Metaphors are direct comparisons using neither of these words: a moth is a piece of satin. Passages of description often contain comparisons; in fact, every comparison—or static equation—could be considered a sentence or two of description.

The sestet, or last six lines, of the sonnet is composed of three questions, and a hypothesis. Though it uses many of the details mentioned in the octave, it is not descriptive but reflective. The poet thinks over the implications of the scene for himself and others.

There are few literary genres based on description. Classical and Renaissance "characters," and modern "character sketches" are partly static descriptions of persons, but they also use other modes. In certain periods of English poetry, poets attempted longer descriptive exercises, but these have never become standard genres of literature. One critic points out that the ancient epic poet Homer never spends very long describing anything and when he does he gives the description a narrative basis: instead of describing his hero Achilles, Homer tells the "story" of how he dresses himself for battle. In most modern writing, description remains subservient to some other mode or modes.

Narration

Here's a fragment of a story from Kafka's diaries. He never finished it, as far as we know, but it's a fascinating, odd little piece in itself. You'll enjoy it, I think, and also be a bit puzzled by it.

(January 19, 1915)

I had agreed to go picnicking Sunday with two friends, but quite unexpectedly slept past the hour when we were to meet. My friends, who
knew how punctual I ordinarily am, were surprised, came to the house
where I lived, waited outside awhile, then came upstairs and knocked on
my door. I was very startled, jumped out of bed and thought only of
getting ready as soon as I could. When I emerged fully dressed from my
room, my friends fell back in manifest alarm. "What's that behind your
head?" they cried. Since my awakening I had felt something preventing
me from bending back my head, and I now groped for it with my hand.
My friends, who had grown somewhat calmer, had just shouted "Be
careful, don't hurt yourself!" when my hand closed behind my head on
the hilt of a sword. My friends came closer, examined me, led me back
to the mirror in my room and stripped me to the waist. A large, ancient
knight's sword with a cross-shaped handle was buried to the hilt in my
back, but the blade had been driven with such incredible precision between my skin and flesh that it had caused no injury. Nor was there a
wound at the spot on my neck where the sword had penetrated; my
friends assured me that there was an opening large enough to admit the
blade, but dry and showing no trace of blood. And when my friends now
stood on chairs and slowly, inch by inch, drew out the sword, I did not
bleed, and the opening on my neck closed until no mark was left save a
scarcely discernible slit. "Here is your sword," laughed my friends, and
gave it to me. I hefted it in my two hands; it was a splendid weapon,
Crusaders might have used it.

Who tolerates this gadding about of ancient knights in dreams, irre-
sponsibly brandishing their swords, stabbing innocent sleepers who are
saved from serious injury only because the weapons in all likelihood
glance off living bodies, and also because there are faithful friends
knocking at the door, prepared to come to their assistance?

Again put down any questions or observations on this passage. You may have a few more questions of your own on this one, but here are a few to think about.

1. How much of this passage can you attribute to the attempt to present visual sensations—to describe—as in the last selection? Note the sentence on the sword. What would you call the rest of the passage? How would you differentiate the parts in quotation marks from those not in quotation marks? How does the last sentence—a question—differ from all the other sentences?

2. Note the persons and tenses in this passage. Which personal pronoun (I, you, he, etc.) is used by the speaker for himself and which for his friends? How many friends are there and are they differentiated from each other? What is the prevailing tense of this passage? What are the implications of this tense? Note the second word of the passage, "had," which suggests "at an earlier time than the time I'll be mainly speaking of."

3. Of course, the big question is, what do you make of the sword? Why has Kafka included such an obviously impossible event in his little story? Other than the sword, do you see anything else preposterous in the story of the friends who have agreed to go on a picnic? Remember the fly in Dickinson's poem about death—does the sword serve a similar function or how does it differ?

4. Is there something about storytelling that seems to call for periodic surprises—though not usually quite so surprising as the sword in this one? Do you see any other surprises in this story? Is laughter what you would expect from the friends when they remove the sword so neatly? And what about the grimly humorous response of the speaker himself, who seems mainly annoyed at the extraordinary privileges and irresponsibility of knights who go about stabbing innocent sleepers? What would happen if their weapons glanced off nonliving bodies—would they kill those already dead? Would you call this story a fantasy, a dream, or what?

For a creative response, think of a continuation of this story. What would the three friends do now—go on their picnic? Or do an entirely new but similar story of someone who finds something odd has happened while he or she slept.

□   □   □

A brief passage of narration may cover a long or a short passage of the characters' time. If you say "He looked for her," it might have been for a year or a minute of his time. Some passages of narration are remote, or cover long stretches of time in each sentence and between sentences; some passages are minute, blow-by-blow accounts. The longest time a passage of narration can cover is great but normally restricted by a lifetime: "During her reign the queen ruled well." The shortest time a passage of narration can cover is seldom shorter than the time it takes to read about it: "She opened the door." The more minute narration becomes the closer it gets to drama.

Here's a brief, typical passage of narration by Ernest Hemingway:

> Two of our Basques came in and insisted on buying a drink. So they bought a drink and then we bought a drink, and then they slapped us on the back and bought another drink. Then we bought, and then we all went out into the sunlight and the heat, and climbed back on top of the bus.

The subjects of narration are usually persons, or animals and things treated as persons—that is, names or the third-person pronouns *he, she,* or *they,* which replace them. In "first-person narration" *I* also occurs, and in "epistolary narration" (a story told in the form of letters) *you,* but many other third persons usually occur alongside them. The example above uses "our" and "we" (first person plural) alongside "they" for the Basques. The usual predicates of narration are the vivid or lively verbs, the "words of action" as they are called in old grammars, such as *run, fall, hit, kill,* or quieter verbs like *walk, enter, sit, write.* In the example above the verbs are "came," "insisted," "bought," "slapped," "went out," and "climbed." The usual tense of verbs in narration is past, which suggests that the action occurred only once at some given point in the past. But narration sometimes occurs in present tense for a colloquial effect, or in future for a prophetic effect.

That is how separate sentences in narration are constructed. The connections between sentences of narration have to be complicated enough to make constant adjustments between the time of the story, which may proceed by fits and starts, or go backwards or forwards, and the time of the reader, which is pretty steady and straightforward from sentence to sentence. The most simple and typical connective is *then,* which results in this typical formula for narration: "I hit him, then she ran in," or "They bought a drink and then we bought a drink." In this formula *then* may be replaced by *afterwards, later, next,* or *thereafter.* These terms vary the formula somewhat: "*after* (or *once, when*) I hit him, she ran in"; and "I hit him *before* (or *scarcely had* I hit him *when*) she ran in." The following terms show that two actions occurred simultaneously: *as, while, meanwhile.* The terms *since* and *till* contrast a single or minute action with a prolonged or remote action: "since he had left, she worked"; and "she did not work till he left." (Her working is prolonged, his leaving single.) Two verbal constructions are necessary for previous and for instantaneous actions: *had* with the past participle, as in "He had written the letter the day before"; *was* with the present participle, as in "When I came in he was writing."

In the little narrative poem below, Frost tells the results of a battle on the birds and insects and plants of the countryside before any soldiers have been hit. Bullets "rent" or cut a cobweb with beads of dew on it and hit a flower, which bends over double. A bird nearby returns to its nest; a butterfly hesitates and finds the bent-over flower; a spider thinks the bullet was a fly hitting its "wheel of thread" or web, which it has constructed between stalks of mullein, a tall plant with a yellow flower. The spider seems sullen or angry to have found no fly there.

Range-Finding

The battle rent a cobweb diamond-strung
And cut a flower beside a ground bird's nest
Before it stained a single human breast,
The stricken flower bent double and so hung.
And still the bird revisited her young.   5
A butterfly its fall had dispossessed
A moment sought in air his flower of rest,
Then lightly stooped to it and fluttering clung.
On the bare upland pasture there had spread
O'ernight 'twixt mullein stalks a wheel of thread   10
And straining cables wet with silver dew.
A sudden passing bullet shook it dry.
The indwelling spider ran to greet the fly,
But finding nothing, sullenly withdrew.

The actors in the story told by this poem are not human, but they are responding to the human actions of the battle, and their actions are reported as in children's books, as if they were human. The "persons" or subjects are the words "battle," "it" (line 3), "flower" (line 4), "butterfly," "bullet," "spider." The objects or complements are "cobweb," "flower" (line 2), "breast," "young," "flower" (line 7), "it" (line 11), "fly." The verbs or predicates are "rent," "cut," "stained," "bent," "revisited," "sought," "stooped," "clung," "shook," "ran," "withdrew." The connectives are "before," "still," "then." The sentence in lines 9–11 uses the construction "there had spread," which carries the story back in time to the night before; but since the sentence is nearly static, it might also be considered descriptive.

Narration may well be the central or crucial mode in literature. Some critics have felt that, because narration moves along in time just as literature itself does, literature should always be primarily narrative. If you recall from some time in the past a literary experience you have had—a movie or play, a song, or a description—it will very likely come back to you as an anecdote or story.

Certainly the majority of literary genres are narrative; stories exist in all languages, and in all sizes and shapes. There are the very short forms—joke, anecdote—which are told for the relish of the story itself; the fable and parable, which are told so as to point up a moral or theme. Then there are myth, legend, chronicle, which may be of any size, but take as their subjects a god, saint, or king. These may be in verse or prose. Some genres are always in verse, like the ballad, a brief folk story. Many critics think the highest point of narration in verse was reached in the classical epic, a story in twenty-four or twelve books about a great national hero. In the ancient Greek poet Homer, as in his many imitators, the epic includes a number of additional techniques or devices: an invocation to a muse, or patron goddess of the poet; beginning in the midst of the action, or *in medias res;* an elevated style, including "epic similes," extended or narrative comparisons; and gods watching over the hero's actions. You may have read Homer's *Odyssey* or *Iliad,* both of which demonstrate these qualities.

In longer prose fiction the standard distinction is that of the American novelist Nathaniel Hawthorne (1804–64) between the romance and the novel. The novel aims at a "minute fidelity," a daylight scrutiny, of everyday experience; the romance occurs in a moonlit "neutral territory, somewhere between the real world and fairy-land, where the Actual and Imaginary may meet, and each imbue itself with the nature of the other" (Preface to *The House of the Seven Gables* and the Introduction to *The Scarlet Letter*). Northrop Frye suggests two additional long forms, the confession or autobiography, examples of which are *Moll Flanders* by Daniel Defoe (1660–1731) and *A Portrait of the Artist as a Young Man* by James Joyce (1887–1941); and the anatomy or satire, examples of which are *Gulliver's Travels* by Jonathan Swift (1667–1745) and *Brave New World* by Aldous Huxley (1894–1963). Each of these longer forms has a matching short form in Frye's scheme: the short story and the tale are the shorter forms of the novel and the romance; and the essay and the dialogue are the shorter forms of the confession and the anatomy. (See *Anatomy of Criticism,* pp. 303–13). Works of intermediate length are the novelette or novella, the short novel; and the saga, or prose epic.

Clearly, then, narrative works may be of any length. One critic cites this single sentence by the ancient Greek poet Bion as a story: "The boys throw stones at the frogs in sport, but the frogs die not in sport but in earnest" (Randall Jarrell in the Introduction to *The Anchor Book of Stories*). But the most memorable and monumental examples are, of course, the long ones, and all the longest literary works are predominantly narrative: the *Iliad,* the *Odyssey,* the *Divine Comedy* by the Italian poet Dante (1265–1321), *Don Quixote* by the Spanish writer Miguel de Cervantes (1547–1616), *The Faerie Queene* by the English poet Edmund Spenser (1552–99), and *War and Peace* by the Russian novelist Leo Tolstoy (1828–1910). Some critics consider such works too long and prefer dramatic and poetic genres, which never get to be as long. Aristotle says about the length of a literary work that you must "be able to consider together the beginning and ending" (*Poetics,* ch. 24), which means that a play is about the right length and that a narrative work should never get to be longer than a novelette. The American poet Edgar Allan Poe (1809–49) says that a literary work should be no longer than what can be read "at one sitting"

("The Philosophy of Composition"). Both comments suggest that it is desirable to be able to see or review the whole literary work at once, like a painting or a design. Despite the objections of Aristotle and Poe, however, many of the greatest narrative works of literature are longer.

Drama

Here are a few entries from Kafka's diaries. The first entry may or may not be an early sketch for the longer one that follows. The middle entry tells a story, if it is a story, as strange as the last one, but strange in different ways. The third entry is very likely a comment on what he has just written; the first sentence seems to be a comment addressed to the characters of the middle entry; in the second sentence he comments on what he has written. For once, he feels he may be able to write. You may be pleasantly surprised to learn that the journals and diaries of famous authors are full of complaints about their inability to write.

(May 6, 1914)

The landlady of the rooming house, a decrepit widow dressed in black and wearing a straight skirt, stood in the middle room of her empty house. It was still perfectly quiet, the bell did not stir. The street, too, was quiet; the woman had purposely chosen so quiet a street because she wanted good roomers, and those who insist on quiet are the best.

(May 27, 1914)

The landlady dropped her skirts and hurried through the rooms. A cold, haughty woman. Her projecting lower jaw frightened roomers away. They ran down the steps, and when she looked after them through the window they covered their faces as they ran. Once a gentleman came for a room, a solid, thickset young man who constantly kept his hands in his coat pockets. It was a habit, perhaps, but it was also possible that he wanted to conceal the trembling of his hands.

"Young man," said the woman, and her lower jaw jutted forward, "you want to live here?"

"Yes," the young man said, tossing his head upward.

"You will like it here," the woman said, leading him to a chair on which she sat him down. In doing this she noticed a stain on his trousers, kneeled down beside him and began to scrape at the stain with her fingernails.

"You're a dirty fellow," she said.

"It's an old stain."

"Then you are an old dirty fellow."

"Take your hand away," he said suddenly, and actually pushed her away. "What horrible hands you have." He caught her hand and turned

it over. "All black on top, whitish below, but still black enough and"—
he ran his fingers inside her wide sleeve—"there is even some hair on
your arm."

"You're tickling me," she said.

"Because I like you. I don't understand how they can say that you are
ugly. Because they did say it. But now I see that it isn't true at all."

And he stood up and walked up and down the room. She remained on
her knees and looked at her hand.

For some reason this made him furious; he sprang to her side and
caught her hand again.

"You're quite a woman," he then said, and clapped her long thin
cheek. "It would really add to my comfort to live here. But it would
have to be cheap. And you would not be allowed to take in other roomers. And you would have to be faithful to me. I am really much younger
than you and can after all insist on faithfulness. And you would have to
cook well. I am used to good food and never intend to disaccustom myself."

Dance on, you pigs; what concern is it of mine?

But it has more reality than anything I have written this past year.
Perhaps after all it is a matter of loosening the joint. I shall once more be
able to write.

You probably will have lots of comments to make on these entries. Put
them all down and keep on thinking about them partly along these lines:

1. Think of the previous story by Kafka, about the sword. How does this story resemble that one and how does it differ? That story had three characters, the sleeper and his "friends," not really differentiated from each other. This one concentrates on just two, clearly differentiated characters and gives us as much of their conversation as of their actions. Without bothering to count words or sentences (you may if you like, of course), which strikes you as more important here, their actions or their conversation? If you omitted all of one or the other, which remainder would best capture the essence of the passage? What would you envisage as a performance of this piece—a recitation by one storyteller or an enactment by two actors?

2. Look closely at the personal pronouns of the conversational parts alone; you will see lots of the second person (you) and of the first (I), and a certain unspecified "they." Which do you see most of and which seems most indicative of conversation? Note also the tenses used in their conversation—which seems most important and most indicative of conversation? Now also look at the pronouns and tenses of the non-conversational parts—which do you see most of there?

3. Now look at the context of their conversation. The first exchange is expected enough—on whether he wants a room there and whether he will like it. What about the exchange on his stain and her hands—could you possibly have expected those? What do they reveal about the characters speaking? Note the underlying sexuality in these exchanges. What do you think of the conditions he sets up in his last speech? Why does he stress faithfulness in her (what right does he have to bring that up?) and why does he think his youthfulness can demand it?

4. From this passage, fragmentary though it is, are you most absorbed by what will happen between them (events) or by just what their individual personalities are like and what their relationship is to be? Or are these questions inseparable?

For a creative response, continue their conversation for a while. Would they go on to look at the room, or continue making observations about each other? Or do an entirely new piece, perhaps about someone engaging a room and what is said between that person and the one offering the room.

□ □ □

The relationship between the time of the story and the time of the reader or spectator is most striking, or dramatic, in the mode of drama, since the two times are the same. In drama the time is always the present, and so is the place: it happens right before you, and as you are watching or reading it. Every page of drama takes the same length of time to happen as it takes to read or recite it. This equivalence partly explains why drama is usually considered the most emotional of the modes, and why the word *dramatic,* in one of its senses, is synonymous with effective or exciting.

Here is a brief, typical passage of drama from Ernest Hemingway:

> "How'd you like the bulls?"
> "Grand. It's grand the way they bring them out."
> "To-morrow come the Miuras."
> "When does the fiesta start?"
> "Day after to-morrow."
> "We've got to keep Mike from getting so tight. That kind of stuff is terrible."
> "We'd better get cleaned up for supper."
> "Yes. That will be a pleasant meal."
> "Won't it?"

Since drama is what one person says to another, the subjects of the sentences of drama are nearly always persons, though persons may also occasionally talk about things: in the example above the speakers talk about themselves and one Mike, but also about the bulls and the fiesta. Names in the form of "direct address" are the commonest subjects. All three personal pronouns occur in drama, but the commonest, and the one most distinctive of drama, is *you:* the speaker in a line of drama speaks of himself as *I,* and sometimes speaks about *him,* but he speaks to a *you,* a listener: in the example above each speaker is an *I* to himself and his listener is a *you.* The usual predicates of drama include the vivid verbs of narration, but also, and especially, verbs of feeling such as *like, love, hate, want, forget.* The usual tense of these verbs is present, not the general indefinite present of description, but an actual present, often "present progressive" or "imperative": for example, "You are forgetting it," or "Forget it!" If the person of drama remains third, and the tense past, apparently some narration, not drama, is being spoken, as the messengers, sentinels, and shepherds do in classical drama. If the person of drama becomes first, and the tense future, apparently some reverie, not drama, is being spoken, as in the soliloquy of Elizabethan drama.

The example below is part of a Frost poem in which a wife speaks to her husband about a beggar who has just gone away from their door and is now walking down the road. The husband's "role" is left for us mostly to surmise. The genre of the poem is the "dramatic monologue," which might be placed somewhere between drama and reverie.

THE HILL WIFE
Her Word

I didn't like the way he went away.
That smile! It never came of being gay.
Still he smiled—did you see him?—I was sure!

Perhaps because we gave him only bread
And the wretch knew from that that we were poor.   5
Perhaps because he let us give instead
Of seizing from us as he might have seized.
Perhaps he mocked at us for being wed,
Or being very young (and he was pleased
To have a vision of us old and dead).
I wonder how far down the road he's got.   10
He's watching from the woods as like as not.

This poem is mostly in the first person, but many of the first persons are plural (*we, us*) and so suggest a *you* as well as an *I*. Most of the poem is a series of speculations about something that has just happened, a beggar stopping at the house of a young couple. If you drop the plurals and also especially drop line 3, there's no reason the mode couldn't be considered reverie. The plurals and the direct second person of line 3 make the poem dramatic—that is, suggest that it is spoken out loud to some other person there to hear it and respond to it. The role of the second person here, the husband, is not very pronounced—just a nod of assent at the second dash in line 3.

There are four possible connections between the separate statements of drama. If there had been a more direct exchange between the characters in this poem you could more clearly see these possible connections. Supposing they had said: "He smiled strangely." "Yes, he smiled strangely." That would show one possible connection between sentences in drama—repetition. Supposing they had said: "You saw him smile." "Yes, I saw him smile." That would show repetition as well as another connection, a switch of person from *you* to *I*. Normally if one character continues speaking, the person does not change. Supposing they had said: "Did you see him smile?" "Yes, I saw him smile." That would show repetition and a switch of person as well as another connection—question and answer. Normally if one character continues speaking she does not ask and answer questions. Note in the example from Hemingway above the asking and answering of questions. Now, supposing the characters in Frost's poem had said: "He smiled." "No, he didn't." That would show the fourth connection—disagreement. Normally if one character continues speaking, she does not disagree with herself; or if she does, you might say she is dramatizing two different attitudes.

All of these connections show a certain conflict from sentence to sentence—a knot or interference of smooth progress—which prevents you from thinking that only one character is speaking to herself or to others. Drama is often defined as conflict, meaning conflict in the overall pattern of the play; but there's also conflict line by line in any passage of drama. The poem above is vaguely "dramatic" by suggesting that some other particular person is there listening; but a passage becomes most clearly dramatic when there are speeches or lines unmistakably spoken back and forth by two or more characters.

Note that in the example from Hemingway above the speakers answer each other, but also respond with their own concerns. Where one seems to be worried about Mike getting tight, the other responds with plans for supper. In classical drama you will find passages of *stichomythia,* where each line of drama is allowed only one line of verse (or print); and the spectator watches the speakers bat the conversational ball back and forth as if watching a tennis match. In modern drama the separate speakers so often go off on their own tangents they seem to be paying little attention to each other.

Drama has sometimes been condemned on account of its moral influence, and sometimes praised on account of its emotional appeal. The ancient Greek philosopher Plato (427–348 B. C.) wanted to ban it from his ideal state because it encourages the author, the actor, and the spectator to impersonate—to become persons other than themselves or the selves they are supposed to be. In epic poems like the *Iliad* and the *Odyssey,* Plato would censor all the "lies" about the gods and he would rewrite most of the dramatic passages in the mode of narration. But Aristotle, Plato's pupil, after considering the rival claims of epic and tragedy (or narration and drama) decided that tragedy was superior, since it can do anything epic can do better—more economically and more vividly (*Poetics,* ch. 26). In works of fiction the most effective or exciting or revealing spots are usually in the mode of drama; a play, which is mostly in the mode of drama, is often expected to be more consistently moving or exciting than a story.

The forms of plays are much more uniform than the forms of stories, since no play is longer than the time an audience can be expected to stay together, rarely more than two hours. Some Greek and Elizabethan plays have survived in groups of three, called trilogies, on related and continuous subjects; but the long intermissions necessary between each play suggest that they are separate if related plays. The smaller units that make up a play are also more uniform than the disparity between the conventional editorial divisions would suggest: Greek plays had episodes and odes, while modern plays have acts and scenes. But aside from the choral odes or songs unique to Greek drama, plays in any age proceed by relatively short and separate confrontations between two or more characters.

The number of characters in a passage of drama is also rather consistent. Aristotle says that the tragedian Sophocles (496–06 B. C.) raised the number of actors (at a time) to three, as if it were quite an achievement (ch. 4); and in fact it was, since three characters are about as many as a passage of drama can accommodate: *I, you, she* or *he.* If there is a fourth character he often constitutes a chorus (a gathering of citizens as commentators who sing and dance), or the passage is transitional or a "crowd scene," where it doesn't matter very much who says what. Nowadays the song-and-dance routine, or chorus, is restricted to light plays, musical comedies; but serious plays also sometimes introduce a narrator or commentator, as in *Our Town* by Thornton Wilder (1897–1975) who takes over the serious function of a classical chorus without the singing or dancing. In classical drama the chorus also serves as the equivalent of a curtain on the modern stage—a break in the play to suggest a shift of time or place. As for the number of units (episodes, scenes, acts, confrontations) in a play, the insistence of Horace (65–8 B. C.) that plays be in five acts, rather than any other number, remained until the nineteenth century a law, instead of what it is, an arbitrary preference (*Art of Poetry* ll. 189–190). More recent plays are in three acts (occasionally in one or two or four), or in any number of separate scenes.

In view of the consistency of dramatic form, the various genres are mostly based on the different plots that can be used: tragedy, or an unfortunate plot usually ending in death; comedy, or a fortunate plot usually ending in marriage; and tragicomedy, or a combination of the two in that order. Melodrama and farce are tragedy and comedy reduced to gross simplifications for sensational effects. The modern problem play is one in which theme, usually a social theme, takes precedence over plot and character. Regardless of plot, plays may be in verse or prose, or in combinations of the two.

Literary critics often disparage the various short forms of drama, and it has been said there is no such thing as a one-act play—that is, a play one-third the length of a regular play. Nevertheless there have been such short forms as the mystery-play, the masque, and the mime—plays based on the Bible, classical mythology, or everyday conversation. In more recent times, plays written for television usually need to be one-hour or even half-hour scripts.

Reverie

Here's a single entry from Kafka's diaries. It appears to be directly about himself to himself (or is he thinking a little about polishing it up, to be seen, if only by himself, as "literature"?). His tangled and tormented relationship with his fiancée Felice Bauer (called "F" in the entry) has reached the point where he considers suicide.

Incidentally, he did not execute his plan that night. He died of tuberculosis ten years later at the age of forty-one.

(February 14, 1914)

There will certainly be no one to blame if I should kill myself, even if the immediate cause should for instance appear to be F.'s behavior. Once, half asleep, I pictured the scene that would ensue if, in anticipation of the end, the letter of farewell in my pocket, I should come to her house, should be rejected as a suitor, lay the letter on the table, go to the balcony, break away from all those who run up to hold me back, and, forcing one hand after another to let go its grip, jump over the ledge. The letter, however, would say that I was jumping because of F., but that even if my proposal had been accepted nothing essential would have been changed for me. My place is down below, I can find no other solution, F. simply happens to be the one through whom my fate is made manifest; I can't live without her and must jump, yet—and this F. suspects—I couldn't live with her either. Why not use tonight for the purpose, I can already see before me the people talking at the parents' gathering this evening, talking of life and the conditions that have to be created for it—but I cling to abstractions, I live completely entangled in life, I won't do it, I am cold, am sad that a shirt collar is pinching my neck, am damned, gasp for breath in the mist.

After putting down your own observations, think about these questions as well:

1. Note the personal pronouns—which by far dominates the passage? There is also a "she" and some other third persons—"they." Do you see any second person—you? If there were a "you" here, who would it be?
2. What are the tenses of most of the verbs—or, what is the time written about in relation to the time of the writer writing? Some of the events mentioned are just possible ones; without bothering about technical terms, how would you characterize the verbs for these possible events? Toward the end of the passage the verbs change to another tense—what is it, and why the change?
3. You have encountered sentences that describe, sentences that tell a story, and sentences spoken by characters back and forth. How do these sentences differ? What would you call them? Do any of them resemble the kinds of sentences mentioned above? What would you call writing of this kind? The title of the chapter that follows is just one possible term for this kind of writing. Perhaps you'd prefer "thinking sentences" or "thought" or "reflection" or "meditation" or "speculation"—or another term of your own.

4. Note the details occurring here—the letter, the balcony, the ledge, and
that shirt-collar pinching his neck. What do these details add to the passage? Do you find your thoughts grasping such details?

For a creative response, you might develop Kafka's entry, adding details
of your own. Or write your own new passage, speculating on a certain course
of action (not suicide, let us hope, but that topic—or any other—certainly
can't be forbidden) and why you probably won't take it.

☐   ☐   ☐

If it's true that you can review your life in a moment just before death by
accident, or plan in intricate chess-like strategy during a conversation, or see
in a flash of insight how to handle a complicated situation—then it follows
that reverie covers less time than any of the other rhetorical modes. A page of
reverie, which is a literary report of somebody's reverie—the word is used
both for the thoughts and the report of the thoughts—may cover only the
time it takes her to open a door or light a cigarette. So there is a gradual reduc-
tion in the time covered by the successive modes. No story time passes during
a description, even though it comes at a given point in the story; description
covers space instead of time. Narration covers time, anywhere from a very
long time to as short a time as it takes to read or recite it, which is the time of
drama. In drama, stage time and audience time passing are equal or are hinted
at being equal. In reverie the time passing is even less.

Here's a brief, typical passage of reverie by Ernest Hemingway. Note its
concern with the feelings of the thinker, the *I*. Also note the mingling of the
past (the war) and the "present," the situation in which the thinker finds himself.

It was like certain dinners I remember from the war. There was wine, an
ignored tension, and a feeling of things coming that you could not prevent happening. Under the wine I lost the disgusted feeling and was
happy. It seemed they were all such nice people.

The various modes are often separate from each other but also often
mixed. Narration generally partakes of some description. Drama generally
partakes of some narration as well as description. And reverie, when it appears, often seems to dominate the other modes it's mixed with. A person
thinking may think about the scene before her and that will put some description in her thoughts; she may think over some past events and that will put
some narration in her thoughts. She may review a conversation she has had
and that will put some drama in her thoughts. But here a problem arises, for
anything anyone puts down on paper naturally comes from that person's
thoughts. If you're reading a story, even a first-person story, and encounter
mixed description, narration, and drama along the way, there is no need to
call any of it reverie. At most, if one central character is narratively present

during all the scenes, events, and conversations, you may say the story is written from that character's "point of view," a concept I take up more fully near the end of this section. The following paragraph from "The Kiss" by Anton Chekhov (1860–1904) is in several modes:

> At the end of the way the path went uphill, and, skirting the church enclosure, turned into the road. Here the officers, tired with walking uphill, sat down and lighted their cigarettes. On the other side of the river a murky red fire came into sight, and having nothing better to do, they spent a long time in discussing whether it was a camp fire or a light in a window, or something else. . . . Ryabovitch, too, looked at the light, and he fancied that the light looked and winked at him, as though it knew about the kiss.

The paragraph passes easily from description to narration and description mingled, to some drama reported as "indirect discourse," since it's not important just what was said. The last sentence is reverie and binds all the others to Ryabovitch's "point of view": apparently you are to assume that the other modes are also filtered through his consciousness; but without the reverie there would be no need to make the assumption. A later paragraph in the story is entirely in the mode of reverie, though it glances at descriptive and narrative effects along the way:

> "All I am dreaming about now which seems to me so impossible and unearthly is really quite an ordinary thing," thought Ryabovitch, looking at the clouds of dust racing after the General's carriage. "It's all very ordinary, and everyone goes through it. . . . That General, for instance, has once been in love; now he is married and has children. Captain Vahter, too, is married and beloved, though the nape of his neck is very red and ugly and he has no waist. . . . Salmanov is coarse and very Tatar, but he has had a love affair that has ended in marriage. . . . I am the same as everyone else, and I, too, shall have the same experience as everyone else, sooner or later. . . ."

What is especially notable here is the use of the first person and the mixed tenses, especially the future. Even if you put a simple description or narration or conversation in the future you make it reverie, for somebody must be imagining or planning the scene or event or talk in his mind. And the use of the first person is almost always an invitation to reflectiveness, or reverie. The "I" who is writing is free to think about any time, and his mixture of times, while keeping himself the center of his thoughts, is what identifies the passage as reverie.

Drama is marked by a steadiness of tense—the present—and a switching of persons; reverie is marked by a steadiness of person—the first—and a switching of tenses. But just as the second person is most special to drama, since it doesn't usually occur in any other mode, so the future tense and other hypothetical or speculative forms of the verb are most special to reverie. In modern literature, drama, and especially reverie, may be composed of abrupt, halting, disconnected statements, sometimes confusingly run into each other; and many modern writers feel that this is a close approximation of how people actually talk and think. This disconnectedness is a sign of reverie (or drama), but not an unmistakable sign. In older literature, even though all the sentences are beautifully finished, and sometimes in elegant verse as well, the modes switch just as easily as in modern literature. And you can determine those switches by the handling of times and persons, as given above.

The connections between statements in reverie may then be as conflicting as those in drama; but they may also be logical or pseudo-logical or psychological. Logic is the study of ideal statements and the ideal connections between them. Reverie sometimes makes use of everyday or lowdown logic, by parodying or making fun of the syllogism, here somewhat adapted to show differences of tense: "If (since, because, as) Socrates is a man, and all men have formerly died, then (so, hence, therefore, accordingly, consequently) Socrates too will die."

In the Frost poem below, the poet explores his feelings, in and out of his house, when a roaring wind seems to suggest that someone must know he is there all alone. (The word "bereft" means "left alone.")

Bereft

Where had I heard this wind before
Change like this to a deeper roar?
What would it take my standing there for,
Holding open a restive door,
Looking down hill to a frothy shore?   5
Summer was past and day was past.
Somber clouds in the west were massed.
Out in the porch's sagging floor,
Leaves got up in a coil and hissed,
Blindly struck at my knee and missed.   10
Something sinister in the tone
Told me my secret must be known:
Word I was in the house alone
Somehow must have gotten abroad
Word I was in my life alone,
Word I had no one left but God.   15

The past tense of this poem gives it a narrative effect, and the four middle lines of the poem (lines 7–10) are descriptive-narrative. But in the rest of the poem the persistence of the first person, and the variation of verb forms, suggests reverie. The past perfect in line 1 compares one past with an earlier past. The next verb "would . . . take" is speculative, and so reflective. The overall syllogistic structure might run like this: "If that scene was so ominous, and all previous hope was over, then I might fear the worst." Though no future tense actually occurs in the poem, the entire effect is a brooding over what might soon happen.

The usual genre of reverie is the lyric poem, defined as a short emotional expression of the poet himself; the genre is often considered the highest mode of literary expression, synonymous with the term poetry, when that term is used to mean noble and elevated utterance. It is so highly pitched it can't last long. At least Poe says there is no such thing as a long poem, one much over a hundred lines: "all intense excitements," he says, "are, through a psychal necessity, brief" ("The Philosophy of Composition").

Lyric poems come in more intricately devised forms than do stories or plays. This may be because poets feel they should put their most beautiful sentiments in the most beautiful designs. Or it may be because they feel the most uncontrollable emotions must be most rigidly controlled in form. Even modern "free verse" poets find their poems falling into certain designs, sometimes unexpectedly. Most lyric poems are so brief that you can easily see whatever ornamental or symmetrical design they have on the single page. The classification of lyric poems is by the design or the subject—the form or content—or by both. For instance, the Japanese haiku, probably the shortest lyric genre ever devised, is in three lines of seventeen syllables, with five, seven, and five syllables in the three lines. But the haiku is also usually a poem descriptive of a scene or seasonal effect, with a stated or suggested philosophical observation in response to the scene. In the following translation of a haiku by Matsuo Bashō (1644–94), the translator, Harold G. Henderson, has used even fewer syllables (fourteen) than those allowed in Japanese:

> On a withered branch   (5)
> a crow has settled—   (5)
> autumn nightfall.   (4)

The most popular and best-known brief lyric genre is the fourteen-line sonnet, in one of two rhyme-schemes: the Italian, whose octave rhymes *abba abba,* and with various rhyme-schemes in the sestet; and the English, which usually rhymes *abab cdcd efef gg.* The sonnet is also often, though not necessarily, on the subject of love. For an example of a sonnet with the Italian rhyme-scheme, and not on the subject of love, see Frost's "Design" in the section on Description above. Longer lyric genres vary in design and are classified primarily according to subject. These include the elegy, hymn, and ode, which usually commemorate or celebrate a particular death, a petition to God, or an occasion or idea.

Lyric genres are in verse, even if it is "free" verse. In prose the only recognized genre for reverie is the personal essay, the reflective ramble in the style of the French writer, often considered the creator of the personal essay, Michel de Montaigne (1533–92). The English essayist Charles Lamb (1775–

1834) follows in the tradition of Montaigne. Note that in the passage below Lamb is as concretely reflective as poets usually are:

> I am now as if I had never been other than my own master. It is natural to me to go where I please, to do what I please. I find myself at eleven o'clock in the day in Bond Street, and it seems to me that I have been sauntering there at that very hour for years past. I digress into Soho, to explore a book-stall. Methinks I have been thirty years a collector. There is nothing strange nor new in it. I find myself before a fine picture in the morning. Was it ever otherwise? What is become of Fish Street Hill? Where is Fenchurch Street?
>
> *("The Superannuated Man")*

Fiction, from Homer on down, has always included some reverie. But you will find the most extensive use of reverie in those modern works called "stream of consciousness" novels—the novels of Marcel Proust (1875–1922), James Joyce (1882–1941), Virginia Woolf (1882–1941), and William Faulkner (1897–1962). A question of classification arises about the "novels" of these authors. If they are predominantly reflective or lyric works, then maybe the notion of the short verse lyric needs revamping—especially Poe's dictum that there is no such thing as a long lyric. Proust's *Remembrance of Things Past* may be the longest literary work ever written, and all "stream of consciousness" novels are the usual length of novels. On the other hand, if these works are rightly called novels, they must be primarily fictional or narrative works.

Such a question as this about "stream of consciousness" novels is the kind raised by rhetorical analysis, which, though it deals with the surface of a literary work, can hint at basic qualities of genre. Sometimes in a creative writing course a student sets out to write a play, and the teacher says it should be a story instead; she means that the basis of the writer's conception lends itself more easily to narration than to drama. And some finished plays come closer to fiction than others do. George Bernard Shaw (1856–1950), who was in some sense a frustrated novelist, accompanied his plays with elaborate commentary and fictional endings and beginnings; and his stage-directions are often clearly novelistic. But even plays not written to be read sometimes come close to stories. Try reading a play, imagining the stage directions as descriptive-narrative passages between the dialogue; or try reading a short novel imagining the dialogue as really staged, and the descriptive-narrative passages reduced to stage directions. Such transformations occur when a fictional work is adapted to the stage or screen; and critics sometimes complain of such adaptations that the original work was not basically suited to such adaptation, or that the adapter has not sufficiently reconstituted the work to suit it for its new medium. Many original moviescripts, such as those of the Swedish director Ingmar Bergman (born 1918), are, apart from technical cinematic marks, rhetorically equivalent to short novels. Rhetorical analysis will allow you to assess the rhetorical flavor of a work apart from such merely typographical indications as quotation marks, parentheses and brackets, and italics.

Rhetorical analysis is also a convenient approach to the question of "point of view," or the way the reader is led by the writer to see the action; this term may be applied to drama and poetry, but usually applies just to fiction. The different possible points of view are usually divided into objective and subjective, or into first-person and third-person, including "omniscient" (all-knowing) and "limited." The first two sentences of Chekhov's "The Kiss" are purely narrative and consequently objective.

> At eight o'clock on the evening of the twentieth of May all the six bat-teries of the N—— Reserve Artillery Brigade halted for the night in the village of Myestetchki on their way to camp. When the general commo-tion was at its height, while some officers were busily occupied around the guns, while others, gathered together in the square near the church enclosure, were listening to the quartermasters, a man in civilian dress, riding a strange horse, came into sight around the church.

A little later in the story Ryabovitch's point of view is introduced, and these two sentences are clearly subjective.

> At first, on going into the room and sitting down to the table, he could not fix his attention on any one face or object. The faces, the dresses, the cut-glass decanters of brandy, the steam from the glasses, the moulded cornices—all blended in one general impression that inspired in Ryabo-vitch alarm and a desire to hide his head.

Here the mingling of reverie with the narration and description indicates Rya-bovitch's subjective point of view. If Ryabovitch were telling his own story using "I" the point of view would be first-person. In "The Kiss" the point of view is "limited" to Ryabovitch; if Chekhov had entered anybody else's mind, especially the minds of many others, the point of view would be "omni-scient."

Description, narration, and drama, then, are usually "objective," and only reverie "subjective": description is like a photograph, narration like a si-lent motion picture, and drama like a tape-recording of voices. Reverie is sub-jective, and there is no objective machine to grasp the sequence of thoughts inside the mind. The point of view is usually "objective," then, when there is no reverie, no access to any character's mind. The point of view is "omni-scient" when there is the reverie of more than one character. The point of view is "limited" when there is the reverie of only one character, and he is also sup-posed to be present during all description, narration, and drama. "First-per-son narration" is almost a contradiction in terms, since the use of the first person almost always results in reverie; "third-person narration" is almost re-petitive, since all narration has some third persons. The only rhetorical differ-ence between these two is according to whether the character with the reverie is talking in first person or talked about in third person.

Rhetorical analysis serves to confirm formal analysis. Just as there is a closer focus of time in the sequence of modes, so there is a closer restriction on a character or person. If you take typical formulas for the modes—description, *it is;* narration, *he ran;* drama, *you love;* reverie, *I will*—you get closer and closer to the center of everything, the self. This progression may explain why each mode is dominant over its predecessor: a passage of narration within a description will give the whole passage a narrative heightening; a passage of drama in narration a dramatic heightening; a passage of reverie in drama a reflective heightening. This successive dominance will give a certain rise in Freytag's pyramid, or the "curve of emotion." The pyramid rises as the mode switches from description to remote and then minute narration, and then to drama and sometimes to reverie. In older stories, with little reverie and a great deal of remote narration, the high point was usually minutely narrative or dramatic; in more modern Chekhovian-Joycean stories, composed largely of minute narration and drama, the high point is an "epiphany" or a passage of reverie in which the main character has an illumination, or sees the light. The "epiphany" of "The Kiss" is the passage quoted on page 142. Between drama and reverie the heights are very close; drama will often be more exciting, reverie more moving. After the highest point of the story has been reached, the "curve of emotion" will begin falling as the mode switches from minute or blow-by-blow narration back to remote narration. Some stories even end the way many stories begin, with description.

Finally, rhetorical analysis suggests an approach to the analysis of elements. Though the correspondence is never exact, there is a suggestive correspondence between modes and elements; for plot is most easily rendered by narration, character by drama, theme by reverie, and setting by description. But since any mode can actually render any element, more than a rhetorical analysis is needed to arrive at an analysis of elements.

3

Analysis of Elements

The two longer Frost poems below tell stories of the New England countryside, which is the setting of most of his poems. In the first, "The Death of the Hired Man," a farm couple, Mary and Warren, talk about the return of their sometime hired man Silas now that winter is coming. Mary has already received him and talked to him and made up his bed. Warren, returning with supplies, does not want to keep him. As the two talk over the meanings of home and where else Silas might go, Warren's attitude toward Silas seems to soften. But when Warren goes to talk with him, he finds the hired man dead.

The second poem tells a story about a witch—and also a ghost. In "The Witch of Coös," a traveller visits with a mother and son, who begin telling the visitor of the mother's abilities as a witch, and she tells him about the dead in general and mother and son gradually begin telling him about a ghost supposedly in the attic. They refer to the ghost as "Bones—a skeleton," and sometimes refer to "they" for bones, "it" for the skeleton, and sometimes to "he," when they think of the ghost as a person. The witch tells of how the bones once rose up from the cellar where they were buried, assembled as a skeleton, and climbed to the upstairs bedroom, where she and her husband, now deceased, coaxed them up to the attic and nailed the door shut after them. The witch also tells of the earlier relationship between herself, her husband, and the person whose bones are now presumably in the attic.

These two poems are well worth reading over and over in themselves, and they will also form the basis for a discussion of the six elements of literature through an analysis of the combination of elements in them. Now that you've got into the habit of putting down your observations after reading, see what you can make of these poems on your own. Before attempting the exercises and discussions that follow, put down your own impressions and observations, and ask yourself the kinds of questions you have so far learned to ask, so that you are ready for a further analysis of the poems in the six sections based on them below.

The Death of the Hired Man

Mary sat musing on the lamp-flame at the table
Waiting for Warren. When she heard his step,
She ran on tip-toe down the darkened passage
To meet him in the doorway with the news
And put him on his guard. "Silas is back."   5
She pushed him outward with her through the door
And shut it after her. "Be kind," she said.
She took the market things from Warren's arms
And set them on the porch, then drew him down
To sit beside her on the wooden steps.   10

"When was I ever anything but kind to him?
But I'll not have the fellow back," he said.
"I told him so last haying, didn't I?
If he left then, I said, that ended it.
What good is he? Who else will harbor him   15
At his age for the little he can do?
What help he is there's no depending on.
Off he goes always when I need him most.
He thinks he ought to earn a little pay,
Enough at least to buy tobacco with,   20
So he won't have to beg and be beholden.
'All right,' I say, 'I can't afford to pay
Any fixed wages, though I wish I could.'
'Someone else can.' 'Then someone else will have to.'
I shouldn't mind his bettering himself   25
If that was what it was. You can be certain,
When he begins like that, there's someone at him
Trying to coax him off with pocket-money,—
In haying time, when any help is scarce.
In winter he comes back to us. I'm done."   30

"Sh! not so loud: he'll hear you." Mary said.

"I want him to: he'll have to soon or late."

"He's worn out. He's asleep beside the stove.
When I came up from Rowe's I found him here,
Huddled against the barn-door fast asleep,   35
A miserable sight, and frightening, too—
You needn't smile—I didn't recognize him—
I wasn't looking for him—and he's changed.
Wait till you see."

                    "Where did you say he'd been?"

"He didn't say. I dragged him to the house,   40

And gave him tea and tried to make him smoke.
I tried to make him talk about his travels.
Nothing would do: he just kept nodding off."

"What did he say? Did he say anything?"

"But little."
     "Anything? Mary, confess   45
He said he'd come to ditch the meadow for me."
"Warren!"

    "But did he? I just want to know."

"Of course he did. What would you have him say?
Surely you wouldn't grudge the poor old man
Some humble way to save his self-respect.   50
He added, if you really care to know,
He meant to clear the upper pasture, too.
That sounds like something you have heard before?
Warren, I wish you could have heard the way
He jumbled everything. I stopped to look   55
Two or three times—he made me feel so queer—
To see if he was talking in his sleep.
He ran on Harold Wilson—you remember—
The boy you had in haying four years since.
He's finished school, and teaching in his college.   60
Silas declares you'll have to get him back.
He says they two will make a team for work:
Between them they will lay this farm as smooth!
The way he mixed that in with other things.
He thinks young Wilson a likely lad, though daft   65
On education—you know how they fought
All through July under the blazing sun,
Silas up on the cart to build the load,
Harold along beside to pitch it on."

"Yes, I took care to keep well out of earshot."   70

"Well, those days trouble Silas like a dream.
You wouldn't think they would. How some things linger!
Harold's young college boy's assurance piqued him.
After so many years he still keeps finding
Good arguments he sees he might have used.   75
I sympathize. I know just how it feels
To think of the right thing to say too late.
Harold's associated in his mind with Latin.
He asked me what I thought of Harold's saying
He studied Latin like the violin   80

Because he liked it—that an argument!
He said he couldn't make the boy believe
He could find water with a hazel prong—
Which showed how much good school had ever done him.
He wanted to go over that. But most of all   85
He thinks if he could have another chance
To teach him how to build a load of hay—"

"I know, that's Silas' one accomplishment.
He bundles every forkful in its place,
And tags and numbers it for future reference,   90
So he can find and easily dislodge it
In the unloading. Silas does that well.
He takes it out in bunches like big birds' nests.
You never see him standing on the hay
He's trying to lift, straining to lift himself."   95

"He thinks if he could teach him that, he'd be
Some good perhaps to someone in the world.
He hates to see a boy the fool of books.
Poor Silas, so concerned for other folk,
And nothing to look backward to with pride,   100
And nothing to look forward to with hope,
So now and never any different."

Part of a moon was falling down the west,
Dragging the whole sky with it to the hills.
Its light poured softly in her lap. She saw   105
And spread her apron to it. She put out her hand
Among the harp-like morning-glory strings,
Taut with the dew from garden bed to eaves,
As if she played unheard the tenderness
That wrought on him beside her in the night.   110
"Warren," she said, "he has come home to die:
You needn't be afraid he'll leave you this time."

"Home," he mocked gently.

                    "Yes, what else but home?
It all depends on what you mean by home.
Of course he's nothing to us, any more   115
Than was the hound that came a stranger to us
Out of the woods, worn out upon the trail."

"Home is the place where, when you have to go there,
They have to take you in."

                    "I should have called it
Something you somehow haven't to deserve."   120

Warren leaned out and took a step or two,
Picked up a little stick, and brought it back
And broke it in his hand and tossed it by.
"Silas has better claim on us you think
Than on his brother? Thirteen little miles   125
As the road winds would bring him to his door.
Silas has walked that far no doubt today.
Why didn't he go there? His brother's rich,
A somebody—director in the bank."

"He never told us that."

                        "We know it though."   130

"I think his brother ought to help, of course.
I'll see to that if there is need. He ought of right
To take him in, and might be willing to—
He may be better than appearances.
But have some pity on Silas. Do you think   135
If he'd had any pride in claiming kin
Or anything he looked for from his brother,
He'd keep so still about him all this time?"

"I wonder what's between them."

                          "I can tell you.
Silas is what he is—we wouldn't mind him—   140
But just the kind that kinsfolk can't abide.
He never did a thing so very bad.
He don't know why he isn't quite as good
As anybody. Worthless though he is,
He won't be made ashamed to please his brother."   145

"*I* can't think Si ever hurt anyone."

"No, but he hurt my heart the way he lay
And rolled his old head on that sharp-edged chair-back.
He wouldn't let me put him on the lounge.
You must go in and see what you can do.   150
I made the bed up for him there tonight.
You'll be surprised at him—how much he's broken.
His working days are done; I'm sure of it."

"I'd not be in a hurry to say that."

"I haven't been. Go, look, see for yourself,   155
But, Warren, please remember how it is:
He's come to help you ditch the meadow.
He has a plan. You mustn't laugh at him.
He may not speak of it, and then he may.

I'll sit and see if that small sailing cloud   160
Will hit or miss the moon."

               It hit the moon.
Then there were three there, making a dim row,
The moon, the little silver cloud, and she.
Warren returned—too soon, it seemed to her,
Slipped to her side, caught up her hand and waited.   165
"Warren?" she questioned.

                        "Dead," was all he answered.

The Witch of Coös

I staid the night for shelter at a farm
Behind the mountain, with a mother and son,
Two old-believers. They did all the talking.

MOTHER. Folks think a witch who has familiar spirits
She could call up to pass a winter evening,   5
But won't, should be burned at the stake or something.
Summoning spirits isn't "Button, button,
Who's got the button," I would have them know.

SON. Mother can make a common table rear
And kick with two legs like an army mule.

MOTHER. And when I've done it, what good have I done?   10
Rather than tip a table for you, let me
Tell you what Ralle the Sioux Control once told me.
He said the dead had souls, but when I asked him
How could that be—I thought the dead were souls,   15
He broke my trance. Don't that make you suspicious
That there's something the dead are keeping back?
Yes, there's something the dead are keeping back.

SON. You wouldn't want to tell him what we have
Up attic, mother?

MOTHER. Bones—a skeleton.   20

SON. But the headboard of mother's bed is pushed
Against the attic door: the door is nailed.
It's harmless. Mother hears it in the night
Halting perplexed behind the barrier
Of door and headboard. Where it wants to get   25
Is back into the cellar where it came from.

MOTHER. We'll never let them, will we, son! We'll never!

SON. It left the cellar forty years ago

And carried itself like a pile of dishes
Up one flight from the cellar to the kitchen,
Another from the kitchen to the bedroom,
Another from the bedroom to the attic,
Right past both father and mother, and neither stopped it.
Father had gone upstairs; mother was downstairs.
I was a baby: I don't know where I was.   35
MOTHER. The only fault my husband found with me—
I went to sleep before I went to bed,
Especially in winter when the bed
Might just as well be ice and the clothes snow.
The night the bones came up the cellar-stairs   40
Toffile had gone to bed alone and left me,
But left an open door to cool the room off
So as to sort of turn me out of it.
I was just coming to myself enough
To wonder where the cold was coming from,   45
When I heard Toffile upstairs in the bedroom
And thought I heard him downstairs in the cellar.
The board we had laid down to walk dry-shod on
When there was water in the cellar in spring
Struck the hard cellar bottom. And then someone   50
Began the stairs, two footsteps for each step,
The way a man with one leg and a crutch
Or a little child, comes up. It wasn't Toffile:
It wasn't anyone who could be there.
The bulkhead double-doors were double-locked   55
And swollen tight and buried under snow.
The cellar windows were banked up with sawdust
And swollen tight and buried under snow.
It was the bones. I knew them—and good reason.
My first impulse was to get the knob   60
And hold the door. But the bones didn't try
The door; they halted helpless on the landing,
Waiting for things to happen in their favor.
The faintest restless rustling ran all through them.
I never could have done the thing I did   65
If the wish hadn't been too strong in me
To see how they were mounted for this walk.
I had a vision of them put together
Not like a man, but like a chandelier.
So suddenly I flung the door wide on him.   70
A moment he stood balancing with emotion,
And all but lost himself. (A tongue of fire
Flashed out and licked along his upper teeth.

Smoke rolled inside the sockets of his eyes.)
Then he came at me with one hand outstretched, 75
The way he did in life once; but this time
I struck the hand off brittle on the floor,
And fell back from him on the floor myself.
The finger-pieces slid in all directions.
(Where did I see one of those pieces lately? 80
Hand me my button-box—it must be there.)
I sat up on the floor and shouted, "Toffile,
It's coming up to you." It had its choice
Of the door to the cellar or the hall.
It took the hall door for the novelty, 85
And set off briskly for so slow a thing,
Still going every which way in the joints, though,
So that it looked like lightning or a scribble,
From the slap I had just now given its hand.
I listened till it almost climbed the stairs 90
From the hall to the only finished bedroom,
Before I got up to do anything;
Then ran and shouted, "Shut the bedroom door,
Toffile, for my sake!" "Company?" he said,
"Don't make me get up; I'm too warm in bed." 95
So lying forward weakly on the handrail
I pushed myself upstairs, and in the light
(The kitchen had been dark) I had to own
I could see nothing. "Toffile, I don't see it.
It's with us in the room though. It's the bones." 100
"What bones?" "The cellar bones—out of the grave."
That made him throw his bare legs out of bed
And sit up by me and take hold of me.
I wanted to put out the light and see
If I could see it, or else mow the room, 105
With our arms at the level of our knees,
And bring the chalk-pile down. "I'll tell you what—
It's looking for another door to try.
The uncommonly deep snow has made him think
Of his old song, *The Wild Colonial Boy,* 110
He always used to sing along the tote road.
He's after an open door to get outdoors.
Let's trap him with an open door up attic."
Toffile agreed to that, and sure enough,
Almost the moment he was given an opening, 115
The steps began to climb the attic stairs.
I heard them. Toffile didn't seem to hear them.
"Quick!" I slammed to the door and held the knob.

"Toffile, get nails." I made him nail the door shut,
And push the headboard of the bed against it.   120
Then we asked was there anything
Up attic that we'd ever went again.
The attic was less to us than the cellar.
If the bones liked the attic, let them have it.
Let them stay in the attic. When they sometimes   125
Come down the stairs at night and stand perplexed
Behind the door and the headboard of the bed,
Brushing their chalky skull with chalky fingers,
With sounds like the dry rattling of a shutter,
That's what I sit up in the dark to say—   130
To no one any more since Toffile died.
Let them stay in the attic since they went there.
I promised Toffile to be cruel to them
For helping them be cruel once to him.

SON. We think they had a grave down in the cellar.   135

MOTHER. We know they had a grave down in the cellar.

SON. We never could find out whose bones they were.

MOTHER. Yes, we could too, son. Tell the truth for once.
They were a man's his father killed for me.
I mean a man he killed instead of me.   140
The least I could do was to help dig their grave.
We were about it one night in the cellar.
Son knows the story: but 'twas not for him
To tell the truth, suppose the time had come.
Son looks surprised to see me end a lie   145
We'd kept all these years between ourselves
So as to have it ready for outsiders.
But tonight I don't care enough to lie—
I don't remember why I ever cared.
Toffile, if he were here, I don't believe   150
Could tell you why he ever cared himself. . . .

She hadn't found the finger-bone she wanted
Among the buttons poured out in her lap.
I verified the name next morning: Toffile.
The rural letter box said Toffile Lajway   155

Plot

Here's another entry from Kafka's diaries. It's a sketch for another odd
story—or perhaps you'll think this one not quite so odd as some you've already
seen.

(*July 29, 1914*)

I was in great perplexity. Only a moment ago I had known what to do. With his arm held out before him the boss had pushed me to the door of the store. Behind the two counters stood my fellow clerks, supposedly my friends, their gray faces lowered in the darkness to conceal their expressions.

"Get out!" the boss shouted. "Thief! Get out! Get out, I say!"

"It's not true," I shouted for the hundredth time; "I didn't steal! It's a mistake or a slander! Don't you touch me! I'll sue you! There are still courts here! I won't go! For five years I slaved for you like a son and now you treat me like a thief. I didn't steal; for God's sake, listen to me, I didn't steal."

"Not another word," said the boss, "you're fired!"

We were already at the glass door, an apprentice darted out in front of us and quickly opened it; the din coming in from what was indeed an out-of-the-way street brought me back to reality; I halted in the doorway, arms akimbo, and, as calmly as I could despite my breathlessness, merely said, "I want my hat."

"You'll get it," the boss said, walked back a few steps, took the hat from Grassmann, one of the clerks, who had jumped over the counter, tried to throw it to me but missed his aim, and anyway threw it too hard, so that the hat flew past me into the street.

"You can keep the hat now," I said, and went out into the street. And now I was in quandary. I had stolen, had slipped a five-gulden bill out of the till to take Sophie to the theater that evening. But she didn't even want to go to the theater; payday was three days off, at that time I should have had my own money; besides, I had committed the theft stupidly, in broad daylight, near the glass window of the office in which the boss sat looking at me. "Thief!" he shouted, and sprang out of the office. "I didn't steal," was the first thing I said, but the five-gulden bill was in my hand and the till open.

Put down your observations and questions as before. Also think about these questions:

1. This story has some similarity to the story about the landlady and the prospective lodger, though this one is a "first-person" account and that one was a "third-person" account. Both stories combine conversation and nonconversation. Is the proportion of these the same, or is there less conversation here? Also note the quality of the conversation—what it's like. Does the conversation serve to indicate the distinctive relationship between the characters (what is special about the boss as boss and the employee as employee) or to express out loud the events that have occurred and are occurring, as the characters see them? Consider what kind of knowledge the answers to the following questions would reveal about

the characters involved: Why is a young man attracted to an older woman with hands he himself considers horrible? Has a certain employee stolen money from the till or hasn't he?

2. Note the pronouns and tenses of the story. You will see that the conversational parts have the same characteristics you have already noted in previous conversations, and that the nonconversational parts have the same characteristics you have seen in such parts before, except that the main character here is "I" (as in the story about the sword)—unlike the "he" in the story about the landlady and lodger. But note that in this story the boss, the fellow clerks, and the apprentice are third persons.

3. What chiefly absorbs your attention here—such questions as these: Has the employee stolen or not? Why has he stolen? What is he going to do now that he's fired? Or such questions as these: How exactly does he feel about his boss? Why do his friends not come to his support? Why has he stolen so close to payday? Why does he want to buy theater tickets when he knows his girlfriend doesn't want to go? Or are all of these questions of equal importance?

4. Think again of the story about the landlady and the lodger in comparison to this one. Both are fragments and lead you to wonder more, but more of what? In the previous story, do you want to know more of what led up to the taking of the room and what events will follow, or what special attitudes the characters have and will have toward each other? In this story, do you wonder more about what events led up to and what events will follow the theft, or about the special relationship of this employee to this boss?

5. In this story, did you know all along that the employee had stolen, or did you accept his denial up to the point where he reveals his guilt? Is the author playing on your interest in his character's individuality, or playing on your interest in what the events are and how they come about? Is your interest in the events what propels you to read, or your interest in the characters?

6. When the narrator says that only a moment before he had known what to do, does he mean his theft or his denial, which he says he made a hundred times? Why does he want and then not want his hat? Like the young man in the story about the landlady, we learn some pretty strange and revealing things about him. Which of the two characters, the thief or the lodger, do you think you get to know better—or do you know the two equally well?

For a creative response, see if you can add some details to this story that might explain some of the unanswered questions above. Or write a new story about someone else who does something dangerous when he doesn't even seem to need or want the result of his dangerous act.

□   □   □

Making an analysis of the elements in a work of literature, I said earlier, is like trying to tell what's happening inside a live body. So you will have to know what the condition and functioning of the body reveals about its insides. No wonder analysis of elements turns out to be more difficult than formal analysis or rhetorical analysis. But much in an analysis of elements can be demonstrated beyond any reasonable doubt, and good estimates can be made of the remainder.

Literary works—stories, plays, and poems—apparently existed long before anyone tried to analyze their elements. The first analysis on record comes form Aristotle's *Poetics,* written around 360–55 B.C., shortly after he joined the Academy headed by his teacher Plato. Plato speculated a great deal about literature, but we have no record that he tried to analyze its elements. When Aristotle broke tragedy down into six elements, he may have been operating out of a Greek tradition of literary analysis, but there is no sign it is anyone's work but his own. Some 2335 years of criticism have not significantly improved it; and it has been adapted and extended from tragedy, which was Aristotle's main concern, to literature as a whole.

Aristotle lists the elements in the order of his preference: plot or fable (*mythos*), character or nature (*ethos*), theme or thought (*dianoia*), diction or style (*lexis*), sound or song (*melos*), setting or costuming or spectacle (*opsis*). Of these, Aristotle considers the first two most important and the last two least important—the separate contributions made to a stage show by music and costumes (ch. 6). But in another place (ch. 26) he says you can sense the sound and setting even if you read the work to yourself, and I am here considering these elements as integrated with the other elements in every literary work. Plot and character Aristotle sees in close rivalry for the first place, and he gives a series of arguments for preferring plot over character; that is, he wishes writers to keep a clear progression of action, and a clear dominance of plot over characterization.

Some modern literature, and some modern critics, confirm Aristotle's preference of plot over other elements. But some modern literature, and also some critics, have preferred character over plot. One of Aristotle's arguments for the importance of plot over character is this analogy from painting: "if you smear the most beautiful colors at random you will not please so much as with an outline on a white ground." The smearing of colors without sharp outlines suggests several sytles of modern painting. Like modern literature, modern painting has not entirley upheld Aristotle's preference.

I have slightly adapted and rearranged Aristotle's elements, following Northrop Frye. Just as literature occupies a central position between the arts of time and space, or of the ear and the eye, so the elements of literature may be structured in units of three, character central between plot and theme, diction central between sound and setting. Frye considers plot, character, and theme the primary elements; and sound, diction, and setting the secondary elements.

The rhetorical modes of literature may now be reduced to three—description assimilated by the others, mainly by reverie—and seen in the same structure: narration the best agency of plot and sound; drama the best agency of character and diction; reverie the best agency of theme and setting. In this section you will find general definitions of each of the elements of literature; some rules or conditions for determining its possible emphasis in any given work and especially in "The Death of the Hired Man" and "The Witch of Coös"; and some further classification of qualities found within the element.

Every literary work contains all six elements, but you usually cannot see them right on the surface. Like the four ancient elements of pottery (earth, air, fire, water), they are fused in the finished product and difficult to differentiate. Some critics deny that they can be distinguished at all. Henry James, the American novelist (1843–1916), in a celebrated comment, says: "What is character but the determination of incident? What is incident but the illustration of character?" ("The Art of Fiction"). James is speaking of a condition—possibly an ideal condition—in which plot and character are so well fused they cannot be separated. But some stories or plays, or some parts of them, come so close to single-minded pursuit of plot that the characterization seems thin; and other stories or plays, or parts of them, come so close to characterization alone that the sense of what's happening, the progression of plot, is at least temporarily suspended. Sometimes the plot is simply the result of the expression of character and seems to have little propulsion of its own.

Any element may be emphasized in any literary work, or in any part of one, and one element comes into prominence usually at the expense of others. A passage mainly devoted to storytelling will not be very expressive of character; a passage mainly devoted to characterization will not advance the plot very far. Some literary works seem to maintain a balance between elements, at least between the primary ones, but they are not necessarily better works on that account. Analysis of elements will not give you a sure way to judge literature, but it will better show you how each work is put together and so insure a sounder judgment.

Aristotle defines plot as "the arrangement of the incidents"; another definition might be the progression of the action—how the story gets told. The English novelist E. M. Forster (1879–1969) says that a plot necessarily tells or suggests why the incidents proceed as they do (*Aspects of the Novel,* ch. v)—a sensible precaution to keep in mind when analyzing plot. Many critics see the formal development of a work, with its "pyramids" or "curves of emotion" as essentially equivalent to the plot; and there is no doubt that both trace the work through time and try to account for some of the reader's excitement (or lack of it) in the course of the reading. A brief account of a plot is called a plot-summary. No two people would give exactly the same plot-summary of a given work, but most would agree on the main incidents. For "The Death of the Hired Man" most readers would probably accept: "One day a farmwife, having earlier welcomed a former hired man to her household, persuades her husband to be hospitable to him, but the husband finds him dead." For "The Witch of Coös" most readers would probably accept: "A traveller spends the night with a mother and son who tell him a strange tale about a skeleton presumably locked up in the attic." Actually both poems tell a story within the overall story and some readers might prefer the internal story as the basis of a plot-summary. For "The Death of the Hired Man" there is the story Mary tells: "A hired man appears at a farm where he has worked off and on, and tells the farmwife disconnectedly how he wants to improve their farm and to teach his skills to a college boy he has formerly worked with." For "The Witch of Coös" there is the story the witch tells: "After her husband has gone to bed, a farmwife thinks she hears someone down in the cellar where they have once buried a lover of the wife's; an apparition of some kind appears when she opens the door and it goes upstairs to the bedroom where they let it go on up to the attic, and then lock the door after it." Some critics use the term "story" for the isolatable external background of the immediate plot—the chronological arrangement of all suggested incidents. The story behind "The Death of the Hired Man" has to do with one respectable and one disreputable brother, and how the disreputable one becomes a homeless hired man; the story behind "The Witch of Coös" has to do with a woman and two men, a farmer and another man, perhaps a peddler, and how she chooses the farmer and lets him kill the other. In this book I use "plot" to mean the sequence of action page by page, rather than any suggested previous "story."

Once you have determined the plot of a work the next step is to determine its emphasis in the work. The first sign to look for is extensiveness of narration. Normally the more extensive the narration the more important is the plot. But even if a work is extensively narrative, plot is not necessarily the dominant element, for narration, especially minute narration, can render character, and narration can also render theme, or other elements. The two Frost poems appear to be primarily dramatic, but in fact the principal speakers, Mary and the witch, are also storytellers, and so there is a fair amount of narration in both works. In "The Death of the Hired Man" lines 40–103 and in "The Witch of Coös" lines 40–134 are primarily narrative.

Another sign of emphasis on plot is the insistence of the question "What will happen next?" as you are reading. But this question arises in all literary work, even in those emphasizing other elements. The question is, how much are you wondering what will happen next? Works emphasizing plot are likely to arouse suspense as you pass from one incident to another and surprise at the incidents themselves. In "The Death of the Hired Man" you are wondering whether Warren will decide to keep the hired man, and how the hired man will respond to his treatment, but these questions are not as insistent as, in "The Witch of Coös," whether the apparition will try to strike the woman or her husband, how they will respond to it, or whether there really is any apparition at all: the greater the suspense and surprise aroused, the greater the importance of plot in a given work.

Another sign of emphasis on plot is a large extent of story time, for a writer will usually extend the time of the story in order to accommodate turns of plot. But even within a greater extent of time he may focus on a short span, in order to emphasize character, or he may use a greater extent of time to express a theme. The time of "The Death of the Hired Man" is largely one day, the afternoon on which Warren comes home, though it also refers back to the last haying season. The time of "The Witch of Coös" is considerably greater, between the night on which the skeleton appears and the night the traveller visits the mother and her son, who has grown up in the meantime. If you consider story time by itself, then, it would seem "The Witch of Coös" has a greater opening for an emphasis on plot.

Another sign of emphasis on plot is the importance of sequence itself, of how important it is that things should happen exactly in the order they do. Of course, the sequence in any good literary work is unalterable, even in a work whose plot is slight. The question is, could certain incidents or passages almost be otherwise arranged? In "The Death of the Hired Man" it is necessary that Silas appear at the farmhouse before he dies, but the body of the work, the exchange of attitudes between Mary and Warren, might almost have been inspired simply by a report that Silas has been around, or by the news of his death. In "The Witch of Coös" the sequence of actions by the apparition, its ascent up the two flights of stairs and what happens between the farmer and his wife as a result, seems more tightly bound. Both poems close with a turn of plot, the death of Silas and the revelation of who the dead man was; but the death of Silas is no special surprise, while the story of the witch's lover uncovers a whole plot of the past and illuminates the story of the apparition. Cross-references of time—omens, prophecies, and other anticipations of future action; confessions, flashbacks, and other recollections of past action— call further attention to the sequence of the plot. The future tense, whether it occurs in the mode of drama or reverie, always suggests some possibility of plot, is always teasing your expectation of what might happen later.

Another sign of emphasis on plot is a plot more intricate or contrived than usual. Any literary plot will be carefully constructed, of course. The question is, how neatly or elaborately has the plot been contrived? Coincidence is a term for the neat pairing of incidents required by an intricate plot. "The Death of the Hired Man" would seem more contrived if a telegram arrived from Silas's brother just before his death and revived him, or just after his death when it was too late; or if Harold Wilson appeared and gave in to his argument at the last minute; or if Silas turned out to be Mary's or Warren's father. "The Witch of Coös" would seem more contrived if the witch turned out to have killed her husband and buried him in the cellar; or if the son turned out to be the lover's instead of the husband's. Some critics do not approve of such coincidences and may call them by unflattering terms such as contrivances, devices, or gimmicks, but such coincidences are found in Aristotle's favorite plots in Greek tragedies and also in many classical and modern comedies. Complicated plots are often supported by "props" (from properties used on the stage)—inanimate objects on which the plot turns. Letters and wills, rings and caskets, swords and guns, birthmarks and deformities, are often the props an intricate plot hinges on. "Plots" in the colloquial sense—hoaxes within the work contrived by the characters themselves—also contribute to an emphasis on plot. So do "sub-plots": in general, the more plots, and characters to execute them, the greater the importance of plot in relation to other elements.

The major question in determining the emphasis on plot is which elements are subservient to which other element or elements. This question can be better answered after considering the separate claims of character and theme, but may be at least broached now. How much of the plot happens without any corresponding revelations of character or theme? In "The Death of the Hired Man," if you consider what happens between the three characters, the answer is none. In "The Witch of Coös" possibly her striking of the skeleton's hand, or his seeking an open door, might be considered incidents introduced primarily for the excitement they arouse, but they also help to characterize the witch and her dead lover, and so they are not very clearly isolated from characterization. So far it would seem that plot is in both poems subservient to some other element, though it seems of greater importance in "The Witch of Coös."

There have been numerous attempts to list all the possible plots of literature. Aristotle differentiates between those changing from bad to good fortune and those from good to bad, presumably comic and tragic plots (ch. 7). Frye enlarged Aristotle's scheme of two basic plots to four: comic, romantic, tragic, ironic—metaphorically related to the seasons spring, summer, autumn, winter. The comic and tragic represent an opposition between the happy and unhappy, the romantic and ironic between the ideal and the actual. These plots Frye locates on two concentric circles, which make up the wheel of fortune of myths or plots: one circle is bisected up and down between right and left, tragic plots going down, comic ones coming up; the other is bisected between upper and lower, romantic plots passing from the upper half of comedy to the upper half of tragedy, ironic plots passing from the lower half of tragedy to the lower half of comedy. The top of the circle looks up to heaven, the bottom down to hell; *The Divine Comedy* of Dante (1265–1321) covers the full semi-circle of comedy and rises from hell to heaven, whereas the heroes of a divine tragedy like Satan or Adam fall from heaven to hell or earth. Every literary work presumably is at some point or arc of one of these two circles.

In the typical comic myth or plot, a young man pursues a young woman, and she also wishes to pair off with him, but some obstacle, usually set up by a parent or some other member of the older generation, prevents them from coming together, until by some twist or twists of the plot, they pair off happily in the end, and often bring along with them other pairing couples and parents or older people who also form a union suggestive of a happily-ever-after

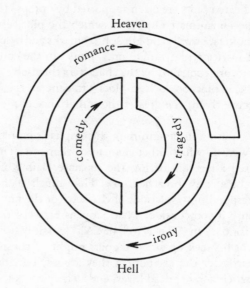

Frye's mythic wheel of fortune

society. Examples of the comic plot may be found in Shakespeare's comedies, and the novels of Henry Fielding (1707–54), Jane Austen (1775–1817), and Charles Dickens (1812–70).

The typical romantic plot as laid out by literary critics has no necessary similarity to the type of drugstore romance or soap opera we're all familiar with; that type of romance is closer to the typical plot of comedy above, although it may have some darker implications suggestive of the tragic plot. The literary plot of romance is one of a knight in shining armor, or similar hero, who has a series of trials or labors to overcome, often including giants or dragons or evil kings. After successfully completing his labors, the hero earns a reward of treasure or property, which may also include a young maiden— but she is not as necessary in this plot as she is in the comedic plot. Usually the hero kills his foe, but he may also die himself, and the ending is not as important as the adventures along the way. Examples of the romantic plot may be found in the exploits of King Arthur, *The Faerie Queene* by Edmund Spenser (1552–99), and more recently in the stories of J. R. R. Tolkien (1892–1973).

Aristotle gives a series of hints on writing tragedies which partially constitute a general account of the tragic plot. He says that the change of fortune in a tragedy is from good to bad, of a character not perfectly good or bad but in a state of good fortune and susceptible to an error which brings about his downfall (ch. 13). Frye offers some elaborations on Aristotle. More so than the comic hero, who is part of a pleasant domestic society, the tragic hero is alone or nearly alone, confronting a power outside himself which forces him to recognize a law of nature, which is sometimes called fate. Aristotle says the tragic hero has some flaw in character, and his tragic end—usually his death and often the death of others associated with him—comes about sometimes through his flaw and sometimes by his struggling against but succumbing to the law outside himself. One frequent example of law is the hero's discovery that he must revenge a former evil or crime; in the course of executing his revenge he meets his own downfall. Examples of tragic plots are Aristotle's favorite, *Oedipus the King* by Sophocles, and other classical tragedies by Sophocles, Aeschylus, and Euripides. Outside the plays of ancient Greece, the most highly respected tragedies are those by Shakespeare, such as *Hamlet, Macbeth,* and *King Lear.*

The ironic or satiric plot requires a prior understanding of irony and satire. Irony occurs when we perceive something contrary to expectation. It may occur in words (often called sarcasm or verbal irony) as someone saying the opposite of what is meant; or it may occur in events as a turn or twist of plot the opposite of what the characters or the readers know or expect. Satire is a literary technique whereby an author makes fun of a given situation or group of people in society in order to suggest some correction of existing evils or follies.

The typical ironic or satiric plot usually functions by making fun of the typical romantic plot, by setting in motion expectations of heroism and achievement and showing that the results fall far short. The "heroes," instead of appearing heroic, turn out to look silly. In *Don Quixote* by Cervantes (1547–1616), the Don fights against a windmill instead of a real foe. In *Gulliver's Travels* by Jonathan Swift (1667–1745), Gulliver becomes a giant tied down by a society of little people and then he becomes a childlike little person in a society of giants.

The two poems by Frost are neither of them clearly identifiable examples of the comic, romantic, or tragic plots. Both are perhaps suggestive of tragedy, in the death of the hired man, in the haunting by the ghost of the murdered man. Silas is no great tragic hero, but he sees himself as an avenger against Harold Wilson, who has vanquished him at least in conversation. Nor is the witch an impressive tragic heroine, but she struggles against the apparition that rises apparently to get even with those who have killed him. Actually both plots seem reversals of romantic or tragic expectations and so are best considered, like most modern literary works, ironic.

Character

Below is an entry from the travel diary Kafka kept during a trip he took with Max Brod, his friend and future editor, from August to September, 1911. In it he tells of the slight misunderstandings occurring between friends.

Beginning of our Parisian misunderstandings. Max came up to my hotel room and was upset that I wasn't ready. I was washing my face, whereas I had previously said that we should just wash up a little and leave at once. Since by "washing up a little" I had only meant to exclude washing one's whole body, and on the other hand it was precisely the washing of my face that I had meant by it, which I hadn't finished yet, I didn't understand his complaints and went right on washing, even if not with quite the same solicitude; while Max, with all the dirt of the night's journey on his clothes, sat down on my bed to wait. Whenever Max finds fault with someone he has the trick of knitting his mouth and even his whole face together in a sweet expression, he is doing it this very moment, as if on the one hand he intended by this to make his reproaches more understandable, and as if he wanted to indicate on the other hand that only the sweetness of his present expression keeps him from giving me a box on the ear. In the fact that I force him into a hypocrisy unnatural to him there is contained a further reproach which I feel him to be expressing when he falls silent and the lines of his face draw apart in a contrary direction—that is, away from his mouth—in order to recover from the sweetness they had expressed, which of course has a much stronger effect than did his first expression. I, on the other hand, out of weariness can retreat so deeply inside myself that these various expressions never reach to me (such was the case in Paris); which is why I can then behave in so lordly a fashion in my misery (out of a feeling of completest indifference and without a trace of guilt) as to apologize at once. This pacified him at the time in Paris, or so at least it seemed to, and he stepped out on the balcony with me and remarked on the view, chiefly on how Parisian it was. What I really saw was only how fresh Max was; how assuredly he fitted into a Paris of some sort that I couldn't even perceive; how, emerging from his dark back room, he stepped out on a Paris balcony in the sunlight for the first time in a year and knew that he was deserving of it, while I, unfortunately, was noticeably more tired than when I had first come out on the balcony shortly before Max. And my tiredness in Paris cannot be got over by sleep, but only by going away. Sometimes I even consider this one of the characteristics of Paris.

This was really written without ill will, but he was at my heels at every word.

Put down your observations again and think also about these questions:

1. Is this a story with Franz and Max as characters (like the stories about the boss and employee or the landlady and lodger), or just a sketch or diary entry which we don't need to think of another term for? We would normally say the previous entries were "fiction" or "made up" and this one "nonfiction" or "based on real life." But maybe we shouldn't make too much of these distinctions either? The "made-up" story may well ex-

press an essential problem of the author's psychology, whereas the one "based on real life" may, even if written hurriedly under the pressure of being watched, have a literary heightening, as if the characters were on the way to becoming characters in a story. Or what do you think?

2. Note the persons and tenses of this piece. Don't we have a third and first person—like the boss and employee? Don't we have an extensive use of the past tense, as in other stories? There is a fairly long middle section not in the past tense, beginning "Whenever Max finds fault with someone," ending "so as to apologize at once" and including the immediate "he is doing it this very moment." How does this passage alter the whole? But if most of the passage has the expected constituents of a story, why isn't it one, if it isn't? What does it lack?

3. See if you can make the most of this piece as a story. What happens in it? Where are the friends going? Why should Max be annoyed at the delay? What does the previous episode on the balcony in Paris have to do with the present occasion? What can you imagine as happening next, or isn't that an appropriate question?

4. What is revealed about the friends and their relationship here? Why is Max apparently annoyed at Franz's necessity for cleanliness, and Franz apparently annoyed at the dirt on Max's clothes? Why should Max take on a sweet expression when he is annoyed? Why should he become further annoyed at being forced to seem hypocritically sweet? Why should Franz be at once weary, lordly, indifferent, and unguilty? Why should Max seem so fresh and assured to Franz—so "deserving" of the Parisian scene? Isn't Franz deserving of it? Is Franz really without ill will, as he says, and does Max's inspection of what Franz is writing suggest some sort of ill will? Remember that these are good friends but also both practicing writers—sometimes working in collaboration but also in possible competition with each other. Were such qualities as these as closely noted in the previous entries from Kafka's diaries? What does this passage have more of that others had less of?

For a creative response, see if you can add some details to the relationship depicted, in keeping with those given. Or treat the piece as the beginning of a story and continue it for a bit. Or do an entirely new piece indicating a close and slightly strained relationship between friends.

□   □   □

Aristotle suggests that character is shown in the statement of a choice or the choice itself—in words or in action without words—or you might call it the psychological inclinations of all the characters in a given work. Many critics find conflict to be the basis of plot—an external conflict in events and the connections between them; other critics find internal conflict within the characters the basis of characterization; and a character in a conflict or dilemma must make a choice, which brings us back around to Aristotle's discovery of character in choice.

In "The Kiss," Chekhov characterizes his main character when first introduced in the story with explicit commentary, using description and reverie:

> The most ill at ease of them all was Ryabovitch—a little officer in spectacles, with sloping shoulders and whiskers like a lynx's. While some of his comrades assumed a serious expression, while others wore forced smiles, his face, his lynx-like whiskers, and spectacles seemed to say: "I am the shyest, most modest, and most undistinguished officer in the whole brigade!"

But he is probably better characterized at the very end of the story when he has a chance to return to the General's house in which occurred the accidental kiss that has obsessed him throughout the story; and he chooses not to go:

> For an instant there was a flash of joy in Ryabovitch's heart, but he quenched it at once, got into bed, and in his wrath with his fate, as though to spite it, did not go to the General's.

At this point of the story he has an important choice to make; he can return to the scene of the accidental kiss that he has dreamt of recapturing, or he can admit to himself that he has been chasing an idle fantasy and carry on his life with more humdrum but more likely expectations. He makes the more realistic, less romantic, choice and reveals the distinctiveness of his character better in that choice than anywhere else in the story. As Aristotle said, the choices made by characters characterize them.

In "The Death of the Hired Man" Mary chooses to keep Silas but Warren is doubtful whether to accept him, and Silas has chosen to go to their farm rather than elsewhere; most readers would probably agree as a result of these choices that Warren is hardheaded and practical but humane, Mary is kindly and sympathetic but levelheaded, and Silas is "just the kind that kinsfolk can't abide" or, as Mary finally admits, "worthless." In "The Witch of Coös" the witch has chosen, in the prior action, first her lover, then her husband, and she chooses to lock up the lover-ghost when he chooses to return, while the choices of her husband Toffile and her son are not presented. Most readers would probably agree that the witch is strong and quick and her son is weak and slow; her husband and her lover are not characterized, but as one was apparently a farmer and the other a peddler, the lover may have been more adventurous, the husband more domestic.

You should be able to tell what the characters are like even if character is not what the author was most interested in; and you can test your ability at this kind of analysis by writing character-sketches of the chief characters; these are capsules of the element of character, just as a plot-summary is a capsule of the element of plot. A more difficult analytic problem is determining just how much the disposition of the work as a whole is weighted toward characterization. I said above that there is a tendency for drama and dramatic passages to characterize more than passages in other modes. But this is an overall tendency and cannot necessarily be relied on in brief, given passages. Drama can be used to convey narrative events (plot) or abstract ideas (theme); in a play, for instance, all the elements must be almost wholly conveyed through drama. Characters in a play sometimes tell each other stories, and in those passages they are helping to develop the plot; and they sometimes argue about ideas, and in those passages they are helping to develop the theme. But in a passage like the following one, from *Man and Superman* by the Irish playwright George Bernard Shaw (1856–1950), the characters are obviously talking to sharpen their distinctive conflicts toward each other. Tanner mistakenly thinks Ann will marry Tavy; he does not yet know, as she does, that she will marry him:

> TANNER. Oh, I know you don't care very much about Tavy. But there is always one who kisses and one who only allows the kiss. Tavy will kiss; and you will only turn the cheek. And you will throw him over if anybody better turns up.
>
> ANN [*offended*]. You have no right to say such things, Jack. They are not true, and not delicate. If you and Tavy choose to be stupid about me, that is not my fault.
>
> TANNER [*remorsefully*]. Forgive my brutalities, Ann. They are levelled at this wicked world, not at you. [*She looks up at him, pleased and forgiving. He becomes cautious at once*]. All the same, I wish Ramsden would come back. I never feel safe with you: there is a devilish charm—or no: not a charm, a subtle interest [*she laughs*]—Just so: you know it; and you triumph in it. Openly and shamelessly triumph in it!
>
> ANN. What a shocking flirt you are, Jack!
>
> TANNER. A flirt!! I!!!

Tanner insults Ann, which makes Ann become offended, which makes Tanner remorseful, which pleases Ann, which makes him cautious, which makes her laugh and call him a flirt, which horrifies him. Drama, unless it is being used primarily to convey plot or theme, calls for constant, successive changes of attitude in the characters. The small changes lead to larger changes—and that is why the mode of drama is usually more revealing of character than other modes are.

Both Frost poems seem to be dramatic, at least typographically, though "The Death of the Hired Man" is set up as a narrative with quotation marks and *said's*, and "The Witch of Coös" as a play with speech-tags instead of quotation marks and *said's*. A large part of both poems is actually narrative, but drama also occurs in the longer, apparently narrative speeches. In "The Death of the Hired Man" there is the conversation reported by Warren, lines 14–24, between himself and Silas; there is also the conversation reported by Mary, lines 79–85, between Silas and Harold Wilson. In "The Witch of Coös" there is the conversation reported by the witch, lines 93–113, between herself and Toffile. Beyond these reported conversations there are the immediate ones between Mary and Warren and between the witch and her son, which are often revealing of character. In "The Death of the Hired Man" the drama sharpens the sympathetic and unsympathetic attitudes toward Silas: " 'Sh! not so loud: he'll hear you,' Mary said. / 'I want him to: he'll have to soon or late.' " (31–32) and " 'Yes, I took care to keep out of earshot.' " (70) As well as:

> "What did he say? Did he say anything?"
> "But little."
>   "Anything? Mary, confess
> He said he'd come to ditch the meadow for me."
> "Warren!"
>   "But did he? I just want to know."
> "Of course he did. What would you have him say . . ." (44–48)

In "The Witch of Coös" this line sharpens the roles of dominance and submissiveness: "We'll never let them, will we, son! We'll never!" (27)

If plot is sequential, character is pretty constant. Once you have an idea of what a character is like she doesn't usually surprise you much. Of course, some characters change in the course of the work, and are therefore called dynamic characters, as opposed to static characters, who do not change. Another interesting distinction is E. M. Forster's between round and flat characters. A round character "is capable of surprising in a convincing way. If it never surprises, it is flat" (*Aspects of the Novel,* ch. iv). At any rate, works in which dynamic or round characters occur would seem to be more character-oriented than works in which only static or flat characters occur, which are more likely to be plot-oriented. In a character-oriented work, what the characters are like remains a continuing question, by means of the changes in character that take place. These changes can be as important as Ryabovitch's decision not to return to the General's house at the end of "The Kiss," or can be as small as the changes of attitude revealed, for instance, in the passage from *Man and Superman* above.

In "The Death of the Hired Man" the major change in character is in Warren's attitude toward Silas. At the beginning he can't be bothered with the nuisance of having Silas around. But after Mary tries to change his mind, "As if she played unheard some tenderness / That wrought on him beside her in the night," he finally reveals a new, more sympathetic attitude toward Silas, as he says in this quietly dramatic climax of the poem: "*I* can't think Si ever hurt anyone." The corresponding passage from "The Witch of Coös" is the one in which the witch finally decides to reveal her secret:

> SON. We think they had a grave down in the cellar.
> MOTHER. We know they had a grave down in the cellar.

SON. We never could find out whose bones they were.
MOTHER. Yes, we could too, son. Tell the truth for once. (135–138)

Of course, changes of character cannot occur unless the author is focusing on a few characters: a smaller cast of characters offers more opening for a stress on character, just as a larger cast does for a stress on plot.

Distinctiveness, rather than typicality, of character also indicates a swing toward character. I mean, of course, literary or artistic distinctiveness; distinctive characters in books may strike you as familiar characters in life, and vice versa. When a distinctive character appears in literature, the reader's first response may be "How lifelike." But such familiar characters in literature as giants and super-heroes are certainly not familiar in life. The question of literary distinctiveness depends on whether such characters have appeared in former literary works. And this distinctiveness is hard to demonstrate, for all characters are somewhat typical: even the witch might be considered rather typical of witches. Distinctiveness of character is then a matter of degree, and is better seen in vivid and novel touches than in a character so immediately distinctive he may not even be recognizably human.

In the Frost poems, Mary and Warren may be a typical farm couple, and Silas a typical stray hired hand; the witch and her son may be typical of a dominant mother and a submissive son. But both poems show vivid touches of characterization. In "The Death of the Hired Man" occurs the following: "I'll sit and see if that small sailing cloud / Will hit or miss the moon" (160–161), which reveals a special tenderness for nature in Mary. Warren's account of how Silas builds a load of hay (88–95) helps characterize both men. In "The Witch of Coös" occur the following: "Mother can make a common table rear / And kick with two legs like an army mule:" (9–10) "I had a vision of them put together / Not like a man, but like a chandelier." (68–69) As in these examples, comparisons are a way of revealing the distinctiveness of the speaker and the one spoken of: one becomes the special kind of character who sees the matter that special way, the other the character the comparison specially applies to.

In balancing the overall significance of character with other elements, the question is, which element governs the others? Do all the derivable traits of character emerge only to keep the plot in motion, or does the plot exist as a slight pretext for getting the character expressed? A work governed by character is Chekhov's "The Kiss." Early in the work Ryabovitch is accidentally kissed in a dark room; but all the plot-possibilities of this coincidence—which might have been exploited by a swashbuckling thriller—never develop, and Chekhov carries Ryabovitch through his dull military routine primarily to see what effect the kiss has on his character. It is almost as if Chekhov is saying: "That coincidence I began with was only the given I needed to show you what my character is like. For imagine a man so shy his first adolescent kiss occurs after he has become an officer, and even then only by accident—a man who could be kissed only by mistake in the dark."

In the Frost poems, the question of the governing element has been partly answered in the discussion of plot above: plot in both poems seems subservient to some other element. The question remains, can the characters be shown to govern the plot? In "The Death of the Hired Man" the plot demands of the characters only the return and death of the hired man to a farm he has formerly worked at; the characters of Mary and Warren, and the change she works on him, are all independent of the plot, though they form something of a plot themselves, which also serves mainly to show what Mary and Warren are like as characters. In "The Witch of Coös" the actions of the apparition (or the witch's imaginings about them) have a certain novelty or intricacy in themselves, but they serve also, perhaps mainly, to show how the witch as a character responds to them; and her recounting of the story brings her to a more honest revelation of the past. The actions of the past are a part of the plot; her willingness to reveal them now is a revelation of her character. If anything, the characters seem to take precedence over the plot in both poems.

There have been numerous attempts, psychological and critical, to list all the possible characters of literature. Frye derives typical characters from classical criticism and ethics. Two of these are the excess and the defect of the Aristotelian virtue of truthfulness—the boaster (*alazon*) and the ironist (*eiron*). The boaster talks at length and enlarges the truth in order to praise himself— he is always less than he appears to be. The ironist keeps silent or minimizes his role in events—he is always more than he seems to be. These characters are, according to Frye, the heroes typical of tragedy (the boaster) and comedy (the ironist)—keeping in mind that the typical may not be readily apparent in individual cases. Two additional characters may be derived, though Frye does not do so, from the excess and the defect of the Aristotelian virtue of courage—the rash man (*thrasys*) and the cowardly (*deilos*), who may serve as the heroes of romance and irony. In tragedy the hero boasts of himself while the source of his doom is an ironic commentator; in comedy the hero minimizes himself while his (or his girlfriend's) parent lords it over him; in romance the hero acts very bravely, perhaps even overacts, while his foe, often very powerful, takes unfair advantage of him; in irony the hero is feeble while the people or forces around him bully and overwhelm him. But all four characters—those who boast more or less than is moderate, and those who act more or less than is moderate—turn up in nearly every plot. In tragedy and comedy, where the over-talker and the under-talker take primary roles, the secondary characters are not so much courageous and cowardly as encouraging or discouraging to the hero. In romance and irony, where the over-doer and under-doer take primary roles, the secondary characters talk to swell or shrink not themselves, but the hero.

These contrasting possibilities of characterization are helpful in trying to see literature as a whole, but they are rarely adequate to given characterizations in a story, play, or poem. When you look at literature from some distance, many works resemble each other and broad classifications of plots and characters seem appropriate; when you look at individual works of literature up close, the most minute distinctions between plots and characters seem more significant. The broad classifications are helpful in getting a start on more detailed analysis of character.

In "The Death of the Hired Man" it's clear that the conversation between Mary and Warren is one between encourager and discourager, while the contest between Silas and Harold Wilson, however abbreviated, is one between boaster and ironist. In "The Witch of Coös" it's clear that the witch is rash compared with the ghost, and boastful compared with her son; and Toffile is discourager, if not coward. Because both plots or poems are ironic, however, all the characters seem relatively helpless in their environments, and none of the characters are pure representatives of their types but more like mocking imitations of their originals in tragedy or romance or comedy.

Theme

Here's another of those fragmentary sketches from Kafka's diaries. It's a story, or something like a story. See what you can make of it. (The word "singular" means odd or peculiar, a good word for this fragment.)

(July 22,1916)

A singular judicial procedure. The condemned man is stabbed to death in his cell by the executioner without any other person being permitted to be present. He is seated at the table finishing a letter or his last meal. A knock is heard, it is the executioner.

"Are you ready?" he asks. The content and sequence of his questions and actions are fixed for him by regulation, he cannot depart from it. The condemned man, who at first jumped up, now sits down again and stares straight before him or buries his face in his hands. Having received no reply, the executioner opens his instrument case on the cot, chooses the daggers and even now attempts to touch up their several edges here and there. It is very dark by now, he sets up a small lantern and lights it. The condemned man furtively turns his head toward the executioner, but shudders when he sees what he is doing, turns away again and has no desire to see more.

"Ready," the executioner says after a little while.

"Ready?" screams the condemned man, jumps up and now, however, looks directly at the executioner. "You're not going to kill me, not going to put me down on the cot and stab me to death, you're a human being after all, you can execute someone on a scaffold, with assistants and in the presence of magistrates, but not here in this cell, one man killing another!" And when the executioner, bent over his case, says nothing, the condemned man adds, more quietly: "It is impossible." And when the executioner even now says nothing, the condemned man goes on to say: "This singular judicial procedure was instituted just because it is impossible. The form is to be preserved, but the death penalty itself is no longer carried out. You will take me to another jail; I shall probably have to stay there a long time, but they will not execute me."

The executioner loosens a new dagger from its cotton sheath and says: "You are probably thinking of those fairy tales in which a servant is commanded to expose a child but does not do so and instead binds him over as apprentice to a shoemaker. Those are fairy tales; this, though, is not a fairy tale."—

Again put down your observations and questions and think about these questions too.

1. Note the pronouns and verbs here. The pronouns are those we would expect of a story, but what about the verbs? What is the effect of that choice of tense? Is this a story about one condemned man and one executioner, or about any, a generalized, condemned man and his executioner? Note that he is "finishing a letter or his last meal." If an individual man is intended, wouldn't we learn which of these he was doing—surely not both, at the moment of the executioner's knock? Note also "stares straight before him or buries his face in his hands." Wouldn't an individual man be doing just one of these? Do we seem to be learning how several such men have behaved or might behave? What is the effect of such generalizing? If the "condemned man" is any such man or many such men, are we to assume that the ensuing conversation occurs every single time? Note that the piece begins by calling itself a "procedure," and that "the content and sequence" of the executioner's questions "are fixed for him by regulation." If this piece isn't a story, what do you want to call it, a "procedure," or what?

2. Look more closely at the conversation. If you recall the conversation in the story about the landlady and lodger, does this conversation resemble theirs at all? Are the speakers here speaking out of their individual, personal relationship toward each other, or according to their assigned, generalized roles as condemned man and executioner? Has what they say to do with them as individuals or as types? Note the condemned man's protest against the "singular judicial procedure" and apparently also against the entire "death penalty." Note also the unsympathetic, or brutal, response to his objection.

3. What about the odd procedure? If such an impossible procedure were ever possible, how would it differ from any other kind of execution you have heard of? Does this look more like ordinary murder? Why is it in private, and individually performed, instead of the expected public and ceremonial execution? How does the public and societal ceremony seem to carry more of a moral sanction—to excuse the society from blame for the execution? How does this account insist that we look upon a society's presumption in judging or executing anyone?

4. What was the condemned man's crime? If "he" is any condemned man, presumably his crime could have been almost any. Does the omission of any mention of guilt in the condemned man suggest he may be innocent, that he might almost be any one of us? Would we take a more kindly attitude toward the executioner and the society that puts him up to it if we knew that the condemned man was guilty of murder or treason?

5. Apart from his disbelief in the nature of his execution and his protest against it, which we would certainly expect from anyone in his position, do you see any signs of individuality in the condemned man? Or what about his story? Can we surmise anything about his life before he got to this point? And what would be the ending of his story? Do you think it possible that a servant will somehow find a way to spare him, as in a fairy tale?

6. What does the account do to our possible belief or disbelief in a "death penalty," or capital punishment? Does the account permit us to continue thinking, "Well, for certain capital offenses, no punishment can be too inhumane?" Or is the story primarily set up to undermine a belief in capital punishment? Note that the tense of the story suggests an ongoing, existing procedure—are we going to let it continue? True, most capital punishment isn't this bad, but doesn't it amount to murder, and does any society have a right to murder?

For a creative response, continue this account for a while, probing the meaning of condemnation and punishment a little further. Or do a completely new procedure—slightly fantastic, like this one—which gives us a new insight on some commonly accepted practice in society.

□   □   □

Aristotle says theme is found wherever characters "show that something is or is not, or declare something general" (ch. 6); or you might call it all the general implications of the work. The word *theme* is also used in English for the subject of a work, as the death of a hired man and the haunting of a ghost are subjects. In this discussion theme refers only to the general ideas of literature. Aristotle, instead of defining theme, tells where it is found, as if it's easier to locate than to define. At least it's easy to locate the general statements in an otherwise particular work. Mary says, "How some things linger!" (72). She has been talking about Silas's recollections, but now it is clear she is talking about recollections in general for anyone. A few lines later she says, "I know just how it feels / To think of the right thing to say too late" (76–77). That is how Silas feels and how she feels, but again it's a statement generally true for anyone.

One sign of emphasis on theme is extensiveness of reverie, for works largely reflective are likely to prove thematic. But even in works extensively reflective, theme is not necessarily the most prominent element, for reverie can also render both plot and character. Since the general passages in a work are as easy to locate as the reflective ones, it's probably wiser to begin by locating them. In "The Death of the Hired Man," in addition to the statements above, the most notable general passage is this one near the ending:

> "Home is the place where, when you have to go there,
> They have to take you in."
>   "I should have called it
> Something you somehow haven't to deserve." (118–120)

These are two different definitions of home; while they help also to characterize the speakers, Warren and Mary, they are purely general statements. The discussion is no longer about Silas or about their farm in particular: the "you" refers to anyone; the "home" to any home. In "The Witch of Coös" the most prominent general passage in this one coming near the beginning:

> He said the dead had souls, but when I asked him
> How that could be—I thought the dead were souls,
> He broke my trance. Don't that make you suspicious
> That there's something the dead are keeping back?
> Yes, there's something the dead are keeping back. (14–18)

These general statements serve as hypotheses the apparition seems to come to prove. Again the passage is general: "the dead" refers not simply to the dead lover (he hasn't yet been mentioned) but to all the dead. General statements can be differentiated from particular ones by the use of plural nouns, as here, instead of singular ones, or by *a, any* preceding nouns, instead of *the, this;* by the indefinite *you, one, we;* and by the general or indefinite present tense, as in all the examples above.

Another sign of emphasis on theme is a certain prompting in the way the work is written, by discussion among the characters or by the apparent urging of the author behind them, towards the question, "What is the author getting at?" or "What should I conclude in general?" as you are reading. Many students read works of literature this way almost exclusively, as if every story, play, or poem were trying to be an essay arguing opinions. Two cautions need to be offered: first, to be sure to discover whatever themes a work expresses or suggests; second, to be sure that all other elements are given their full weight in the total ensemble of the work. Though all literary works can be shown by analysis to suggest ideas, many—I might even safely say most—are not primarily thematic. It's a very lopsided kind of analysis that looks for themes to the exclusion of other elements.

In the two Frost poems, as in all literary works, there would be some expression of ideas even if there were no general passages at all. Nor is it wise to assume that the prominent general passage of a work automatically expresses the theme of the work. It may or may not be the best statement of the overall theme. Is the whole point of "The Death of the Hired Man" to arrive at a satisfactory definition of home, and of "The Witch of Coös" to prove that the dead may have a physical state? These would seem rather trivial goals. The question is, how much are you wondering what the author is getting at even in the particular or concrete passages? Certainly "The Death of the Hired Man" seems to be raising a question about what responsibility relative strangers have to act as their brothers' keepers, and "The Witch of Coös" seems to be asking what responsibility sinners have toward those they have sinned against.

Theme, like character, does not change in the course of the work as markedly as does the plot, but a certain emphasis on theme may be shown by an important change of opinion occurring in a work. In fact, one sign of emphasis on theme is that the ideas of the work are not pat but are kept alive by questioning them throughout the work. In "The Death of the Hired Man" Warren comes round somewhat to Mary's opinion, and the witch no longer sees any reason to hide her sins. These are concrete changes of character, but they also have general implications. Such significant changes of opinion, which reflect on both character and theme, are likely to come near the end of a work.

Another sign of emphasis on theme is the author's suggestion that single characters stand not just for themselves but for a larger class of people like themselves; the larger the class the character represents the more general the applicability of the story. Aristotle observes that poetry is more philosophical than history (ch. 9)—suggesting that it's more general or abstract than history; but Frye adds that it's also more historical than philosophy. This puts literature in the central or paradoxical position between history and philosophy sometimes called the "concrete universal": it offers concrete examples with general implications. Of course, all characters are partly distinctive and partly typical and may seem different from different perspectives: Mary may seem more typical as a wife than as a hostess of hired men; the witch may seem more typical as a sweetheart and wife than as a hostess of apparitions.

The major question for determining the emphasis on theme is the same as that for plot and character: namely, which elements are subservient to which other element or elements? How conveniently do plot and character serve to illustrate a fairly clearcut theme? Suppose the point of "The Death of the Hired Man" had been the rewards of brotherly love, and Mary and Warren had found a million dollars on the dead man. Suppose the point of "The Witch of Coös" had been the punishment of murder and the skeleton had killed the witch's baby. Then the plot would have been clearly contrived in order to justify the neat thematic conclusion, and plot would clearly be working in the service of theme. If plot and theme are not so neatly tied, does the theme, such as it is, issue from the spontaneous and independent development of plot and character? If so, one of those two elements would take precedence over theme. In the two Frost poems, there is undoubtedly some thematic interest, but in both theme seems in the end subservient to character.

The themes of literature are usually ethical (from *ethos* or character)—related, that is, to the arts and sciences of human nature: politics, psychology, sociology, anthropology, economics, history, and ethics itself, the study of the moral choices humans make in their relationships with each other. Excluded would be the exact sciences, where opinion is of little importance compared with fact; opinions on how to live your life are always subject to argument, to varying viewpoints, and so to literary exemplification. Aristotle, instead of giving any elaborations of theme in his *Poetics,* refers the reader to his *Rhetoric* (ch. 19), where he treats general arguments and opinions more fully. Some, but not many, literary works can be studied as examples of orations or demonstrations of opinions; the more theme governs plot and character the more you would be tempted to call a given work philosophical rather than literary. In fact, one way to differentiate literature from philosophy is to restrict literature to works in which plot and character are of at least equal importance with the theme. Questions of theme may be fascinating in showing how literature opens out into the world of ideas at large, but readers and critics who pursue ideas should remember that they are getting further and further away from the work as a work of literature.

Frye observes that the plot or myth a writer has chosen, or habitually chooses, will to a large extent determine the themes his works express. Tragedy will be full of gloom and catastrophe and its characters, especially toward the end, will stand around talking about the uncertainties of happiness and the inescapability of fate. Comedy will be full of pleasantly unexpected good fortune, especially toward the end, and its characters will stand around talking about miraculous discoveries and harmonies, and the gratitude and joy we feel for the mercies life provides us. Romantic plots are not usually as expressive of theme, for the interest of the reader will be caught up mainly in the adventures themselves as they come along so quickly; but the romantic plot as a whole will urge a heroic view of life, will urge ordinary readers to measure themselves against super-heroes and super-struggles. The ironic or satiric plot, in contrast to the romantic, urges an unheroic or anti-heroic view of life, forcing readers to see themselves as feeble puppets in an absurd and apparently purposeless universe.

In order to locate precisely all the passages in a given work expressive of theme, you might now reconsider the rhetorical modes of literature and note as a refinement on the study of theme four additional modes which are parallel to those mentioned above in the section on rhetorical analysis. The surface of literature is normally concrete or particular, in the modes of description, narration, drama, or reverie; but when general passages occur in a work, its surface may be general or abstract, in the modes of definition, process, dialogue, or persuasion. In order to illustrate these modes I cite over the next few pages brief passages from the Frost poems, and slightly fuller ones from "Poetry," an essay by E. B. White (born 1899).

Definition is abstract description, or discourse structurally the same as description, in which the terms are abstract instead of concrete. The formula of static equations is common to both modes, to concrete descriptions and to such abstract definitions as, Home is "Something you somehow haven't to deserve." Here is a passage of definition from White:

> There are many types of poetical obscurity. There is the obscurity that results from the poet's being mad. This is rare. Madness in poets is as uncommon as madness in dogs. A discouraging number of reputable poets are sane beyond recall. There is also the obscurity that is the result of the poet's wishing to appear mad, even if only a little mad. This is rather common and rather dreadful. I know of nothing more distasteful than the work of a poet who has taken leave of his reason deliberately, as a commuter might of his wife.

White is defining and distinguishing between two types of poetical obscurity. Notice how, as in description, almost every verb is a form of *to be,* and the result is static, not moving. But the terms between the verbs here are all general or abstract, instead of concrete. The passage closes with a rather concrete analogy.

Process is abstract narration, or discourse structurally the same as narration, in which the terms are abstract instead of concrete. The formula, "I hit him, then she ran in," is common to both modes, except that process is usually in the indefinite present tense, while narration is in the past. A temporal formula is the basis of concrete narration and of such abstract processes as "when you have to go there / They have to take you in." Here is a passage of process from White:

> Sometimes a poet becomes so completely absorbed in the lyrical possibilities of certain combinations of sounds that he forgets what he started out to say, if anything, and here again a nasty tangle results. This type of obscurity is one that I have great sympathy for: I know that quite frequently in the course of delivering himself of a poem a poet will find himself in possession of a lyric bauble—a line as smooth as velvet to the ear, as pretty as a feather to the eye, yet a line definitely out of plumb with the frame of the poem. What to do with a trinket like this is always troubling to a poet, who is naturally grateful to his Muse for small favors. Usually he just drops the shining object into the body of the poem somewhere and hopes it won't look too giddy.

White is going on to define another type of poetical obscurity, as he indicates at the beginning of the second sentence. But otherwise he is considering the process of writing a poem as a source of one type of obscurity. The development of the passage is chronological as in narration, but the poet, the "he," is not a particular person, but the general concept of any poet. In the middle of the passage White again includes some concreteness—two similes and the metaphor ("plumb . . . frame").

Philosophic dialogue, or dialectic, is abstract drama, or discourse structurally the same as drama, in which the terms are abstract instead of concrete.

The sentence-by-sentence conflicts of repetition, switch of person, question
and answer, and disagreement are common to both modes, to concrete drama
and to such abstract dialogue as the combination of the two sentences just
quoted, showing disagreement:

> "Home is the place where, when you have to go there,
> They have to take you in."
>   "I should have called it
> Something you somehow haven't to deserve."

Here is a passage of dialogue from White:

> "I wish poets could be clearer," shouted my wife angrily from the next
> room.
>   Hers is a universal longing. We would all like it if the bards would
> make themselves plain, or we think we would. The poets, however, are
> not easily diverted from their high mysterious ways. A poet dares be just
> so clear and no clearer; he approaches lucid ground warily, like a mariner
> who is determined not to scrape his bottom on anything solid. A poet's
> pleasure is to withhold a little of his meaning, to intensify by mystifica-
> tion. He unzips the veil from beauty, but does not remove it. A poet
> utterly clear is a trifle glaring.

The dialogue between husband and wife is only partly reported; the husband's
answer is restated. Still it is clear that the first two sentences of his comment
are in agreement with her, are elaborations of what she has said. The third
sentence introduces his answer to her—his disagreement with her, as the word
"however" indicates—which is elaborated in the rest of the passage. Again he
includes a concrete simile ("mariner . . . bottom"), and a metaphor ("unzips
the veil"). Apart from those, the subject and the terms are all general or abstract, and the anger of his wife is directed at the general subject. If she had
been angry at her husband, drama might have resulted instead of general dialogue.
    Persuasion is abstract reverie, or discourse structurally the same as rever-
ie in which the terms are abstract instead of concrete. The syllogism is the
basic structure of both, but is stricter in persuasion, more haphazard in reverie. In the following example the first two lines are reported dialogue, but the
relationship between them and the following lines is syllogistic, or "if—then"
reasoning.

> He said the dead had souls, but when I asked him
> How could that be—I thought the dead were souls,
> He broke my trance. Don't that make you suspicious
> That there's something the dead are keeping back?
> Yes, there's something the dead are keeping back.

In syllogistic form it might run: if the dead cannot be said to be souls but to
have souls, then they must have something other than souls, perhaps bodies or

skeletons. The last line in the passage might be called a thesis, a position or case to be argued—a term often used interchangeably with "theme," but is normally restricted to the main idea of essays or abstract works of non-fiction in which theme overwhelms any lurking plots or characters.

Below is a passage of persuasion from White. In it, he mentions two poets not so well known today. Edgar Guest (1881–1959) was a widely popular poet syndicated in many newspapers, whose simple verses expressed folksy and sentimental ideas. His most famous sentence: "It takes a heap o' livin' in a house t' make it home." Gertrude Stein (1874–1946) was an experimental poet whose writing was to many readers bafflingly repetitive. Her most famous sentence: "A rose is a rose is a rose is a rose."

> Some poets are naturally clearer than others. To achieve great popularity or great fame it is of some advantage to be either extremely clear (like Edgar Guest) or thoroughly opaque (like Gertrude Stein). The first poet in the land—if I may use the word poet loosely—is Edgar Guest. He is the singer who, more than any other, gives to Americans the enjoyment of rhyme and meter. Whether he gives also to any of his satisfied readers that blinding, aching emotion that I get from reading certain verses by other writers is a question that interests me very much. Being democratic, I am content to have the majority rule in everything, it would seem, but literature.

White is differentiating between clear and opaque poets, but not simply to define them. He pretends at first to offer a formula for success, which is a kind of persuasive recommendation. Later he suggests that only poets who give a "blinding, aching emotion" should be considered great; and he closes by denying any democratic majority the right to rule in literature—his persuasive thesis. In syllogistic form the passage might run: since the poets best known and liked by the majority are not the best poets, the majority cannot be allowed to rule in literature.

Sound

We return to Emily Dickinson. Here are two of her best known and best loved poems: one about how she gets drunk on air, the other about how she loves to watch the railroad train. The drinking poem has a few references that may be unusual to you: "inebriate" and "debauchee" are words for drunkard; the last stanza anticipates the speaker's arrival in heaven. In the poem about the train, "prodigious" means impressive, great, marvelous; "supercilious" means haughty or disdainful. Boanerges is a loud-voiced preacher, literally "sons of thunder." "Docile" and "omnipotent" are almost opposite in meaning: "docile"—humble, yielding; "omnipotent"—all powerful.

(214)

I taste a liquor never brewed—
From Tankards scooped in Pearl—
Not all the Vats upon the Rhine
Yield such an Alcohol!

Inebriate of Air—am I—   5
And Debauchee of Dew—
Reeling—thro endless summer days—
From inns of Molten Blue—

When "Landlords" turn the drunken Bee
Out of the Foxglove's door—   10
When Butterflies—renounce their "drams"—
I shall but drink the more!

Till Seraphs swing their snowy Hats—
And Saints—to windows run—
To see the little Tippler   15
Leaning against the—Sun—

(585)

I like to see it lap the Miles—
And lick the Valleys up—
And stop to feed itself at Tanks—
And then—prodigious step

Around a Pile of Mountains—   5
And supercilious peer
In Shanties—by the sides of Roads—
And then a Quarry pare

To fit its Ribs
And crawl between   10
Complaining all the while
In horrid—hooting stanza—
Then chase itself down Hill—

And neigh like Boanerges—
Then—punctual as a Star   15
Stop—docile and omnipotent
At its own stable door—

Put down any observations you have to make on these poems. Think also
about these questions.

1. Do you see any signs of "story" in either poem? Is there a progression
   about the happy drunkard who finally arrives, admired by all, in heav-

en? Is there a story of the train going through its various adventures and then arriving home? What about ideas here? Does either poem prove anything? Is there an implied moral to either poem? Drink air, if you must drink? Since machines have come out so impressively, let's get all the pleasure from them we can? What about characterization? Isn't the first poem largely a self-characterization—of the person who takes such joy in nature? Isn't the second poem also, though less directly, a self-characterization, of the person who loves to watch such a show?

2. You won't see much of narration here, but what about description? See if you can add up all the descriptive details in both poems, though we could hardly say either poem aims chiefly to describe a scene at rest. What about conversation—is the poet talking to anyone, or is anyone answering her? Aren't we left with what we usually find in poems, the poet expressing thoughts and reflections?

3. Think about comparisons in these poems. Why are the tankards she drinks from in her imagination "scooped in Pearl"—what could that mean? In the middle section of the poem, note the series of expressions comparing herself to a drunkard reeling home from an inn. The bee and butterflies are also drunkards, but the bee has been "bounced" or turned out the door and the butterflies have renounced their "drams"—or given up their portions of drink—while she still drinks. In that final stanza, when the residents of heaven come to the window and swing their hats to celebrate her arrival, she is leaning like a drunkard, not against a wall or door, but the sun. In the second poem, she compares the train extensively to a horse—note all the terms by which she does so. That word "stanza" also makes of the train, or the horse, something of a poet, hooting out its verses.

4. Now consider the music of these poems. See if you can tap out their rhythm—it's the same in both poems, and very regularly kept up, with a few exceptions. If you are measuring out the rhythm carefully, you will see that you are missing a beat after the words "Tippler," "Mountains," "Stanza," and "Boanerges"—pronounced BO - an - ER - ges. Is the rhythm of these poems one you know? Clue: many nursery rhymes are in this rhythm—try "The queen of hearts" or "Mary had a little lamb." You may know the song "The yellow rose of Texas" (though not its words); see if you can "sing" a few stanzas in that tune. All in all, what is the effect of this rhythm, quite apart from any meaning the words put into it might have? Do you get a rollicking, joyous sense of bounce as you listen to it, very appropriate to the joyous content of these two poems? Would it be appropriate for poems expressing sad or grim thoughts? Think of some of the entries from Kafka—would it do to put some of those thoughts in stanzas like these? Think, for instance, of the entry about Kafka's potential suicide, which is structurally very similar to "I taste a liquor never brewed," ending up with an anticipation of the

effect of his arrival and actions at a house—would anyone want to put those thoughts in this bouncing rhythm? Don't the stanzas, by their sound effects, seem to demand a certain delight in the contents of them?

For a creative response, see if you can add a stanza in the same rhythm to either poem. Or do a new poem, expressive of some special pleasure you take in nature, or in watching some machine going through its actions.

□   □   □

Aristotle says that the sense of song-making (*melopoiia*) is perfectly clear, and then he drops the subject (ch. 6). He implies that it is what musicians add to a musical stage-show, but I take sound as a literary element to be everything the ear hears, apart from what the mind understands, however "musical" or "unmusical" it may seem. You might say sound is what you would hear at a recitation or chanting of a literary work in a language you didn't know. Even if you were hearing it for the first time, you could probably tell the difference between regular progressions of sound, or verse, and irregular progressions of sound, or prose. These definitions of verse and prose are quite different from the typographical ones I gave above under formal anlaysis. Verse has an uneven right margin in print because it's broken into separate lines according to its measurements of sound. An apparent exception is "free verse," which appears to be as irregular as prose from the standpoint of sound but is nonetheless printed in broken lines. Some might call it prose in arbitrarily broken lines; others might insist that no verse is really "free," but governed by sound effects other than those usually recognized.

As literary elements, both plot and sound are concerned with rhythmic progressions in time. Nowadays storytellers are not so often singers as silent writers, but their stories are no less based on "musical" development of plot. Naturally, both dramatic and lyric works can emphasize sound considerably, but it is the epic or narrative poet, in modern as in ancient times, who best captivates his audience's ear in time. The modern media of movies and television distort this emphasis somewhat, for we often hear plays and songs recited or sung out loud, but not stories, except around campfires.

Whether speaking, chanting, or singing, the human voice can differentiate according to quality (formation of sounds in the mouth), volume (loud or soft), pitch (high or low), tempo (fast or slow), and duration of sound or silence (long or short). Though every language, and every speaker, makes use of all of these variations somehow, verse may be measured by exploiting some and disregarding others. Classical poetry counts primarily on duration, modern English poetry on volume; quality counts hardly at all in classical poetry, but has taken on considerable importance in modern languages. Though modern English speech (including poetry) uses both pitch and duration, poetry takes no special notice of them; it counts only on volume and quality.

Whatever a particular poetry or poem may be like, the basic unit of most verse is the syllable, or a sound made by one opening of the mouth, composed of a vowel, an open or free sound, and whatever consonants, or constricted sounds, surround it. Other units of meaning or grammar, such as the word or phrase or sentence, have no metrical status unless they somehow influence the number of syllables, the loudness or softness of them, and the quality of sounds in the syllables. In reading a poem for purposes of scansion, or analysis of its sound-effects, you must in fact train yourself to disregard grammar and meaning temporarily in order to hear the sound alone, syllable by syllable. The larger units of sound—feet, or brief gatherings of syllables, and lines, or longer gatherings of syllables—are not entirely reliable as basic units of measurement. Some verse is devised entirely according to arrangements of syllables—Japanese, French, and some modern syllabic poetry in English. But in most verse the syllable is the basic unit in determining meters, or ideal arrangements of syllables. Rhythm, or actual arrangements of syllables, at most approximates meter.

In order to begin hearing some of the typical sounds of poetry in English, consider the following poem. Read it aloud several times as you would to a child, possibly stressing the rhythm with movements of the hand or arm.

The queen of hearts
She made some tarts
All on a summer's day.

The knave of hearts
He stole the tarts,
And took them clean away.

The king of hearts
Called for the tarts
And beat the knave full sore.

The knave of hearts
Brought back the tarts
And vow'd he'd steal no more.

If you're still having trouble, try it this way:

The QUEEN of HEARTS
She MADE some TARTS
ALL on a SUM-mer's DAY.

The KNAVE of HEARTS
He STOLE the TARTS
And TOOK them CLEAN a-WAY.

Repeat these lines until you sense their rhythm. You will have learned one of the most basic rhythms of English poetry, often called "common measure," "common meter," "ballad stanza," or "fourteeners"—note that each stanza has fourteen syllables. Common measure has eight syllables or four feet (a foot in this case having two syllables) followed by six syllables or three feet, with the even syllables stressed—2, 4, 6, 8, etc. Frequently common measure is set up in print as four-foot lines alternating with three-foot lines, and the short lines rhyme, as in the poem above: "day" and "away," and "sore" and "more." Actually, "The queen of hearts" has additional rhymes which seem to split the four-foot line into two lines of two feet each: "hearts" and "tarts." You might note a few exceptions to the meter in the rhythm of the poem: "All on" and "Called for" and "Brought back" have a loud first syllable though the meter calls for a loud second syllable; in "Brought back" the two syllables are about equally loud or stressed. Two such loud syllables together make up a unit called a "spondee."

If you're having a hard time telling how many syllables there are in words, and which of them are louder or softer, you can test yourself on longer words by guessing and then looking up the words in a dictionary which divides the words into syllables and indicates which are louder or stressed. If eventually you can improve your guesses at least on the number of syllables, you might try saying the word (aloud or to yourself), making each syllable in turn extra loud—and choosing whichever distortion is least wrong-sounding. For instance, the word "literature" has four syllables—lit-er-a-ture—and its first and last syllables are louder than the middle two. The word "analysis" also has four syllables—a-nal-y-sis—and its second and fourth are louder than the first and third. For purposes of scansion, of determining and marking syllables as soft or loud, stressed (or loud) syllables are marked ´ and unstressed (or soft) syllables are marked ˘. For instance: ă nál y̆ sís ŏf lít ĕr ă túre.

Here is another familiar poem in "common measure," scanned:

Máry̆ hád ă líttlĕ lámb
    Ĭts fleéce wăs whíte ăs snów;
Ănd éverȳwhére thăt Máry̆ wént
    Thĕ lámb wăs súre tŏ gó.

Ĭf fóllŏwed hér tŏ schoól ŏne dáy
    Whĭch wás ăgaínst thĕ rúle;
Ĭt máde thĕ chíldrĕn laúgh ănd pláy,
    Tŏ sée ă lámb ăt schoól.

This poem is normally printed as here in two stanzas, or recurring, similarly shaped gatherings of lines—here two quatrains (four-line stanzas), with the second and fourth lines rhyming: "snow" and "go" and "rule" and "school." The second stanza also introduces a rhyme between the first and third lines: "day" and "play." Note that the first line of this poem seems to be missing its first soft syllable; the beginning of a poem, or stanza, or line, often distorts the meter slightly.

The terms used for English meters are Greek, where they were used for differences of duration, alternations of short or long syllables. In English these terms are used for differences of volume, alternations of soft and loud syllables. Iambic, a soft syllable followed by a loud one, is the commonest conversational meter for both verse and prose. It is often observed that all English prose is basically iambic, and when Frost says that English has virtually but two meters, strict iambic and loose iambic ("The Figure a Poem Makes"), he includes almost all English discourse, whether in prose or verse. In English verse, iambs usually run three or four or five to the line—iambic trimeter, iambic tetrameter, and iambic pentameter—or an iambic sequence with the end of a line coming every six, eight, or ten syllables or so.

The next meter, trochaic, is only iambic reversed, a loud syllable followed by a soft one; a line of trochaic is an iambic line with the first, soft syllable moved to the end, or replaced by a pause. In the next poem the first two lines are trochaic and the third and fourth are iambic; the two meters combine very easily.

> Pétĕr, Pétĕr, púmpkĭn-eátĕr,
> Hád ă wífe ănd couldn't keép hĕr.
> Hĕ pút hĕr ĭn ă púmpkĭn shéll,
> Ănd thére hĕ képt hĕr vérў wéll.

This poem makes a quatrain or two couplets (pairs of rhyming lines). Note that the rhyme in the first couplet is not quite exact: "eater" and "keep her." A perfect rhyme would be between "eater" and "beat her." The approximate rhyme is called a half-rhyme or a "slant" rhyme; (I have also called it a "near" or "partial" rhyme.) Note that in the third line the word "in," according to the meter, calls for a stress; but most readers would not stress that word, unless they were beating out the meter for a child. Little irregularities in the rhythmic or actual approximation of the ideal meter are common in both children's poetry and in poetry for adults.

Other than iambic and trochaic, the only meters that occur—and not very commonly—in English are groupings of three syllables each. In dactyllic meter, a first loud syllable is followed by two soft ones, as in the first line below:

> Dáffў-dŏwn-díllў hăs cóme ŭp tŏ tówn
> Iń ă yéllŏw péttĭcoăt ănd ă greén gówn.

The second line is not as regular as the first. Instead of the first dactyl it seems to have two trochees. Also the word "green" would probably be loud, though the meter calls for a soft syllable. If this poem is to be considered a dactyllic couplet, with four feet to the line, note also that the last dactyl of each line has its two weak syllables missing—replaced by rests or pauses, perhaps.

The fourth meter is anapestic, a grouping of two soft syllables followed by a third loud one. The next poem is largely anapestic.

Thĕre wás ăn ŏld wómăn whŏ líved ĭn ă shoé
Shĕ hád sŏ mánў chíldrĕn shé dídn˘t knŏw whát tŏ dó.
Shĕ gáve thĕm sŏme bróth wĭthoút ănў breád;
Shĕ whípped thĕm ăll sóundlў ănd pút thĕm tŏ béd.

This poem is anapestic, except that the first foot of every line is iambic instead of anapestic. Otherwise lines one, three, and four are anapestic except for a missing syllable (replaced by a pause) after "broth." Lines one and four have eleven syllables (count them) and line three has ten. But the second line is very irregular and has extra syllables adding up to a total of fourteen syllables. The pattern of four stresses to a line would probably give us as the loudest syllables "had," "child-," "did-," "do." Where we expect two soft syllables, according to the meter, we have three—"so many"—or four—"n't know what to," and we would probably also stress the word "what."

Mother Goose poems, in fact, seem to combine the various meters without much difficulty. In a poem like the following, the analyst might be puzzled to determine which meter is the primary one:

Líttlĕ Jăck Hórnĕr
Sát ĭn ă córnĕr
Eátĭng ă Chrístmăs pié.

Hĕ pút ĭn hĭs thúmb
Ănd púlled oŭt ă plúm,
Ănd criéd, "Whăt ă goód bŏy ăm Í."

The first two lines of this poem are made up of one dactyl and one trochee. The third line is the same with an added loud syllable at the end, which might be considered the beginning of another trochee or a dactyl with its soft syllable(s) replaced by a pause. The last three lines seem to switch to iambic and anapestic; lines 4 and 5 have one iamb followed by one anapest. The last line has an iamb followed by two anapests. The extra syllables in the last line seem to insure that the poem will close with a bang; most readers would raise their voices there. Note also that this poem seems to be a variation on the "common measure," the basic pattern of a four-stress line followed by a three-stress line, with extra syllables and rhymes thrown in here and there.

Some students may be able to sense meters better by a musical analysis of verses into "measures," or roughly equal units of time. In the chart below, some familiar verses are broken down into roughly equal measures, four to a line, with stresses coming at the end or beginning of each measure. Note that when many syllables are combined into a measure, there is a tendency to rush them in, and that when measures are lacking some syllables, pauses or "rests" occur.

'Twăs thĕ níght	bĕfŏre Chríst	măs whĕn áll	throŭgh thĕ hoúse
Nŏt ă creá	tŭre wăs stír	ríng nŏt ĕ́	vĕn ă moúse
thĕ stóck	ĭngs wĕre húng	bў̆ thĕ chím	nĕy wĭth cáre
ĭn hópes	thăt Sĭ́. Ních	ŏ lăs soón	woŭld bĕ thére

Líttlĕ Mĭss	Múf fĕt shĕ	sát ŏn ă	túffĕt
éatīng ŏf	cúrds ănd	whéy;	thĕre
cáme ă bĭg	spí dĕr whŏ	sát dŏwn bĕ	síde hĕr ănd
fríghtĕned Mĭss	Múf fĕt ă	wáy	

Óne	twó	búcklĕ mў̆	shoé
threé	foúr	shút thĕ	doór
fíve	síx	pĭck ŭp	stícks
sé vĕn	eíght	láy thĕm	straíght
níne	tén ă	bíg fát	hén

Threé	blínd	míce	
Seé	hów thĕy	rún	thĕy
áll rŭn	áf tĕr thĕ	fár mĕr's	wífe whŏ
cút ŏff theĭr	taíls wĭth ă	cár vĭng	knífe dĭd yoŭ
ĕ́ vĕr	seé sŭch ă	síght ĭn yoŭr	lífe ăs
threé	blínd	míce	

Beyond the "common measure," the most common arrangements of lines in English are couplets (pairs of rhyming lines) and quatrains (four-line units with the even lines rhyming and often the odd ones too). "Peter, Peter, pumpkin eater" may be considered two couplets or one quatrain with lines one and two and lines three and four rhyming. But sophisticated poets have often used stanzas of five, six, or even more lines. Frost's "Dust of Snow" is a poem in two quatrains, in iambic dimeter, or two iambs to the line, rhyming *abab*—that is, the odd lines rhyme and also the even ones.

> The way a crow
> Shook down on me
> The dust of snow
> From a hemlock tree
>
> Has given my heart
> A change of mood
> And saved some part
> Of a day I had rued.

"A Mood Apart" is also in two quatrains, though not usually so printed, primarily in iambic tetrameter, or four iambs to the line, also rhyming *abab*.

> Once down on my knees to growing plants
> I prodded the earth with a lazy tool

In time with a medley of sotto chants;
But becoming aware of some boys from school
Who had stopped outside the fence to spy
I stopped my song and almost heart,
For any eye is an evil eye
That looks in on to a mood apart.

Both these poems have extra syllables here and there. Try to scan the poems
with the marks ´ and ˘ and see if you can find the extra syllables.

Beyond these patterns of stanzas, the most common short metrical arrangement in English is the sonnet, of which you have already had an example
in Frost's "Design." Here it is again: this time see if you can scan it, mark all
its syllables as loud or soft; and see if you can note all the rhymes, using the
alphabetical system *ab,* etc.

I found a dimpled spider, fat and white,
On a white heal-all, holding up a moth
Like a white piece of rigid satin cloth—
Assorted characters of death and blight
Mixed ready to begin the morning right,
Like the ingredients of a witches' broth—
A snow-drop spider, a flower like a froth,
And dead wings carried like a paper kite.

What had that flower to do with being white,
The wayside blue and innocent heal-all?
What brought the kindred spider to that height,
Then steered the white moth thither in the night?
What but design of darkness to appall?—
If design govern in a thing so small.

Note that the rhyme-scheme seems to bind together the octave, or first eight
lines (perhaps as two quatrains), and the sestet or last six lines.

Longer poems in English, such as "The Death of the Hired Man" and
the "The Witch of Coös," are often in what is called "blank verse," or lines of
about ten syllables in iambic pentameter, or five iambs to the line—called
"blank" because it usually has no rhymes.

On hearing or reading these two longer Frost poems for the first time
you might be aware of blank verse, though Frost's blank verse is often close to
prose. The first sign to look for in determining the emphasis of sound as an
element in a work is the sound calling some special attention to itself. If the
poem is in blank verse, sound calls the least possible attention to itself without being prose or free verse. If, as occasionally in blank verse, you find rhyme
here and there along the way or at the close, sound calls a little more attention
to itself than the minimal sound effect of blank verse.

Besides arrangements in volume, then, English and other modern poetry counts on arrangements of quality, mainly those of rhyme, or like endings, and alliteration, or like beginnings. More precisely, rhyme is an identity of sound between two words or phrases, including the last loud vowel and whatever follows it. In "gray-hay" nothing follows the vowel sound; in "great-hate" a consonant follows the vowel; in "grateful-hateful" a consonant and another syllable follow the vowel; in "greatfulness-hatefulness" a consonant and two syllables follow. The similarity between "gratefulness" and "truthfulness" is not a true rhyme but a partial or "slant" rhyme, because the loud vowels, and the consonants following them, are not the same, even though the last two syllables are identical. Alliteration is an identity of sound between two words, including only the beginning consonant sounds before the first vowel; in Old English poetry all words beginning in vowels were also considered alliterative. Normally, rhyme occurs between the ends of two lines, and alliteration occurs between two or more words of one line.

The two longer Frost poems do not make a considerable use of either effect but both have examples. Of rhyme, within a line: " 'All right,' I say, 'I can't afford to pay . . . (21)' " And at the ends of lines:

"Company?" he said,
"Don't make me get up; I'm too warm in bed." (94–95)

Of alliteration: "to beg and be beholden" (21), "I'll sit and see if that small sailing cloud" (161), and "The faintest restless rustling" (64). The last example also shows consonance, or the same pattern of consonants, with different vowels in between, as in "restl" and "rustl." There is also assonance, or like vowel sounds apart from consonants:

he made me feel so queer—
To see if he was talking in his sleep. (56–57)

The last example also shows the effect of half-rhyme or "slant" rhyme, the various approximations of rhyme at the ends of lines, made up of some consonance or assonance.

All these arrangements of volume and quality occur in prose as well as verse, though not so often. Rhythm, or the actual sound of human talk with its various successions of loud and soft, high and low, long and short, and its various qualities of sound, naturally occurs in prose as well as verse. Indeed, the more you look at careful prose and easy verse, the more the differences between verse and prose begin to seem almost conventional or typographical. The beginning of A Tale of Two Cities by Charles Dickens (1812–70) is more strictly iambic than most of Frost's blank verse:

It was the best of times, it was the worst of times, it was the age of wisdom, it was the age of foolishness, it was the epoch of belief, it was the epoch of incredulity, it was the season of Light, it was the season of Darkness, it was the spring of hope, it was the winter of despair . . .

The major question in determining an emphasis on sound as a literary element in a given passage or work is which elements can be shown to be subservient to it. In the Frost poems, the blank verse calls insufficient attention to itself to draw attention away from other elements.

In the example below, the English poet Algernon Charles Swinburne (1837–1909) is making fun of his own tendency to minimize plot, character, and the other elements in favor of sound:

> From the depth of the dreamy decline of the dawn
>   through the notable nimbus of nebulous noonshine,
> Pallid and pink as the palm of the flagflower
>   that flickers with fear of the flies as they float,
> Are the looks of our lovers that lustrously lean
>   from a marvel of mystic, miraculous moonshine,
> These that we feel in the blood of our blushes
>   that thicken and threaten with throbs through the throat?
>
>   ("Nephelidia")

A poet can call special attention to sound by such catchy or singsong sequences as in the passage above, sometimes called euphony, or beautiful sound; but poets can also call equal or greater attention to sound by harsh and jarring sequences, or cacophony, which Frye argues is more clearly "musical," since "music itself is not a sequence of harmonies at all, but a sequence of discords ending in a harmony" (*Anatomy of Criticism*, p. 256). This is the passage from Robert Browning (1812–89) which Frye cites as "musical."

> I could favor you with sundry touches
> Of the paint-smutches with which the Duchess
> Heightened the mellowness of her cheek's yellowness
> (To get on faster) until at last her
> Cheek grew to be one master-plaster
> Of mucus and fucus from mere use of ceruse;
> In short she grew from scalp to udder
> Just the object to make you shudder.
>
>   ("The Flight of the Duchess")

The rhythm of a passage of either verse or prose is always worthy of study, and no good writer writes without due consideration for how the result will sound when read aloud. Even when you read to yourself you "hear" the sounds mentally, and they have some effect on your total response, though you aren't paying strict attention to them. The special sound-effects of verse—meter, rhyme, alliteration, and so on—call special attention to themselves, but good prose is also partly governed by sound.

Diction

Here are two more poems by Emily Dickinson, of special interest because they exist in different versions, leaving us to decide which version we prefer. The first poem is about the dead, in their caskets or tombs, in their cemeteries. The poem is in two stanzas, and for the second stanza we have four possibilities. The variations give us a rare view of the poet at work—and a chance to work as the poet works. The second poem is a simple account of the marvels of spring, presented here at first in just one version. A few words you might not know: "alabaster"—white stone; "stolid"—inactive, unemotional; "sagacity"—wisdom; "Firmaments—row"—skies argue or quarrel; "diadems"—crowns worn by royalty; "Doges"—chiefs of certain republics (pronounced DOE—jez); "hoar"—frosty.

(216)

Safe in their Alabaster Chambers—
Untouched by Morning
And untouched by Noon—
Sleep the meek members of the Resurrection—
Rafter of satin,   5
And Roof of stone.

Light laughs the breeze
In her Castle above them—
Babbles the Bee in a stolid Ear,
Pipe the Sweet Birds in ignorant cadence—   10
Ah, what sagacity perished here!

version of 1859

Safe in their Alabaster Chambers—
Untouched by Morning—
And untouched by Noon—
Lie the meek members of the Resurrection—
Rafter of Satin—and Roof of Stone!   5

Grand go the Years—in the Crescent—above them—
Worlds scoop their Arcs—
And Firmaments—row—
Diadems—drop—and Doges—surrender—
Soundless as dots—on a Disc of Snow—

version of 1861

Additional attempts at a second stanza:

Springs—shake the sills—
But—the Echoes—stiffen—

Hoar—is the window—
And numb the door—
Tribes—of Eclipse—in Tents—of Marble—
Staples—of Ages—have buckled—there—

Springs—shake the Seals—
But the silence—stiffens—
Frosts unhook—in the Northern Zones—
Icicles—crawl from Polar Caverns—
Midnight in Marble—Refutes—The Suns—

(1333)

A little Madness in the Spring
Is wholesome even for the King,
But God be with the Clown—
Who ponders this tremendous scene—
This whole Experiment of Green—
As if it were his own!

Make any observations you like about these two poems, perhaps already
making choices among those offered for the first poem. Think also about these
questions.

1. Let's get the meters straight first of all, because they aren't entirely apparent from the shape of the poems as we see them here. See if you can
   count syllables and note rhymes or partial rhymes. Begin with the
   shorter, second poem. How does the rhythm seem to shape up—do you
   see two eight-syllable lines with four loud syllables each followed by one
   six-syllable line with three loud syllables? Do we really have then two
   similarly shaped stanzas? The first poem is a little trickier, or less regular. Begin with the second stanza, all the versions of it, and stick to
   counting loud syllables—do you get four loud syllables for each of four
   lines, with the second and fourth lines rhyming? (That's what I get,
   with a few extra soft syllables here and there.) In order to clarify this
   pattern we need to imagine these stanzas printed in four lines, by com-
   bining the first and second lines, or the second and third, into single
   lines. Then, if we look at the first stanza, we see that it too is in this
   pattern, if we combine lines two and three, and also combine the last
   two lines of the first version, as she herself did in the second version. The
   third line resulting, "Sleep the meek members of the Resurrection" has
   five loud syllables, perhaps to stress its importance?—"those quietly
   (meekly) waiting to be resurrected." The rhymes of all the versions turn
   out to be "Noon—stone," "Ear—here," "row (pronounced like *now*)—
   Snow," "door—there," "Zones—Suns." Do the differing versions assure us at least that this was the pattern she had in mind for the poem?

Perhaps a squirrel may remain.
My sentiments to share.
Grant me, Oh Lord, a sunny mind
Thy windy will to bear!

Safe in their Alabaster Chambers.
Untouched by morning
And untouched by noon.
Sleep the meek members of the Resurrection
Rafter of satin,
And roof of stone.

Light laughs the breeze
In her Castle above them.
Babbles the Bee in a stolid Ear,
Pipe the Sweet Birds in ignorant Cadence
Ah, what sagacity perished here!

X

Safe in their Alabaster
Chambers -
Untouched by Morning -
And untouched by Noon -
Lie the meek members of
the Resurrection -
Rafter of satin - and Roof
of stone !

Grand go the Years - in the
Crescent - above them -
Worlds scoop their Arcs -
And Firmaments - row -
Diadems - drop - and Doges -
surrender -
Soundless as Dots - on a
Disc of snow -

_____

Springs - shake the sills -
But - the Echoes - stiffen -
Hoar - is the window -

And - numb - the Door-
tribes - of Eclipse - in Tents -
of Marble -
Staples - of Ages - have
buckled - there -

Springs - shake the Seals -
But - the Silence - stiffens -
Frosts unhook - in the
Northern Zones -
Icicles - crawl from Polar
Caverns -
Midnight - in Marble -
Refutes - the Suns -

Note that she does not use here the pattern of "I taste a liquor never brewed" and "I like to see it lap the miles"—would that pattern be appropriate for a poem about the dead? Does this meter call more or less attention to its sound than the other meter?

2. Is the first poem a story? a conversation? Or do you see signs in it of description and reflection, a common combination for poetry? Do you see a plot or characters, other than the generalized dead? A theme? Is the poem an affirmation of her belief in resurrection? Or is that theme just something she assumes in order to give us an impression of them lying there through various seasons? So what do we end up with—an impression, a mood? If the sounds as sounds claim less attention than do the sounds in "I taste a liquor never brewed," then don't we have here a perfect setup for closer attention to the selection of words as an issue in itself? Does the poem, especially in all its versions, give us a stunning display of marvelous words?

3. What about the little poem on spring? This poem gives us two characters, a King and a Clown, but are they individualized, or just any King and Clown, a contrast between somebody very important and somebody very unimportant in society? Is there any story about them, or are they both just enjoying the spring? Is there a theme suggested, about what good it does anyone just to contemplate this new, recurring marvel, and how it belongs equally to the high and low? Do you see any theme so

prominent in the first poem? Consider the last line of the first version of stanza two about the wisdom that has passed on here.

4. Now consider in more detail the four different versions of the second stanza on the dead. We see at once that we are not dealing with minor word-choices for the same ideas, but, between versions one and two, entirely different meanings. The first gives us a spring scene which goes on unnoticed by those sleeping below. Versions three and four both contrast spring and winter, seasons equally unnoticed by the dead; these three stanzas together have a close similarity in intent and meaning. But the second version gives us a larger perspective of the passing years, with huge heavenly and earthly changes—wars in the heavens, crowns of kings falling and chieftains surrendering to their replacements—having no more effect on the dead than "dots—on a Disc of snow." According to Charles R. Anderson, *Emily Dickinson's Poetry: Stairway of Surprise* (New York: 1960), p. 272, the poet was thinking of the Milky Way with the words "Crescent" and "Disc," a crescent as it appears to us, or a full disc if we could see it all.

    Susan Gilbert Dickinson, an old friend of the poet's who became the wife of her brother Austin, had apparently seen both the first two versions, was still not satisfied with the second, and wondered whether the first stanza couldn't stand alone. Of the second version she said, "it does not go with the ghostly shimmer of the first verse as well as the other one"—the first version of stanza two. The poet then attempted two new second stanzas, of which she copies the first in a new note to Susan. We don't know what Susan's response to this (third) version was, but the poet seems to have gone back to the first version, which was later published anonymously in a Springfield, Mass. newspaper.

    The poet seems to have been unsure enough of her second stanza to allow us a choice. Perhaps you would prefer a finished poem of three stanzas, comprised of the first, plus the first and second versions of the second stanza; some editors have preferred the poem in this form. But how do you like versions three and four, in which she tried to match the "ghostly shimmer" of the first stanza somewhat more as she had in the first version? Note the contrast of the seasons with the stiffness and numbness of the dead, the contrast of eclipses above and marble below, and the midnight of the tombs that denies the suns above. The last line of the third version seems an attempted summary of the second version—the permanence among times passing above of those who have buckled down in the tomb.

5. In the spring poem, the poet tried a number of variations on the next to last line. Instead of "whole Experiment" she tried "sudden legacy," as if spring were a surprise inheritance. Then she tried "fair Apocalypse"—a revelation. Then, instead of "fair," she tried "whole," "gay," "bright," "fleet," "sweet," "quick." And, instead of "Apocalypse," she tried "experience," "Astonishment," "Periphery," and then returned to "Experi-

ment" with "wild experiment." These give you plenty to choose among—all quite wonderful choices. Which do you prefer? Or, seeing them all, isn't it difficult to choose and are we tempted to sweep them all up into one gorgeous whole?

For a creative response, you might try a combination among the various versions of the second stanza of the first poem, or, if you really feel bold, an entirely new stanza that might have better satisfied Susan—a hard lady to please, it seems. For the second poem, try out a few of the different versions and see how they work. Or try adding a third stanza to the poem, perhaps beginning, "For spring belongs to high and low—"

□   □   □

Aristotle defines *lexis* as the expression of the meaning in words (ch. 6), which suggests that "style" might be the best translation. I use "diction" (choice of words), since all studies of style include sound as well as diction, and often parts of other elements as well. Whatever elements a literary work contains must be expressed in words; so it's clear that a study of the words will eventually reach into all the other elements. The study of a writer's "world" normally begins with his rhythms and choice of words and ends with his treatment of setting and the primary elements; and the whole study might legitimately be called stylistic.

An important difference between sound and diction is shown in translation, for the original choice of words can usually be well approximated in the new language, while most of the sound effects are completely changed. In studying sound it's of great importance to know the particular language of the literature; what was said above about English under sound will not apply to many other languages. But most of what can be said about choice of words applies to all languages. While the words are different in each language, the relationships between words—the kinds of words, the choices among them, and to some extent the sequences and syntactical constructions of words—are often very similar from one language to another.

Aristotle's view of diction seems to be based on an assumption that there is always one clear choice of a word and one place for it in a given situation, and that writers who make that choice will be unremarkable for diction; in fact, if they choose it always, their diction will be mean, or over-familiar. Diction will only call attention to itself when the writer chooses a stranger word, a word from a different and unexpected area. Clearly there might be some difference of opinion on what the normal word or its place might be, and the number and variety of words available in English would render Aristotle's view simplistic; nonetheless, most analyses of style have followed Aristotle in broad outlines. The Roman orator Cicero (106–43 B. C.) and others amplified this discussion to include three distinct styles and various figures of speech. Diction, according to this view, has a vertical structure (up and down) of high, middle, and low, and a horizontal structure (further and nearer) suitable for the choice of metaphors and other figures.

Lists of words with frequencies (number of times a writer has used a word), eventually becoming concordances, or word-lists with citations of examples, may not seem very subtle or interesting projects for students of literature, but they offer one immediate sign of a writer's diction, which is a basic, if not the basic, literary study. A writer's preference for certain words, and certain kinds of words, will best establish his place on a scale of high or low diction. For the English critic Samuel Johnson (1709–84), literature should relate the actions of noble men and women in general and elevated language— which excludes the lower classes as well as everyday language. The English poet William Wordsworth (1770–1850) found some place in literature for both, and argued that poetry should be written "in a selection of language really used by men" ("Preface" to the *Lyrical Ballads*). Wordsworth's objections to highflown poetic diction sound very much like the objections Aristotle cites against certain tragedians, "because they use phrases no one would say in conversation, such as *the house out of* instead of *out of the house*" (ch. 22).

The high style involves high characters using general and unusual words, as in the classical epic poets. Aristotle seems to suggest that high diction is appropriate to tragedy, and low to comedy, but he hadn't seen any high comedy, the "comedy of manners" of William Congreve (1670–1729) and Oscar Wilde (1854–1900), in which the humor arises partly from the use of highflown terms for lowdown activities; nor had he seen any low tragedy, the tragedy of Henrik Ibsen (1828–1906) and Arthur Miller (born 1915), in which low characters are engaged in serious activities. As for the middle style, perhaps it is best shown in classical historians and modern novelists. The low style, the streetcorner flavor, is just as persistent in literature, from Aristophanes (445–380 B. C) to J. D. Salinger (born 1919). Frost's level, like Wordsworth's, is about middle, but still general enough to satisfy critics who might disapprove of a language too "low" for the dignity of poetry.

In the horizontal structure of diction the choice of words is not so much higher or lower (though it may also be that), as from further or nearer the given topic of discussion. Metaphor means in Greek a transference, a replacing of one word with another from a different area. Instead of the sun *scattering* his rays he is *sowing* his rays (like a farmer), to use Aristotle's example (ch. 21). A simile, a metaphor using *like* or *as*, is really an explanation of a metaphor: the sun shines, as if sowing his rays. Or an example from Frost, speaking of how Silas handles a forkful of hay: "He takes it out in bunches like big birds' nests" (93). To make a metaphor of this you would omit "bunches like." Or, as Frost says in "Design": "a moth / Like a white piece of satin cloth." A metaphor in which the comparison is drawn from an unexpectedly distant area from the basic topic of conversation is called a conceit, as a poet might liken his despair in love to a ship tossed in a storm, or as John Donne (1572–1631) likens his separation from his lady to the separation between the feet of a pair of compasses, forming a circle that always returns where it began. Synecdoche and metonymy are variations of metaphor, various swappings of part and whole or genus and species, as the witch refers to the apparition by its parts as "the bones" (100) or by its attributes as "the chalk-pile" (107). In "Range-Finding," Frost says "The battle rent a cobweb," when it was a bullet that did; he substitutes the whole for the part.

Aristotle includes these figures in his discussion of metaphor without naming them; they are transferences from not so far away as some other metaphors. The structure of all metaphor is the equation $a = b$, a is (or is like) b. Notice that this is the same as the structure of description; so it comes as no surprise that metaphors are often descriptive. The extension of metaphor is the analogy, as Aristotle says, "when the second is to the first as the fourth to the third," a is to b as c is to d. Aristotle's examples are: old age is to life as evening is to day; the sun scattering rays is like someone sowing seed. In "The Oven Bird," Frost offers this analogy: "for flowers / Mid-summer is to spring as one to ten." Or in "The Witch of Coös":

> Brushing their chalky skull with chalky fingers,
> With sounds like the dry rattling of a shutter. (128–129)

That is, the fingers brushing the skull are like the wind rattling the shutter. As this example shows, analogy is halfway between description and narration, and the extension of analogy might be called narrative, or, as it is usually called, the epic simile. It might also be called allegory, except that allegory is sometimes restricted to an extended narrative equation, half of which is thoroughly general. The following from "The Death of the Hired Man" is a miniature allegory:

> Part of a moon was falling down the west,
> Dragging the whole sky with it to the hills.
> Its light poured softly in her lap. She saw it
> And spread her apron to it. She put out her hand
> Among the harp-like morning-glory strings,
> Taut with the dew from garden bed to eaves,
> As if she played unheard some tenderness
> That wrought on him beside her in the night. (103–110)

Whatever she is doing to the strings she is doing to Warren too. Later when she says, "I'll sit and see if that small sailing cloud / Will hit or miss the moon," (161–162) this imagery is extended:

> It hit the moon.
> Then there were three there, making a dim row,
> The moon, the little silver cloud, and she. (162–164)

By now the narrative equation has brought you to equate the moon and cloud with Silas and death. The terms might be called "symbolic," since they are not restricted to one passage, but run through the poem. A symbol is an image or object or event which signifies something larger than itself throughout a literary work.

Parallel to the progression of comparisons—metaphor, analogy, and allegory—is a progression of contrasts or negative comparisons. A negative metaphor is an antithesis, *a is not b but c.* This example from "The Witch of Coös" combines an antithesis with two similes: "Not like a man, but like a chandelier" (69). A pun is a variation of compressed antithesis, in which the *b* and *c* look or sound or are alike, often jokingly explained in a form that shows the antithesis: not *sun* but *son,* not *dye* but *die,* not *lover* but *lubber.* The extension of antithesis is paradox, an antithesis denying received opinion: *a is not as you think b but c,* as the witch's Control tells her that the dead *are* not souls, but *have* souls. The ending of "A Mood Apart" might be considered a paradoxical response to a hint that some snoopiness is friendly: "any eye is an evil eye / That looks in on to a mood apart." Or, for those who think that present prosperity is enough, Frost seems to answer paradoxically, in "Provide, Provide": "No memory of having starred / Atones for later disregard." Irony is an extension of paradox: saying *a is b* (and everything it implies) when you mean *a is not b but c.* As in allegory, half the equation is often suppressed. When Warren asks, "Silas has better claim on us you think / Than on his brother?" (125–26), he is being ironic: he means that Silas has a better claim on his brother than on them. The word "right" in Frost's "Design" is clearly ironic, when Frost says of the white spider, white flower, and white moth, "Assorted characters of death and blight / Mixed ready to begin the morning right." Similarly, the word "soon" in the following poem is clearly ironic.

A diller, a dollar,
A ten o'clock scholar,
What makes you come so soon?
You used to come at ten o'clock
And now you come at noon.

Comparisons are more frequent in literature or fiction, contrasts in philosophy or nonfiction. Aristotle says an eye for metaphors is a sign of genius (ch. 22), but it is probably a sign of poetic genius, whereas an eye for antithesis is a sign of philosophic genius. When the English philosopher John Locke (1632–1704) defines wit and judgment as the arts of finding likenesses and differences, he seems to be naming the tendencies of the poet and the philosopher, respectively (*Essay Concerning Human Understanding,* II, xi).

The view of diction so far given is as static design (up and down or from side to side of a fixed point), but diction can also be seen as temporal development. The sequences or progressions of words involve the grammatical study of syntax, or arrangements of words. The figures of speech above are sometimes called tropes or turns of expression, such as metaphor and simile. There are also the schemes, which have to do with arrangements and rearrangements in the sequences of words. Rhetoricians have noted numerous varieties of repetition or omission or rearrangement of words. A few of these may be seen in the comment of Julius Caesar (100–44 B.C.), "I came, I saw, I conquered," and the familiar phrases of Abraham Lincoln, "of the people, by the people, for the people," which are examples of repetition and syntactical parallelism, perhaps also of climax, the rising to a strong ending. "Little Jack Horner" is also a good example of climax—closing with a bang.

The sequential view of diction also results in further varieties of style, roughly based on the number of different ideas occurring per number of words. As in differentiating between the normal word and a strange or metaphorical word there might be some differences of opinion, so here there might be some difference about how many separate ideas a given passage introduces. But certainly broad differences might be agreed upon, between an ample and lavish style, and a brief and stark one. These are sometimes called, in honor of two of their masters, the Ciceronian and the Senecan, respectively. The Roman orator Cicero (106–43 B.C.) developed a style notable for fullness or expansiveness; the Roman philosopher and playwright Seneca (4 B.C.–65 A.D.) developed a style notable for brevity and curtness. The style intermediate between the two is often mentioned, and praised from Aristotle's *Rhetoric* on, but hard to name, since "middle" is already used for the style between high and low; this one might be called "even," since ideas and words roughly keep pace with each other.

In the following examples from Roger Ascham (1515–68), Francis Bacon (1561–1626), and Joseph Addison (1673–1719), the substance as well as the style, the matter as well as the manner, are respectively Ciceronian, Senecan, and "even."

And as in portraiture and painting wise men choose not that workman, that can only make a fair hand, or a well fashioned leg, but such one, as can furnish up fully, all the features of the whole body, of a man, woman, and child, and withal is able to, by good skill, to give to every one of these three, in their proper kind, the right form, the true figure, the natural color, that is fit and due, to the dignity of a man, to the beauty of a woman, to the sweetness of a young babe: even likewise, do we seek such one in our school to follow, who is able always, in all matters, to teach plainly, to delight pleasantly, and to carry away by force of wise talk, all that shall hear or read him: and is so excellent in deed, as wit is able, or wish can hope to attain unto.

(*Roger Ascham*, The Schoolmaster, II)

Virtue is like a rich stone, best plain set; and surely virtue is best in a body that is comely, though not of delicate features, and that hath rather dignity of presence than beauty of aspect.

(Francis Bacon, Of Beauty*)*

When I read an author of genius who writes without method, I fancy myself in a wood that abounds with a great many noble objects, rising among one another in the greatest confusion and disorder. When I read a methodical discourse, I am in a regular plantation and can place myself in its several centers, so as to take a view of all the lines and walks that are struck from them. You may ramble in the one a whole day together, and every moment discover something or other that is new to you; but, when you have done, you will have but a confused imperfect notion of the place. In the other, your eye commands the whole prospect and gives you such an idea of it as is not easily worn out of the memory.

(Joseph Addison, Spectator 476*)*

Consider the "idea-content" of these three passages, each of them based on an analogy. The first says that it is desirable for a schoolmaster to be able to perform his various tasks well, just as it is desirable for a painter to be able to paint the various parts of the body well. The second says that virtue appears best in a person not beautiful, but comely or dignified, just as a rich stone appears best in a plain setting. The third says that a methodical author is preferable to an unmethodical one, just as an orderly plantation is preferable to a disorderly wood. My restatements of these passages are all of about the same length, but the first and third passages are considerably longer than the second, which it is hard to reduce in length. Then consider what the first and third passages include, missing from my restatements, and how important the inclusions are. The first mentions hand and leg as parts of the body; man, woman, and child as varieties of persons; kind, form, figure, and color as concerns of the painter. It also suggests that it's appropriate for a man to be dignified, a woman beautiful, and a child sweet; and that a schoolmaster should speak and write so as to teach plainly, delight pleasantly, and talk wisely; and that he should behave as well as his wit or wish permits. None of these suggestions is remarkable, or unpredictable; they are fairly obvious elaborations. The writer also has no hesitation in offering slight repetitions or echoes, such as "portraiture and painting"; "fair hand, or a well-fashioned leg"—when "fair hand or leg" would do; "all the features of the whole body"—two phrases when either phrase would be enough alone; the words "proper," "right," "true," "natural"— when any one of them would serve for all; "fit and due" and "always, in all matters"—again double expressions when either would serve alone; and "delight pleasantly"—as much a repetition as "please delightfully."

Certainly it would be easy to express the idea in the second passage at as great or greater length. The first clause, to the word "set," is a metaphorical equation of which one half is left unexpressed, the phrase "best plain set" doing double duty. Bacon could have said, "Truth and virtue in the human character is best and most naturally found in a human body, whose hand and leg—whether in a man, woman, or child, and all the features of the whole body—are fair and well-fashioned rather than delicate and refined"; he could then have gone on at equal length to tell all about varieties of stones, varieties of metals, and shapes for settings. Note too that "dignity of presence" and "beauty of aspect" cannot be thought to echo each other as do "the right form, the true figure," etc., "presence" and "aspect" are as different from each other as are "dignity" and "beauty." Bacon's style, as well as his idea, is "best plain set." The style of the first passage, like the painter and schoolmaster, "can furnish up fully."

The third passage elaborates more than the second, but the elaborations are not so obvious and predictable as those in the first. The similarity between reading authors and walking in nature is not quite so obvious as to need no elaboration. The two metaphors in the first two sentences are parallel to each other (as are the symmetrical halves of a "regular plantation"), and like the metaphorical statement in Bacon, do double duty, for reading and walking. Walking in a wood is exciting but confusing; walking in a plantation is pleasant and orderly. The next two sentences go on to elaborate, but the elaboration is different enough to clarify without repeating or echoing what has already been said: "something or other that is new to you" is not quite the same as "abounds with a great many noble objects"; "a confused imperfect notion of the place" is similar but not the same as "the greatest confusion and disorder." The clause "your eye commands the whole prospect" is a general review, but not a repetition of "can place yourself in its several centers, so as to take a view of all the lines and walks that are struck from them." And the last point, that an orderly experience is remembered longer, is entirely new.

Clearly Addison is writing, as well as encouraging, the "methodical discourse." Bacon might have written this passage more curtly: "A work of genius is, like a wild wood, various and noble; a methodical work is like a plantation, tame and trimmed." Bacon would not necessarily prefer the methodical discourse; and Addison might consider either the Ciceronian or Senecan styles as unmethodical. I will not take the space to give a Ciceronian version of this passage. Most recent writers on style would probably prefer the style of Addison, or possibly of Bacon, to that of Ascham; but I intend here only to differentiate, not to judge them.

The terms Ciceronian, Senecan, and "even" apply to philosophy or nonfiction. But there are also corresponding terms applied to literature or fiction—the lavish baroque style, the stark mannerist style, the intermediate rococo style. In English literature these variations are best found in the Renaissance period. But there is no reason why they cannot be applied to any period or literature where the differences are observed. (See Wylie Sypher, *Four Stages of Renaissance Style*, especially p. 9.) The following examples, describing similar situations, are from John Milton (1608–74), John Donne (1572–1631), and Alexander Pope (1688–1744). The baroque is working for

a lavish splendor, the mannerist for a curious curtness, the rococo for an even
regularity.

> Thus talking, hand in hand alone they passed
> On to their blissful bower; it was a place
> Chosen by the sovran Planter, when He framed
> All things to man's delightful use: the roof
> Of thickest covert was inwoven shade,
> Laurel and myrtle, and what higher grew
> Of firm and fragrant leaf; on either side
> Acanthus, and each odorous bushy shrub
> Fenced up the verdant wall; each beauteous flower,
> Iris all hues, roses, and jessamine
> Reared high their flourished heads between, and wrought
> Mosaic; under foot the violet,
> Crocus, and hyacinth with rich inlay
> Broidered the ground, more colored than with stone
> Of costliest emblem.
>
> (*John Milton,* Paradise Lost, *IV, 689–703)*

> Where, like a pillow on a bed,
>   A pregnant bank swelled up, to rest
> The violet's reclining head,
>   Sat we two, one another's best.
> Our hands were firmly cemented
>   With a fast balm, which thence did spring,
> Our eye-beams twisted, and did thread
>   Our eyes, upon one double string.
>
> (*John Donne,* The Ecstasy, *1–8)*

> Here hills and vales, the woodland and the plain,
> Here earth and water seem to strive again;
> Not Chaos-like together crushed and bruised,
> But, as the world, harmoniously confused:
> Where order in variety we see,
> And where, though all things differ, all agree.
> Here waving groves a chequered scene display,
> And part admit, and part exclude the day;
> As some coy nymph her lover's warm address
> Nor quite indulges, nor can quite repress.
>
> (*Alexander Pope,* Windsor Forest, *12–20)*

In the baroque as in the Ciceronian, note the tendency to elaborate, to
enumerate all the flowers and details; and the scene as well as the style is elaborately ornamented. The content is simply: Adam and Eve entered their beautiful bower. In the mannerist passage the scene, as well as the style, is sparse.

A single bank, like a pillow, holds the violet and the two lovers—or is the violet also a reference to the lady? The last four lines suggest that the lovers are clasping hands and looking into each other's eyes, but these points are accompanied by quite striking metaphors or "conceits." The hands are not clasped but "cemented / With a fast balm"; the eye-beams are as if threaded "upon one double spring." It would be hard to put ideas of this complexity and oddity more briefly; if anything they might be more fully explained. In the lines from Pope the following phrases are similar but different, as in Addison: "harmoniously confused," "order in variety," "though all things differ, all agree." In the first two lines, "hills and vales," "woodland and the plain," "earth and water" are well known to be part of every scene; but they also "seem to strive again," which is a fresher note, a recollection of the formation of the earth. In the closing lines the trees "part admit, and part exclude the day"—a neat pairing, which is given a witty analogy in the last two lines. The style is, like Addison's, orderly and methodical. No doubt Donne would want to cut and complicate this passage, and Milton would want to enlarge and decorate it. All three write in respectable English styles, of course.

Setting

Here is a final entry from Kafka's diaries. In this one he presents a scene of himself in his father's factory observing the girls at work.

(February 5, 1912)

Yesterday in the factory. The girls, in their unbearably dirty and untidy clothes, their hair disheveled as though they had just got up, the expressions on their faces fixed by the incessant noise of the transmission belts and by the individual machines, automatic ones, of course, but unpredictably breaking down, they aren't people, you don't greet them, you don't apologize when you bump into them, if you call them over to do something, they do it but return to their machine at once, with a nod of the head you show them what to do, they stand there in petticoats, they are at the mercy of the pettiest power and haven't enough calm understanding to recognize this power and placate it by a glance, a bow. But when six o'clock comes and they call it out to one another, when they untie the kerchiefs from around their throats and their hair, dust themselves with a brush that passes around and is constantly called for by the impatient, when they pull their skirts on over their heads and clean their hands as well as they can—then at last they are women again, despite pallor and bad teeth they can smile, shake their stiff bodies, you can no longer bump into them, stare at them or overlook them, you move back againt the greasy crates to make room for them, hold your hat in your hand when they say good evening, and do not know how to behave when one of them holds your winter coat for you to put on.

1. Do you see a little bit of a story here, about the young man's visit during the afternoon, and how his attitude toward the girls changes when work ends? A hint of a special relationship between him and the girl who helps him on with his coat? We certainly see something here of characterization, don't we?—the collective characters of the girls, and of the young man who watches them, feeling almost guilty that he can't really see them as human while they work, and then, when they become women again, becomes somehow shy and inferior to them? Do you also see something of theme here, of what working at machines does to humans—of which is serving which? Does he force us to see why the girls should be at the mercy of the machines, why they can't seem to win any control over their petty power?

2. Adding up the total effect of story and characters and ideas, are you satisfied we've covered this passage—or that we have as much of these as we did in earlier passages from Kafka? What do we see here that the others lacked? The sense of what it feels like to be there—at first and when work ends? The whole passage could be seen as descriptive, but description suffused with the viewer's feelings and thoughts. The scene, and what it's like to be there—what can we call this—the atmosphere of the place, a mood piece? Was that so much the issue, for instance, in the story of the landlady and the lodger, or was the point there exactly what they said to each other, whereas here we have none of the words that might have been said by him or by the girls to him or each other? Does the contrast that begins in the middle of the passage with "But" and its change of perspective—do the two perspectives—force us to weigh the effect of perspective itself?

For a creative response, see if you can develop this passage a little, perhaps by adding something in the way of story or characterization, something happening between the young man and one of the girls, perhaps the one who helps him on with his coat. Or begin with a different, similar scene you have been part of and capture the special feeling of that scene.

□   □   □

Aristotle admits that *opsis* or spectacle is striking, but he dismisses it as inartistic, having least to do with the art of poetry (ch. 6). Apparently he considers as spectacle only what the costumer, or the scene-designer and costumer together, add to a stage show. But later he suggests that the vividness contributed by music and painting to a tragedy can be sensed even in reading the work to yourself (ch. 26). At any rate I consider setting the sum of all visual or sensuous references in a work, whether it is staged or not, including everything from place or picture to atmosphere or mood. It is not what the designer adds to a show so much as the basis of what he adds. As the sound of a work eventuates in a musical score, the setting eventuates in a set or scene.

The mode most clearly suggestive of setting is description, which might be considered directions for staging or filming; in scripts of modern plays and movies the descriptive passages are set off in parentheses as asides to the designer and camera people. But description is always on the brink of reverie, and reverie usually includes a considerable amount of description: mood is always hovering between objective and subjective, from what the place looks like to how the person feels who sees it. And the mode of perception and reflection—reverie—encourages both setting and theme: you see the place and you see the point. (See Frye, *Anatomy of Criticism,* p. 77.) Both elements lead you outside the work itself, to the world of physical reality or to the world of ideas. According to this view, then, music, the basis of plot and sound, is more closely identified with literature than painting, the basis of theme and setting, which is always leading you outside the work.

One sign of an emphasis on setting is the insistence of the question "What's the place like?" as you are reading. The answer to this question will give you the external scene of the work, largely in the mode of description. But there is also the question of internal mood, the question, "How do the characters (or how do I the reader) feel about the scene?" The answer to this question will probably be in the mode of reverie. In the two Frost poems, though there are no extensive passages of description, there are certainly many descriptive details, which give you a fairly clear picture of the settings. In "The Death of the Hired Man" you have the "lamp-flame at the table," the stove, the barn-door, the meadow, the upper pasture, the cart, the hazel prong, the "harp-like morning-glory strings," the hound, the "sharp-edged chair-back," the lounge, the bed—in addition to the "moon, the little silver cloud." But probably none of these details convey the mood as clearly as the statement, " 'I can't afford to pay / Any fixed wages, though I wish I could.' " (22–23) In "The Witch of Coös" the setting is about the same, though the details given are somewhat different ones: the "farm / Behind the mountain," the common table, the headboard of the bed, the cellar, kitchen, bedroom, and attic, the "board we had laid down to walk dry-shod on,"

> The bulkhead double-doors were double-locked
> And swollen tight and buried under snow.
> The cellar windows were banked up with sawdust
> And swollen tight and buried under snow. (55–58)

The striking difference of setting here is the supernatural picture of the skeleton:

> (A tongue of fire
> Flashed out and licked along his upper teeth.
> Smoke rolled inside the sockets of his eyes.) (72–74)

But the mood is as clearly conveyed in the statements, "And when I've done it, what good have I done?" (11) and "I don't remember why I ever cared." (149) This poem includes the device of the narrator-observer, whose function, as in *Wuthering Heights* and many other stories in which there is a first-person who does not act, is to heighten the atmosphere: he is like a veil cast before the action, making everything behind it more remote and odd.

The metaphors, including both halves of every literary comparison, also contribute to the imagery, or pictorializing, and hence to the setting of every work, though they may not relate to the given place of action. In "The Death of the Hired Man" the big birds' nests are just the way Silas's bunches of hay look to Warren, but they too are a part of the setting. In "The Witch of Coös" the kicking army mule, the pile of dishes, the chandelier, the "lightning or a scribble," the button-box, the handrail, the tote-road, and the "rural letter-box" with the unusual name Toffile Lajway as well as the details in the following hypothetical passage, also contribute to the setting:

> I wanted to put out the light and see
> If I could see it, or else mow the room,
> With our arms at the level of our knees,
> And bring the chalk-pile down.

The "dry rattling of a shutter," though a metaphor for how the skeleton sounds to the witch, may also be a part of the actual setting—it may be what she really hears. Even from this slight contrast between descriptive and reflective passages, and comparisons, in the two works, it must be clear that setting is emphasized considerably more in "The Witch of Coös," which is to be expected: Gothic, or ghostly, tales regularly emphasize setting.

Another sign of emphasis on setting is distinctiveness, rather than typicality, of setting. Here, both settings are more or less the same typical farm setting. But the ghostly trappings in "The Witch of Coös" certainly give that work some distinctiveness over the other.

The setting of a work is usually pretty constant, but in some longer works, plays and novels, the setting may change, and a change in setting, like changes in other elements, is one way of emphasizing setting. But the major question for determining the emphasis on setting is the same as that for other elements: namely, which elements are subservient to it? Are the places minimally pictured so as to explain where and how the events occur, or to show where the characters live and move? Or do things happen and characters appear primarily to give you the feel of the place? In "The Death of the Hired Man" the coming of Silas and his death are never directly pictured, never utilized in order to picture the place. In "The Witch of Coös" the coming of the apparition is much more functional in picturing the place, and in contributing scary pictures of its own.

The possible settings of literature are all the settings conceivable by the human imagination. And settings, according to Frye, are related to five different levels he finds in literature. He begins with a hint in chapter two of the *Poetics,* that characters may be better or grander than ourselves, worse or lowlier than ourselves, or about the same as ourselves. These three levels he breaks down further into five; actually he adds a first and second level to Aristotle's three.

1. The hero on the first level is so much better than ourselves that he is a god, and the story about him is a myth.
2. On the second level the hero is human, but performs actions impossible for other humans, and the story about him is romantic, including "enchanted weapons, talking animals, terrifying ogres and witches, and talismans of miraculous power."
3. On the third level the hero is a leader—in Aristotle's sense better than ourselves—and the level is the high level of most epic and tragedy.
4. On the fourth level the hero is one of us, and the level is the low level of most comedy and realistic fiction.
5. What is lower than low? If we have the sense of looking down on characters worse than ourselves, "on a scene of bondage, frustration, or absurdity," the level is the ironic level. (For a fuller treatment of these levels, see Frye, pp. 33 ff.)

If these are five conventional levels on which literature operates, it seems appropriate to expect similar settings for different works on the same levels. What kinds of settings—what landscapes and locations—will best put you in the mood to look up to certain characters and stories, down on others, and look at others face to face? Each setting, according to Frye, has its own version of divinity and of humanity in its natural elements of air and earth; of the non-human elements of fire just above and water just below humanity; and of animal, vegetable, and mineral life.

In the first setting divinity is an orderly society of three or more persons (such as the Christian trinity) but may be combined in one benevolent will. Humanity is seen here as an orderly society constituted like a single person. Fire is seen in the sun, moon, and stars, and in fiery or illuminated deities and saints; water is the "water of life," the river of the City of God. Of animal life, there are the lamb and dove. Of vegetable life, the garden, the farm, the grove or the park, often identified as the tree of life or the rose. Of mineral life, there is the shining City, often reduced to a single building, and including the highway or road, the "way." The Biblical Apocalypse is the best example of this setting. In the following passage from Revelation 21 and 22, St. John the Evangelist tells of how an angel brings him to the holy city:

> And he carried me away in the spirit to a great and high mountain, and
> showed me that great city, the holy Jerusalem, descending out of heaven
> from God, having the glory of God: and her light was like unto a stone,

most precious, even like a jasper stone, clear as crystal: And had a wall great and high, and had twelve gates, and at the gates twelve angels, and names written thereon, which are the names of the twelve tribes of the children of Israel. . . . And the twelve gates were twelve pearls; every several gate was of one pearl: and the street of the city was pure gold, as it were transparent glass. . . . And he showed me a pure river of water of life, clear as crystal, proceeding out of the throne of God and of the Lamb. In the midst of the street of it, and on either side of the river, was there the tree of life, which bare twelve manner of fruits, and yielded her fruit every month: and the leaves of the tree were for the healing of the nations.

In the second setting divine creatures are parental, wise magicians. Among human creatures, children are common, and childlike or chaste young women and men. Fire here is a purifying symbol, and the moon, the coolest and hence most chaste heavenly body, has a special place. Water appears in fountains and pools and fertilizing rains. Of animal life, the lamb recurs here, together with the horse and hound, the unicorn, the ass, and birds and butterflies. Of vegetable life, gardens such as the Biblical Garden of Eden belong here, and the tree of life becomes the magician's wand. Of mineral life, the city is rarer here, and the tower or castle, or an occasional cottage, takes its place. The description of the Garden of Eden in *Paradise Lost* by John Milton (1608–74) is one version of the second setting. You may need help with a few unusual words and expressions in this passage:"Hesperian fables"—tales of the far west (Italy or Spain); "irriguous"—well-watered; "umbrageous—shady; "mantling"—covering; "quire"—choir; "vernal airs"—spring breezes; "Pan"—classical god of universal nature; "Graces"—classical goddesses who dispense charm and beauty; "Hours"—classical goddesses of the seasons.

A happy rural seat of various view:
Groves whose rich trees wept odorous gums and balm;
Others whose fruit, burnished with golden rind,
Hung amiable—Hesperian fables true,
If true, here only—and of delicious taste.
Betwixt them lawns or level downs, and flocks
Grazing the tender herb, were interposed,
Or palmy hillock; or the flowery lap
Of some irriguous valley spread her store,
Flowers of all hue, and without thorn the rose.
Another side, umbrageous grots and caves
Of cool recess, o'er which the mantling vine
Lays forth her purple grape, and gently creeps
Luxuriant; meanwhile murmuring waters fall
Down the slope hills dispersed, or in a lake,

That to the fringed bank with myrtle crowned
Her crystal mirror holds, unite their streams.
The birds their quire apply; airs, vernal airs,
Breathing the smell of field and grove, attune
The trembling leaves, while universal Pan,
Knit with the Graces and the Hours in dance,
Led on the eternal Spring.

In the third setting divinity and humanity are closely identified, as seen in the divine right of kings. The fire of the angelic world blazes in the king's crown and the lady's eyes. Water appears in the disciplined river, often ornamented by a royal barge. Of animal life, the eagle and lion, the horse and falcon, the peacock and swan, and the phoenix are common. Of vegetable life and mineral life, the emphasis here is opposite that of the second setting where gardens are near and cities far; now gardens are only formal gardens attached to buildings, and the magician's wand becomes the royal sceptre. The city is a flourishing capital with the court at its center. The tragedies and history plays of William Shakespeare (1516–64) provide examples of this setting. The dying John of Gaunt in Shakespeare's *Richard II* describes England this way:

This royal throne of kings, this scept'red isle,
This earth of majesty, this seat of Mars,
This other Eden, demi-paradise,
This fortress built by Nature for herself
Against infection and the hand of war,
This happy breed of men, this little world,
This precious stone set in the silver sea,
Which serves it in the office of a wall,
Or as a moat defensive to a house,
Against the envy of less happier lands;
This blessed plot, this earth, this realm, this England,
This nurse, this teeming womb of royal kings,
Feared by their breed and famous by their birth,
Renowned for their deeds as far from home,
For Christian service and true chivalry,
As is the sepulchre in stubborn Jewry
Of the world's ransom, blessed Mary's son. . . .

In the fourth setting, the images are the ordinary images of experience. Divinity has little real place and humanity customarily turns its back to heaven in order to work on earth. Fire is often ironic and destructive, and water too is the destructive sea, with some capsizable boat on it. Of animal life, tigers and apes occur. Of vegetable life, there are only farms for men to work. Of mineral life, the city now becomes the labyrinthine and lonely modern metropolis. Most modern fiction and much modern poetry provide examples of this setting. The following is the opening of "Michael" by William Wordsworth (1770–1850), describing a typically modern farm setting. Unusual words here are "tumultuous"—noisy; "kites"—birds of prey; "dell"—small valley. The significance of the stones at the end of this passage appear in the story of the old man Michael and his son, the main characters in the story the poem tells.

> If from the public way you turn your steps
> Up the tumultuous brook of Green-head Ghyll,
> You will suppose that with an upright path
> Your feet must struggle; in such bold ascent
> The pastoral mountains front you, face to face.
> But, courage! for around that boisterous brook
> The mountains have all opened out themselves,
> And made a hidden valley of their own,
> No habitation can be seen; but they
> Who journey thither find themselves alone
> With a few sheep, with rocks and stones, and kites
> That overhead are sailing in the sky.
> It is in truth an utter solitude:
> Nor should I have made mention of this Dell
> But for one object which you might pass by,
> Might see and notice not. Beside the brook
> Appears a straggling heap of unhewn stones!

In the fifth setting, divinity is an inscrutable and sometimes evil force. Humanity gathers in desperate and joyless groups where individual pleasure is sacrificed to duty. Fire appears in malignant demons or spirits broken from hell, and water in the water of death or spilled blood. Of animal life, there are only monsters or beasts of prey—wolves, tigers, vultures, serpents, and dragons. Of vegetable life, there are sinister forests, heaths, and wastelands; the tree of life is now a tree of death in the form of the cross, the stake, or the gallows. Of mineral life, there are cities of destruction and eternal night, and the "way" becomes the labyrinth. The *Inferno* by Dante (1265–1321) and *1984* by George Orwell (1903–50) provide examples of this setting. The following passage, from Shakespeare's *Titus Andronicus,* describes a hellish setting of imprisonment. Unusual words here are "ticed"—lured, enticed; "urchins"—hedgehogs.

> Have I not reason, think you, to look pale?
> These two have ticed me hither to this place,
> A barren detested vale you see it is;

The trees, though summer, yet forlorn and lean,
Overcome with moss and baleful mistletoe.
Here never shines the sun, here nothing breeds,
Unless the nightly owl or fatal raven:
And when they showed me this abhorred pit,
They told me, here, at dead time of the night,
A thousand fiends, a thousand hissing snakes,
Ten thousand swelling toads, as many urchins,
Would make such fearful and confused cries
As any mortal body hearing it
Should straight fall mad, or else die suddenly.
No sooner had they told this hellish tale
But straight they told me they would bind me here
Unto the body of a dismal yew
And leave me to this miserable death.

For a fuller treatment of these settings, see Frye, *Anatomy of Criticism,*
pp. 141–58. The two longer poems by Frost are both in about the same lower
or fourth setting, but "The Witch of Coös" goes lower, to the cellar—and
perhaps the ghost comes from hell itself—and so comes closer to the demonic,
fifth setting, the setting for fiery monsters from the depths.

Final Comments on "The Death of the Hired Man" and "The Witch of Coös"

If you try, a few years from now, to recall either of these two poems you
have now read and reread and analyzed according to their elements, what is
likely to have remained with you? Perhaps a surprisingly vivid impression of
the whole of both poems, but perhaps by then—new experiences having piled
up on old ones—you will retain only a fragment, a line or two, an image, a
sense of character. What you recall after a long stretch of time from a poem or
movie may sometimes be the very item the author first thought of, the seed or
conception of his inspiration. It may also hint at the "most important" element resulting from a careful analysis of the whole work. You cannot be sure,
of course, that what you recall as outstanding will be what the author was so
struck by he decided to write about it—and also what he ended up stressing in
his finished work, in the ensemble of literary elements making up the whole.
But what remains with you was what most vividly captured your imagination—of that you can be sure.

So think over these two wonderful poems again and to yourself. Close the book at this point and put down, for each poem, the one or several outstanding points you think will remain with you—before you read what I think they are, what I think you may have put down on your paper.

What have you come up with? I decided that I would recall, from "The Death of the Hired Man," perhaps the line about home as something you don't have to deserve, something you have coming no matter what. Or perhaps the striking contrast between the hired man so confident in the past about his ability to put together haystacks "in bunches like big birds' nests," his boastfulness toward the young student he has worked with, versus the terrible comedown of his approaching death when he has no family or loved ones to return to and can count as "home" only the couple he has worked for when he couldn't get higher pay elsewhere. After a long time, I find I have often forgot "endings"—in this case, whether the man really died in the poem, or how he died. I find I better recall the "situation" out of which some ending or other emerged.

For "The Witch of Coös" what have you put down? For me the point that remains is the sense of the witch in the presence of the apparition—presumably the ghost of her former lover—bravely striking at its hand as it comes at her. Perhaps you have put down the idea that the dead *are* not souls but *have* souls, but I'd guess you haven't. That idea (really a tricky expression of the idea that ghosts exist and can take on some physical form) seems more like an addition to the poem and not necessarily its essence. The story the witch tells is one demonstration of the idea, but any other ghost story would also be. The witch seems to have a spunky side that I think would be at the core of the piece; and I think I'd remember her more as an event than an idea.

"The Death of the Hired Man" seems more like a story in which situation and idea are inseparable: the situation of the mostly unwelcome hired hand showing up to die seems ideally suited to the idea that home is the place that has to take you in when you're dying. So for me what is likely to remain of "The Death of the Hired Man" is its idea and the situation (not exactly the story or plot) that fits it so well—and of "The Witch of Coös" its heroine striking at the ghost of a man she wronged, an event in a string of events. In other words, I will probably remember the hired-man poem as a theme and the witch poem as a plot.

What about characters? Yes, I may recall the hired man, but note that he never appears in the poem, only in the talk about him by the couple. I think I will remember the witch as a more lively character because she has center stage in most of the poem. As for rhetorical technique, I think I will remember the poem of the witch as her *mono*-logue (though it isn't) and the hired-man poem as a *dia*-logue between the husband and wife on the meaning of home and what they should do about Silas. So the characters of the hired-man poem are the couple who sympathetically differ with each other on whether they should be their "brother's" keeper.

I think I will recall the setting (what the places may look and feel like) of the two poems as almost the same—somewhat impoverished farms—but the vision of the ghost downstairs and then going upstairs places an importance on picturing the place that the other poem lacks.

In style and sound I think I'd merge these poems, in recollection, with most of Frost's poems as smooth and sparse and simple, the characteristics of the best New England talk, which Frost imitates. In other words, a style that calls minimum attention to itself and maximum attention to what it conveys.

So I come up with high marks for theme in the hired-man poem and high marks for plot and setting in the witch poem. Characterization in both poems is strong—the husband and wife and the hired man; the witch, her husband and son, and the apparition of her lover. At this point, stop and see whether your observations differ from mine; and then see if you can put down some ideas on which poem you might value more and why. Note that I bring up this question only after a conscientious analysis and reconsideration of what the poems mean to me as I read them and how I will think of them in the future.

I think I'd probably end up valuing the hired-man poem more than the other, because that poem puts me in an awkward situation I have been in before (and expect to be in again): whether to welcome an acquaintance who is more of a problem than a friend. And it seems to tell me I should welcome that person, troublesome as welcoming him may be. This poem brings about a change in my attitude, if I weren't already inclined to be a welcoming host.

The witch poem is a jolly good ghost story, and some might like ghost stories better than realistic ones. I might be more fascinated by this tale, and I might dream about people I have wronged returning to haunt me. I will remember this poem as a story vivid in its own right but not as bringing about a major change in my attitude toward life.

Not that I require of literary works that they change my life. That, I think, would seem to require that every literary work be an "essay brought to life"—would give more overall importance to the element of theme than I think it should have. The works I value most seem to speak to me with special urgency of the life I know and have known. I may seem to recognize a person I have known, or myself, in a play or poem—or I may value it because I have never experienced anything quite like what is depicted, yet it seems vital or fascinating. I find I must constantly keep myself open to what literature can do for me, because as soon as I think I have located the secret of literary value, I find a new work I am appreciating for new reasons.

You may, for instance, have had entirely different evaluations of these two poems from mine. Share them with your classmates and teacher. But also come back to these poems in a few months or years and see if you still agree with your present evaluations. I often change my opinions of works later on, and you may too.

Part Two

4

Analyzing Fiction

Two stories, by the Russian writer Anton Chekhov (1860–1904) and the contemporary American writer John Updike (born 1932), initiate the subject of six examples in the following pages: "ways of saying goodbye."

The first, "An Upheaval," tells of the stir caused in a rich Russian household by the loss of a brooch. The chief character is a poor but well-educated girl, Mashenka, serving as a governess in the household, which includes a husband and wife and several servants other than Mashenka—a porter, servant-girls, and footmen. The dinner table includes, besides the husband and wife and Mashenka, visitors and children and the household doctor. The governess is called by her first and last name, but the husband and wife are called by their first and middle names, the customary form of address in Russia. The husband is Nikolay Sergeitch, which means that his father's first name was Sergei; and the wife is called Fedosya Vassilyevna, which means that her father's first name was Vassily. She is also called, in the French style, Madame Kushkin, the family surname.

As is common in Russian households of the period, French comes easily to all the speakers. (Mashenka probably tutors the children in French or English or both.) You will find such expressions as *ma chère* (my dear), *pardon,* and *Tout comprendre, tout pardonner* (To understand all is to forgive all). Even the Russian dish of sturgeon is called by its French name, "*Esturgeon à la russe.*" Mashenka knows her Russian history and thinks of herself in the condition of the Princess Tarakanov (1752–75) who was seduced and imprisoned in St. Petersburg.

The scene of the second story, "A & P," is a modern supermarket near Boston. The main character, Sammy, is a cashier who has worked there long enough to think of the customers as sheep and to know by heart the sounds of his cash register as he punches it. The story tells of the stir caused in the supermarket by the appearance of three girls in bathing suits. Though he has a lowly job, Sammy has a keen perception of the people and scenes he has encountered and, like Mashenka, has a strong sense of his values when they are violated by his boss.

An Upheaval

Anton Chekhov

Mashenka Pavletsky, a young girl who had only just finished her studies at a boarding school, returning from a walk to the house of the Kushkins, with whom she was living as a governess, found the household in a terrible turmoil. Mihailo, the porter who opened the door to her, was excited and red as a crab.

Loud voices were heard from upstairs.

"Madam Kushkin is in a fit, most likely, or else she has quarrelled with her husband," thought Mashenka.

In the hall and in the corridor she met maidservants. One of them was crying. Then Mashenka saw, running out of her room, the master of the house himself, Nikolay Sergeitch, a little man with a flabby face and a bald head, though he was not old. He was red in the face and twitching all over. He passed the governess without noticing her, and throwing up his arms, exclaimed:

"Oh, how horrible it is! How tactless! How stupid! How barbarous! Abominable!"

Mashenka went into her room, and then, for the first time in her life, it was her lot to experience in all its acuteness the feeling that is so familiar to persons in dependent positions, who eat the bread of the rich and powerful, and cannot speak their minds. There was a search going on in her room. The lady of the house, Fedosya Vassilyevna, a stout, broad-shouldered, uncouth woman with thick black eyebrows, a faintly perceptible moustache, and red hands, who was exactly like a plain, illiterate cook in face and manners, was standing, without her cap on, at the table, putting back into Mashenka's workbag balls of wool, scraps of materials, and bits of paper. . . . Evidently the governess's arrival took her by surprise, since, on looking round and seeing the girl's pale and astonished face, she was a little taken aback, and muttered:

"*Pardon.* I . . . I upset it accidentally. . . . My sleeve caught in it. . . ."

And saying something more, Madame Kushkin rustled her long skirts and went out. Mashenka looked round her room with wondering eyes, and, unable to understand it, not knowing what to think, shrugged her shoulders, and turned cold with dismay. What had Fedosya Vassilyevna been looking for in her work-bag? If she really had, as she said, caught her sleeve in it and upset everything, why had Nikolay Sergeitch dashed out of her room so excited, and red in the face? Why was one drawer of the table pulled out a little way? The money-box, in which the governess put away ten kopeck pieces and old stamps, was open. They had opened it, but did not know how to shut it, though they had scratched the lock all over. The whatnot with her books on it, the things on the table, the bed—all bore fresh traces of a search. Her linen-basket, too. The linen had been carefully folded, but it was not in the same order as Mashenka had left it when she went out. So the search had been thorough, most thorough. But what was it for? Why? What had happened? Mashenka remembered the excited porter, the general turmoil which was still going on, the weeping servant-girl; had it not all some connection with the search that had just been made in her room? Was not she mixed up in something dreadful? Mashenka turned pale, and feeling cold all over, sank on to her linen-basket.

A maidservant came into the room.

"Liza, you don't know why they have been rummaging in my room?" the governess asked her.

"Mistress has lost a brooch worth two thousand," said Liza.

"Yes, but why have they been rummaging in my room?"

"They've been searching every one, miss. They've searched all my things, too. They stripped us all naked and searched us. . . . God knows, miss, I never went near her toilet-table, let alone touching the brooch. I shall say the same at the police-station."

"But . . . why have they been rummaging here?" the governess still wondered.

"A brooch has been stolen, I tell you. The mistress has been rummaging in everything with her own hands. She even searched Mihailo, the porter, herself. It's a perfect disgrace! Nikolay Sergeitch simply looks on and cackles like a hen. But you've no need to tremble like that, miss. They found nothing here. You've nothing to be afraid of if you didn't take the brooch."

"But, Liza, it's vile . . . it's insulting," said Mashenka, breathless with indignation. "It's so mean, so low! What right had she to suspect me and to rummage in my things?"

"You are living with strangers, miss," sighed Liza. "Though you are a young lady, still you are . . . as it were . . . a servant. . . . It's not like living with your papa and mamma."

Mashenka threw herself on the bed and sobbed bitterly. Never in her life had she been subjected to such an outrage, never had she been so deeply insulted. . . . She, well-educated, refined, the daughter of a teacher, was suspected of theft; she had been searched like a street-walker! She could not imagine a greater insult. And to this feeling of resentment was added an oppressive dread of what would come next. All sorts of absurd ideas came into her mind. If they could suspect her of theft, then they might arrest her, strip her naked, and search her, then lead her through the street with an escort of soldiers, cast her into a cold, dark cell with mice and woodlice, exactly like the dungeon in which Princess Tarakanov was imprisoned. Who would stand up for her? Her parents lived far away in the provinces; they had not the money to come to her. In the capital she was as solitary as in a desert, without friends or kindred. They could do what they liked with her.

"I will go to all the courts and all the lawyers," Mashenka thought, trembling. "I will explain to them, I will take an oath. . . . They will believe that I could not be a thief!"

Mashenka remembered that under the sheets in her basket she had some sweetmeats, which, following the habits of her schooldays, she had put in her pocket at dinner and carried off to her room. She felt hot all over, and was ashamed at the thought that her little secret was known to the lady of the house; and all this terror, shame, resentment, brought on an attack of palpitation of the heart, which set up a throbbing in her temples, in her heart, and deep down in her stomach.

"Dinner is ready," the servant summoned Mashenka.

"Shall I go, or not?"

Mashenka brushed her hair, wiped her face with a wet towel, and went into the dining-room. There they had already begun dinner. At one end of the table sat Fedosya Vassilyevna with a stupid, solemn, serious face; at the other end Nikolay Sergeitch. At the sides there were the visitors and the children. The dishes were handed by two footmen in swallowtails and white gloves. Every one knew that there was an upset in the house, that Madame Kushkin was in trouble, and every one was silent. Nothing was heard but the sound of munching and the rattle of spoons on the plates.

The lady of the house, herself, was the first to speak.

"What is the third course?" she asked the footman in a weary, injured voice.

"*Esturgeon à la russe,*" answered the footman.

"I ordered that, Fenya," Nikolay Sergeitch hastened to observe. "I wanted some fish. If you don't like it, *ma chère,* don't let them serve it. I just ordered it. . . ."

Fedosya Vassilyevna did not like dishes that she had not ordered herself, and now her eyes filled with tears.

"Come, don't let us agitate ourselves," Mamikov, her household doctor, observed in a honeyed voice, just touching her arm, with a smile as honeyed. "We are nervous enough as it is. Let us forget the brooch! Health is worth more than two thousand roubles!"

"It's not the two thousand I regret," answered the lady, and a big tear rolled down her cheek. "It's the fact itself that revolts me! I cannot put up with thieves in my house. I don't regret it—I regret nothing; but to steal from me is such ingratitude! That's how they repay me for my kindness. . . ."

They all looked into their plates, but Mashenka fancied after the lady's words that every one was looking at her. A lump rose in her throat; she began crying and put her handkerchief to her lips.

"*Pardon,*" she muttered. "I can't help it. My head aches. I'll go away."

And she got up from the table, scraping her chair awkwardly, and went out quickly, still more overcome with confusion.

"It's beyond everything!" said Nikolay Sergeitch, frowning. "What need was there to search her room? How out of place it was!"

"I don't say she took the brooch," said Fedosya Vassilyevna, "but can you answer for her? To tell the truth, I haven't much confidence in these learned paupers."

"It really was unsuitable, Fenya. . . . Excuse me, Fenya, but you've no kind of legal right to make a search."

"I know nothing about your laws. All I know is that I've lost my brooch. And I will find the brooch!" She brought her fork down on the plate with a clatter, and her eyes flashed angrily. "And you eat your dinner, and don't interfere in what doesn't concern you!"

Nikolay Sergeitch dropped his eyes mildly and sighed. Meanwhile Mashenka, reaching her room, flung herself on her bed. She felt now neither alarm nor shame, but she felt an intense longing to go and slap the cheeks of this hard, arrogant, dull-witted, prosperous woman.

Lying on her bed she breathed into her pillow and dreamed of how nice it would be to go and buy the most expensive brooch and fling it into the face of this bullying woman. If only it were God's will that Fedosya Vassilyevna should come to ruin and wander about begging, and should taste all the horrors of poverty and dependence, and that Mashenka, whom she had insulted, might give her alms! Oh, if only she could come in for a big fortune, could buy a carriage, and could drive noisily past the windows so as to be envied by that woman!

But all these were only dreams, in reality there was only one thing left to do—to get away as quickly as possible, not to stay another hour in this place. It was true it was terrible to lose her place, to go back to her parents, who had nothing; but what could she do? Mashenka could not bear the sight of the lady of the house nor of her little room; she felt stifled and wretched here. She was so disgusted with Fedosya Vassilyevna, who was so obsessed by her illnesses and her supposed aristocratic rank, that everything in the world seemed to have become coarse and unattractive because this woman was living in it. Mashenka jumped up from the bed and began packing.

"May I come in?" asked Nikolay Sergeitch at the door; he had come up noiselessly to the door, and spoke in a soft, subdued voice. "May I?"

"Come in."

He came in and stood still near the door. His eyes looked dim and his red little nose was shiny. After dinner he used to drink beer, and the fact was perceptible in his walk, in his feeble, flabby hands.

"What's this?" he asked, pointing to the basket.

"I am packing. Forgive me, Nikolay Sergeitch, but I cannot remain in your house. I feel deeply insulted by this search!"

"I understand. . . . Only you are wrong to go. . . . Why should you? They've searched your things, but you . . . what does it matter to you? You will be none the worse for it."

Mashenka was silent and went on packing. Nikolay Sergeitch pinched his moustache, as though wondering what he should say next, and went on in an ingratiating voice:

"I understand, of course, but you must make allowances. You know my wife is nervous, headstrong; you mustn't judge her too harshly."

Mashenka did not speak.

"If you are so offended," Nikolay Sergeitch went on, "well, if you like, I'm ready to apologize. I ask your pardon."

Mashenka made no answer, but only bent lower over her box. This exhausted, irresolute man was of absolutely no significance in the household. He stood in the pitiful position of a dependent and hanger-on, even with the servants, and his apology meant nothing either.

"H'm! . . . You say nothing! That's not enough for you. In that case, I will apologize for my wife. In my wife's name. . . . She behaved tactlessly, I admit it as a gentleman. . . ."

Nikolay Sergeitch walked about the room, heaved a sigh, and went on:

"Then you want me to have it rankling here, under my heart. . . . You want my conscience to torment me. . . ."

"I know it's not your fault, Nikolay Sergeitch," said Mashenka, looking him full in the face with her big tear-stained eyes. "Why should you worry yourself?"

"Of course, no. . . . But still, don't you . . . go away. I entreat you."

Mashenka shook her head. Nikolay Sergeitch stopped at the window and drummed on the pane with his finger-tips.

"Such misunderstandings are simply torture to me," he said. "Why, do you want me to go down on my knees to you, or what? Your pride is wounded, and here you've been crying and packing up to go; but I have pride, too, and you do not spare it! Or do you want me to tell you what I would not tell as Confession? Do you? Listen; you want me to tell you what I won't tell the priest on my deathbed?"

Mashenka made no answer.

"I took my wife's brooch," Nikolay Sergeitch said quickly. "Is that enough now? Are you satisfied? Yes, I . . . took it. . . . But, of course, I count on your discretion. . . . For God's sake, not a word, not half a hint to any one!"

Mashenka, amazed and frightened, went on packing; she snatched her things, crumpled them up, and thrust them anyhow into the box and the basket. Now, after this candid avowal on the part of Nikolay Sergeitch, she could not remain another minute, and could not understand how she could have gone on living in the house before.

"And it's nothing to wonder at," Nikolay Sergeitch went on after a pause. "It's an everyday story! I need money, and she . . . won't give it to me. It was my father's money that bought this house and everything, you know! It's all mine, and the brooch belonged to my mother, and . . . it's all mine! And she took it, took possession of everything. . . . I can't go to law with her, you'll admit. . . . I beg you most earnestly, overlook it . . . stay on. *Tout comprendre, tout pardonner.* Will you stay?"

"No!" said Mashenka resolutely, beginning to tremble. "Let me alone, I entreat you!"

"Well, God bless you!" sighed Nikolay Sergeitch, sitting down on the stool near the box. "I must own I like people who still can feel resentment, contempt, and so on. I could sit here forever and look at your indignant face. . . . So you won't stay, then? I understand. . . . It's bound to be so. . . . Yes, of course. . . . It's all right for you, but for me—wo-o-o-o! . . . I can't stir a step out of this cellar. I'd go off to one of our estates, but in every one of them there are some of my wife's rascals . . . stewards, experts, damn them all! They mortgage and remortgage. . . . You mustn't catch fish, must keep off the grass, mustn't break the trees."

"Nikolay Sergeitch!" his wife's voice called from the drawing-room. "Agnia, call your master!"

"Then you won't stay?" asked Nikolay Sergeitch, getting up quickly and going towards the door. "You might as well stay, really. In the evenings I could come and have a talk with you. Eh? Stay! If you go, there won't be a human face left in the house. It's awful!"

Nikolay Sergeitch's pale, exhausted face besought her, but Mashenka shook her head, and with a wave of his hand he went out.

Half an hour later she was on her way.

A & P
John Updike

In walks these three girls in nothing but bathing suits. I'm in the third checkout slot, with my back to the door, so I don't see them until they're over by the bread. The one that caught my eye first was the one in the plaid green two-piece. She was a chunky kid, with a good tan and a sweet broad soft-looking can with those two crescents of white just under it, where the sun never seems to hit, at the top of the backs of her legs. I stood there with my hand on a box of HiHo crackers trying to remember if I rang it up or not. I ring it up again and the customer starts giving me hell. She's one of these cash-register-watchers, a witch about fifty with rouge on her cheekbones and no eyebrows, and I know it made her day to trip me up. She'd been watching cash registers for fifty years and probably never seen a mistake before.

By the time I got her feathers smoothed and her goodies into a bag—she gives me a little snort in passing, if she'd been born at the right time they would have burned her over in Salem—by the time I get her on her way the girls had circled around the bread and were coming back, without a pushcart, back my way along the counters, in the aisle between the checkouts and the Special bins. They didn't even have shoes on. There was this chunky one, with the two-piece—it was bright green and the seams on the bra were still sharp and her belly was still pretty pale so I guessed she just got it (the suit)—there was this one, with one of those chubby berry-faces, the lips all bunched together under her nose, this one, and a tall one, with black hair that hadn't quite frizzed right, and one of these sunburns right across under the eyes, and a chin that was too long—you know, the kind of girl other girls think is very "striking" and "attractive" but never quite makes it, as they very well know, which is why they like her so much—and then the third one, that wasn't quite so tall. She was the queen. She kind of led them, the other two peeking around and making their shoulders round. She didn't look around, not this queen, she just walked straight on slowly, on these long white prima-donna legs. She came down a little hard on her heels, as if she didn't walk in her bare feet that much, putting down her heels and then letting the weight move along to her toes as if she was testing the floor with every step, putting a little deliberate extra action into it. You never know for sure how girls' minds work (do you really think it's a mind in there or just a little buzz like a bee in a glass jar?) but you got the idea she had talked the other two into coming in here with her, and now she was showing them how to do it, walk slow and hold yourself straight.

She had on a kind of dirty-pink—beige maybe, I don't know—bathing suit with a little nubble all over it and, what got me, the straps were down. They were off her shoulders looped loose around the cool tops of her arms, and I guess as a result the suit had slipped a little on her, so all around the top of the cloth there was this shining rim. If it hadn't been there you wouldn't have known there could have been anything whiter than those shoulders. With the straps pushed off, there was nothing between the top of the suit and the top of her head except just *her,* this clean bare plane of the top of her chest down from the shoulder bones like a dented sheet of metal tilted in the light. I mean, it was more than pretty.

She had sort of oaky hair that the sun and salt had bleached, done up in a bun that was unravelling, and a kind of prim face. Walking into the A & P with your straps down, I suppose it's the only kind of face you *can* have. She held her head so high her neck, coming up out of those white shoulders, looked kind of stretched, but I didn't mind. The longer her neck was, the more of her there was.

She must have felt in the corner of her eye me and over my shoulder Stokesie in the second slot watching, but she didn't tip. Not this queen. She kept her eyes moving across the racks, and stopped, and turned so slow it made my stomach rub the inside of my apron, and buzzed to the other two, who kind of huddled against her for relief, and then they all three of them went up the cat-and-dog-food-breakfast-cereal-macaroni-rice-raisins-season-ings-spreads-spaghetti-soft-drinks-crackers-and-cookies aisle. From the third slot I look straight up this aisle to the meat counter, and I watched them all the way. The fat one with the tan sort of fumbled with the cookies, but on second thought she put the package back. The sheep pushing their carts down the aisle—the girls were walking against the usual traffic (not that we have one-way signs or anything)—were pretty hilarious. You could see them, when Queenie's white shoulders dawned on them, kind of jerk, or hop, or hic-cup, but their eyes snapped back to their own baskets and on they pushed. I bet you could set off dynamite in an A & P and the people would by and large keep reaching and checking oatmeal off their lists and muttering "Let me see, there was a third thing, began with A, asparagus, no, ah, yes, applesauce!" or whatever it is they do mutter. But there was no doubt, this jiggled them. A few houseslaves in pin curlers even looked around after pushing their carts past to make sure what they had seen was correct.

You know, it's one thing to have a girl in a bathing suit down on the beach, where what with the glare nobody can look at each other much any-way, and another thing in the cool of the A & P, under the fluorescent lights, against all those stacked packages, with her feet paddling along naked over our checkerboard green-and-cream rubber-tile floor.

"Oh Daddy," Stokesie said beside me. "I feel so faint."

"Darling," I said. "Hold me tight." Stokesie's married, with two babies chalked up on his fuselage already, but as far as I can tell that's the only differ-ence. He's twenty-two, and I was nineteen this April.

"Is it done?" he asks, the responsible married man finding his voice. I forgot to say he thinks he's going to be manager some sunny day, maybe in 1990 when it's called the Great Alexandrov and Petrooshki Tea Company or something.

What he meant was, our town is five miles from a beach, with a big summer colony out on the Point, but we're right in the middle of town, and the women generally put on a shirt or shorts or something before they get out of the car into the street. And anyway these are usually women with six chil-dren and varicose veins mapping their legs and nobody, including them, could care less. As I say, we're right in the middle of town, and if you stand at our front doors you can see two banks and the Congregational church and the newspaper store and three real-estate offices and about twenty-seven old free-loaders tearing up Central Street because the sewer broke again. It's not as if we're on the Cape; we're north of Boston and there's people in this town haven't seen the ocean for twenty years.

The girls had reached the meat counter and were asking McMahon something. He pointed, they pointed, and they shuffled out of sight behind a pyramid of Diet Delight peaches. All that was left for us to see was old McMa-hon patting his mouth and looking after them sizing up their joints. Poor kids, I began to feel sorry for them, they couldn't help it.

Now here comes the sad part of the story, at least my family says it's sad, but I don't think it's so sad myself. The store's pretty empty, it being Thurs-day afternoon, so there was nothing much to do except lean on the register and wait for the girls to show up again. The whole store was like a pinball machine and I didn't know which tunnel they'd come out of. After a while they come around out of the far aisle, around the light bulbs, records at discount of the

Caribbean Six or Tony Martin Sings or some such gunk you wonder they waste the wax on, sixpacks of candy bars, and plastic toys done up in cellophane that fall apart when a kid looks at them anyway. Around they come, Queenie still leading the way, and holding a little gray jar in her hand. Slots Three through Seven are unmanned and I could see her wondering between Stokes and me, but Stokesie with his usual luck draws an old party in baggy pants who stumbles up with four giant cans of pineapple juice (what do these bums *do* with all that pineapple juice? I've often asked myself) so the girls come to me. Queenie puts down the jar and I take it into my fingers icy cold. Kingfish Fancy Herring Snacks in Pure Sour Cream: 49¢. Now her hands are empty, not a ring or a bracelet, bare as God made them, and I wonder where the money's coming from. Still with that prim look she lifts a folded dollar bill out of the hollow at the center of her nubbled pink top. The jar went heavy in my hand. Really, I thought that was so cute.

Then everybody's luck begins to run out. Lengel comes in from haggling with a truck full of cabbages on the lot and is about to scuttle into that door marked MANAGER behind which he hides all day when the girls touch his eye. Lengel's pretty dreary, teaches Sunday school and the rest, but he doesn't miss that much. He comes over and says, "Girls, this isn't the beach."

Queenie blushes, though maybe it's just a brush of sunburn I was noticing for the first time, now that she was so close. "My mother asked me to pick up a jar of herring snacks." Her voice kind of startled me, the way voices do when you see the people first, coming out so flat and dumb yet kind of tony, too, the way it ticked over "pick up" and "snacks." All of a sudden I slid right down her voice into her living room. Her father and the other men were standing around in ice-cream coats and bow ties and the women were in sandals picking up herring snacks on toothpicks off a big glass plate and they were all holding drinks the color of water with olives and sprigs of mint in them. When my parents have somebody over they get lemonade and if it's a real racy affair Schlitz in tall glasses with "They'll Do It Every Time" cartoons stenciled on.

"That's all right," Lengel said. "But this isn't the beach." His repeating this struck me as funny, as if it had just occurred to him, and he had been thinking all these years the A & P was a great big dune and he was the head lifeguard. He didn't like my smiling—as I say he doesn't miss much—but he concentrates on giving the girls that sad Sunday-school-superintendent stare.

Queenie's blush is no sunburn now, and the plump one in plaid, that I liked better from the back—a really sweet can—pipes up, "We weren't doing any shopping. We just came in for the one thing."

"That makes no difference," Lengel tells her, and I could see from the way his eyes went that he hadn't noticed she was wearing a two-piece before. "We want you decently dressed when you come in here."

"We *are* decent," Queenie says suddenly, her lower lip pushing, getting sore now that she remembers her place, a place from which the crowd that runs the A & P must look pretty crummy. Fancy Herring Snacks flashed in her very blue eyes.

"Girls, I don't want to argue with you. After this come in here with your shoulders covered. It's our policy." He turns his back. That's policy for you. Policy is what the kingpins want. What the others want is juvenile delinquency.

All this while, the customers had been showing up with their carts but, you know, sheep, seeing a scene, they had all bunched up on Stokesie, who shook open a paper bag as gently as peeling a peach, not wanting to miss a word. I could feel in the silence everybody getting nervous, most of all Lengel, who asks me, "Sammy, have you rung up their purchase?"

I thought and said "No" but it wasn't about that I was thinking. I go through the punches, 4, 9, GROC, TOT—it's more complicated than you think and after you do it often enough, it begins to make a little song, that you hear words to, in my case "Hello (*bing*) there, you (*gung*) hap-py *pee*-pul (*splat*)!"—the *splat* being the drawer flying out. I uncrease the bill, tenderly as you may imagine, it just having come from between the two smoothest scoops of vanilla I had ever known were there, and pass a half and a penny into her narrow pink palm, and nestle the herrings in a bag and twist its neck and hand it over, all the time thinking.

The girls, and who'd blame them, are in a hurry to get out, so I say "I quit" to Lengel quick enough for them to hear, hoping they'll stop and watch me, their unsuspected hero. They keep right on going, into the electric eye; the door flies open and they flicker across the lot to their car, Queenie and Plaid and Big Tall Goony-Goony (not that as raw material she was so bad), leaving me with Lengel and a kink in his eyebrow.

"Did you say something, Sammy?"

"I said I quit."

"I thought you did."

"You didn't have to embarrass them."

"It was they who were embarrassing us."

I started to say something that came out "Fiddle-de-doo." It's a saying of my grandmother's, and I know she would have been pleased.

"I don't think you know what you're saying," Lengel said.

"I know you don't," I said. "But I do." I pull the bow at the back of my apron and start shrugging it off my shoulders. A couple customers that had been heading for my slot begin to knock against each other, like scared pigs in a chute.

Lengel sighs and begins to look very patient and old and gray. He's been a friend of my parents for years. "Sammy, you don't want to do this to your Mom and Dad," he tells me. It's true, I don't. But it seems to me that once you begin a gesture it's fatal not to go through with it. I fold the apron, "Sammy" stitched in red on the pocket, and put it on the counter, and drop the bow tie on top of it. The bow tie is theirs, if you've ever wondered. "You'll feel this for the rest of your life," Lengel says, and I know that's true, too, but remembering how he made that pretty girl blush makes me so scrunchy inside I punch the No Sale tab and the machine whirs "pee-pul" and the drawer splats out. One advantage to this scene taking place in summer, I can follow this up with a clean exit, there's no fumbling around getting your coat and galoshes, I just saunter into the electric eye in my white shirt that my mother ironed the night before, and the door heaves itself open, and outside the sunshine is skating around on the asphalt.

I look around for my girls, but they're gone, of course. There wasn't anybody but some young married screaming with her children about some candy they didn't get by the door of a powder-blue Falcon station wagon. Looking back in the big windows, over the bags of peat moss and aluminum lawn furniture stacked on the pavement, I could see Lengel in my place in the slot, checking the sheep through. His face was dark gray and his back stiff, as if he'd just had an injection of iron, and my stomach kind of fell as I felt how hard the world was going to be to me hereafter.

Commentary

A formal analysis of design and development of these stories indicates that each is in several parts. The story by Chekhov is in three parts, though these are not textually indicated. In the first part Mashenka returns home and learns that a brooch is missing; the rising "curve of emotion" of this part is the conversation with Liza. The high point of this conversation is probably Mashenka's speech: "But, Liza, it's vile . . . it's insulting." The second part of the story is the account of dinner, both while Mashenka is there and after she leaves. There are two small "curves of emotion" in this middle part of the story, with high points at the lines, "I can't help it. My head aches. I'll go away"; and "And you eat your dinner, and don't interfere in what doesn't concern you!" The third part of the story returns to Mashenka's room and rises to a new "curve of emotion" at the climax of the story: "I took my wife's brooch."

The story by John Updike is in two parts; and the text offers a space just before the second part begins with the words, "Now here comes the sad part of the story." The high point of the first part is the excitement of the two cashiers Sammy and Stokesie over the girls in bathing suits: "Darling . . . Hold me tight." The high point of the second part, and the climax of the story, is Sammy's line, "I quit."

The Chekhov story gives us the impression of a rich household of prerevolutionary Russia, but it's not directly described. Two of the chief characters are described. The husband: "a little man with a flabby face and a bald head, though he was not old." The wife: "a stout, broad-shouldered, uncouth woman with thick black eyebrows, a faintly perceptible moustache, and red hands, who was exactly like a plain illiterate cook in face and manners." The main character, Mashenka, is not described, except by implication in the husband's remark that she has the only human face in the house. The story also has a good deal of minute narration, which tells of the comings and going in the house. There is no remote narration, which might tell us of the years before or after the time of the story, for the entire story covers only a day in the

Kushkin household, and of the "ending" we learn only that Mashenka will return to her poor parents in the provinces. Of drama, the story has three principal conversations, Mashenka's with Liza, the dinner conversation, and Mashenka's with Nikolay Sergeitch. The story also has three extensive passages of reverie, all of them presenting Mashenka's thoughts. She reflects on her condition both before and after her conversation with Liza, and again when she returns to her room just before Nikolay Sergeitch enters. Most of the reverie is "indirect," as if a narrator tells us what she is thinking: "What had Fedosya Vassilyevna been looking for in her workbag?" But her reverie is also at one point "direct," using the very words she might have thought: " 'I will go to all the courts and all the lawyers,' Mashenka thought, trembling. 'I will explain to them, I will take an oath. . . . They will believe that I could not be a thief!' " The three passages of Mashenka's reflection follow her discovery that her room has been searched, her conversation with Liza, and the dinner-table conversation. And her reflections reach their own climax with her decision to leave the house: "But all these are only dreams, in reality there was only one thing to do—to get away as quickly as possible, not to stay another hour in this place." Some readers might call this important passage the climax of the story; most modern critics would also call it the "epiphany," a passage in which the main character sees, as if by special insight or illumination, what her or his life amounts to, or the condition she is in. You will note that many of the reflective passages are future in implication: what should Mashenka do from now on because of her humiliation?

Because all the reverie in this story is Mashenka's, we might say the story is written from her point of view; and so it is, except for a brief passage of dinner conversation that occurs after she leaves. So we could call the point of view "third-person restricted"—restricted, that is, to Mashenka, except for a brief switch to "omniscient" or all-knowing viewpoint; or we could call the viewpoint as a whole "omniscient" with a primary focus on Mashenka's thoughts. If we might suppose that Mashenka overhears or imagines the conversation after she leaves the table, we might incorporate this conversation in her viewpoint.

The story by John Updike is written in the "first-person" viewpoint and in a style that captures the conversational quality of the boy's speech. In fact, most of the story seems to be the boy talking, so that the distinction of rhetorical modes is a little more difficult to perceive. We have extensive passages of description, especially of the girls, and the description is often infiltrated by the boy's thoughts. In these two sentences the first is primarily descriptive, though seen as the boy would see it, and the second is entirely his reflective response: "With the straps pushed off, there was nothing between the top of the suit and the top of her head except just *her*, this clean bare plane of the top of her chest down from the shoulder bones like a dented sheet of metal tilted in the light. I mean, it was more than pretty." The actual sentences of narration in this story are isolated and seem slight alongside the description and reverie, but the story of course could not be told without them: "In walks these three girls in nothing but bathing suits." "She kind of led them, the other two peeking around and making their shoulders round." "Lengel comes in from haggling with a truck full of cabbages on the lot . . ."

This story has much less of drama than the other. The only significant passages include the little jokes between the two cashiers, "Oh Daddy . . . I feel so faint." And Stokesie's question to Sammy on social usage, "Is it done?"—that is, is it proper for young people of her class to appear in public in skimpy clothing? Also, the manager scolding the girls, with their responses to him, and Sammy's talk with the manager after his announcement that he is quitting. In addition to this "direct" drama, the story has also some "indirect" drama. "I ring it up again and the customer starts giving me hell." Her exact words are not quoted. The following little exchange, presented as narration, might be considered "indirect" drama or "pantomime"—silent drama. "The girls had reached the meat counter and were asking McMahon something. He pointed, they pointed, and they shuffled out of sight behind a pyramid of Diet Delight peaches." Sammy sees but does not hear the conversation.

As is to be expected from a first-person account, "A & P" is extensively reflective. Almost every sentence is permeated with the boy's thoughts, and the persons and events are presented as he sees them. All the reverie is "direct," or presented in the very words the first-person narrator would say or think. A sentence like the following is descriptive but also has little reflective intrusions: "She had on a kind of dirty-pink—beige maybe, I don't know—bathing suit with a little nubble all over it and, what got me, the straps were down." The expressions "beige maybe, I don't know" and "what got me" are his thoughts; even the "kind of dirty-pink" and the "little nubble all over it" tell what Sammy, rather than another viewer, would notice. The following sentence is narrative but easily slips into the boy's thoughts: "After a while they come around out of the far aisle, around the light bulbs, records at discount of the Caribbean Six or Tony Martin Sings or some such gunk you wonder they waste the wax on, sixpacks of candy bars, and plastic toys done up in cellophane that fall apart when a kid looks at them anyway." The following striking passage looks like narration and description, but it is really reverie, the boy imagining a scene at the home of "Queenie": "All of a sudden I slid right down her voice into her living room. Her father and the other men were standing around in ice-cream coats and bow ties and the women were in sandals picking up herring snacks on toothpicks off a big glass plate and they were all holding drinks the color of water with olives and sprigs of mint in them."

The formal and rhetorical analysis of these two stories provides a good basis for an analysis of their elements. The story-time of both stories is short; in the first, part of a day passes in the Kushkin household, perhaps an afternoon and an evening; in the second story only about half an hour passes in the supermarket. The slightly longer time of the first accommodates a more elaborate plot, partly along the lines of a mystery story or "whodunit." What has become of the brooch, or who has stolen it? The surprise caused by our discovery of the husband's theft, and the girl's decision to depart, point to some importance of plot in that story. The second story has no mystery. The manager scolds the girls and they leave; the "surprise" is simply Sammy's decision to quit, but his hope that the girls will hear him is not realized, as it might have been in a story of plot. In such a story, he might have got to know the girls and perhaps even find that he was related to one of them; or one girl might get him a new job at her father's business, and so forth—but Updike's story stops at Sammy's departure and offers us no further plot of the rest of his life. Both stories have ironic plots dealing with weak, modern people mostly powerless in opposition to the forces of society; as both have to do with separations rather than unions between people, they are a little closer to tragedy than to comedy.

In characterization, the first story gives us briefly a good sense of the characters of Kushkin and his wife. The description of them, and their conversation, show him to be weak and dominated by his vulgar wife. The uproar in the household is caused by her insistence on dominating not only her husband but all the servants; she is a tyrant, while he is not respected by her or anyone in the household. Mashenka's reflection on him when he apologizes to her seems right: "This exhausted, irresolute man was of absolutely no significance in the household. He stood in the pitiful position of a dependent and hanger-on, even with the servants, and his apology meant nothing either." In conversation with his wife, and with Mashenka, he comes across as an apologetic, cringing character without self-respect. Because of the relationship between husband and wife in this rich household, we might expect that the money it is based on has come from her family, but we find instead that it has come from his—he has lost any control over it to his demanding and assertive wife. Mashenka herself is not directly characterized, but we come to see her by implication as a modest person of some intelligence and judgment—and spirit, as seen in her decision to give up her job in return for poverty or insecurity.

The main characters in "A & P" are Sammy and Lengel, the manager, and the three girls. The girl Sammy calls "Queenie" comes across as the proud and attractive leader of the three; she seems to lead them around the market. Lengel is characterized by what he says to the girls and to Sammy, which is in keeping with Sammy's characterization of him as conventionally "proper" but also perceptive: "Lengel's pretty dreary, teaches Sunday school and the rest, but he doesn't miss that much." The most fully realized character in the story is naturally Sammy himself; and the extensiveness of his thoughts presented as he would speak them characterize him far more fully than the third-person viewpoint of Mashenka. Despite his lowly job, we see Sammy as gifted with a considerable perception and a keenness in expressing it. He has his job down pat and he is also good at sizing up his co-workers and his customers. In addition to his observations on the girls and Lengel he speculates imaginatively and generalizes on his customers: "You never know for sure how girls' minds work (do you really think it's a mind in there or just a little buzz like a bee in a glass jar?) . . ." "I bet you could set off dynamite in an A & P and the people would by and large keep reaching and checking oatmeal off their lists and muttering 'Let me see, there was a third thing, began with A, asparagus, no, ah, yes, applesauce!' "; and ". . . an old party with four giant cans of pineapple juice (what do these bums *do* with all that pineapple juice? I've often asked myself) . . ." He also has opinions on the uselessness of records and toys in his market; and he perceives the social distinction between his own household that serves beer and "Queenie's" household that serves, as he imagines it, cocktails and snacks; he notes with admiration a "tony" quality in her voice. He is also an experienced girl-watcher, as his knowing inspection of the girls reveals: "these two crescents of white just under it, where the sun never seems to hit, at the tops of the backs of her legs." Apart from his appreciation of the girls' beauty he also has a human sympathy for them: "Poor kids, I began to feel sorry for them, they couldn't help it." Sammy also has a good sense of humor, as he speculates amusingly that by the time Stokesie becomes a manager, the Russians may have taken over our society.

His character is primarily shown in his decision, like Mashenka's, to abandon such security as his job offers because of an insult to his values. He says to Lengel: "You didn't have to embarrass them," but the modesty of his comment cannot fully account for his objections to the embarrassing of the girls. He seems to think the community's conventional standards of propriety are false, and he also seems to be offended at Lengel's middle-class outrage at the easy, upper-class manners of the girls, especially of "Queenie." Stokesie clearly aspires to a higher job and status, and Sammy too, though not so obviously, very likely aspires to a higher social condition than he has previously known. Our review of plot and character in the two stories seems to indicate that plot is of greater importance in the first and characterization in the second.

The theme of "An Upheaval" is hinted at on the first page: "the feeling that is so familiar to persons in dependent positions, who eat the bread of the rich and powerful, and cannot speak their minds." In case there is any doubt of this theme, Liza later confirms it: "Though you are a young lady, still you are . . . as it were . . . a servant . . . It's not like living with your papa and mamma." As the story develops, so does the theme, though it is suggested, not stated: a person of self-respect will not continue to suffer indignities, but must choose insecurity over insult. "A & P" suggests a theme similar to the theme of "An Upheaval": one must assert real standards of value and propriety against false or trivial ones. As the girls have offended Lengel's values, Lengel has offended Sammy's. When Lengel questions Sammy's decision, Sammy seems to weaken, but he offers us this idea: "it seems to me that once you begin a gesture it's fatal not to go through with it." Sammy hints that his parents later disapprove of his decision to quit, but also hints at a closer alliance of personality with his grandmother, from whom he has picked up the remark, "Fiddle-de-doo," and perhaps some of her values as well. When Lengel says, "It's our policy," Sammy has an ironic reflection: "That's policy for you. Policy is what the kingpins want. What the others want is juvenile delinquency." If we reverse, as we should, this ironic comment, we derive the theme that powerless youth may well have values superior to those of adults in positions in power. Sammy seems to share the values of "Queenie's" family as he perceives them. Mashenka, too, has a sense of values superior to those of her mistress, who, though rich, has the manners, in Mashenka's view, of a cook. The themes of the two stories are, then, similar, though the story by Chekhov insists on its theme more than the other story does, by expressing it twice; the story by Updike leaves us to derive a similar theme.

Sound-effects in the story by Chekhov can be entirely dismissed; as the story is translated we can assume all, or most, of its original sound-effects are lost. The story by Updike has a few hints of expression chosen at least partly for their alliterative sound-effects: "looped loose around the cool tops of her arms," "kind of jerk, or hop, or hiccup," "sad Sunday-school-superintendent stare." Both stories are, of course, in prose, the words of which are chosen usually for varying and inconspicuous sounds.

The styles of the two stories contrast considerably, because the Chekhov seems to be written in unobtrusive word-choices, wheras the Updike seems to have been written with a real attempt at stylistic flair—in this case for a racy but incisive colloquialism. The story by Chekhov has only two similes, both applied to the husband and neither very original: "red as a crab," "cackles like a hen." The story by Updike has a great many striking similes and metaphors: "one of those chubby berry-faces, the lips all bunched together under her nose," "these long white prima-donna legs," "a little buzz like a bee in a glass jar," "this clean bare plane of the top of her chest down from the shoulder bones like a dented sheet of metal tilted in the light," "oaky hair," "her feet paddling along naked," two babies "chalked up on his fueslage," "The whole store was like a pinball machine and I didn't know which tunnel they'd come out of," "Fancy herring snacks flashed in her very blue eyes," "Stokesie, who shook open a paper bag as gently as peeling a peach," "I uncrease the bill, tenderly as you may imagine, it just having come from between the two smoothest scoops of vanilla I had ever known were there," "as if he'd just had an injection of iron."

Of setting, we get a strong impression of the workings of the Kushkin household, but no extensive description of it. The details we pick up—of the dinner table, of the maids and footmen, of Mashenka's room with its whatnot (or set of shelves) and workbasket—seem to come up to account for the progression of the plot; no details seem to be introduced for their own sake. In "A & P," however, we have elaborate descriptions of the market, its aisles, its goods, its workers and its customers; these details are not strictly necessary to follow the plot of the girl and the manager and Sammy, and seem to come into the story simply to vivify the place of its action. The comparison of the super-market to a pinball machine also gives us the feeling of the place as one awaits for a desired person or persons to reappear. As a result we have a much more vivid sense of the supermarket than we have of the Russian household.

Overall in the disposition of elements, though we have found, of course, all the elements in both the stories, we have discovered an emphasis on plot, character, and theme in the story by Chekhov, and on character, style, and setting in the story by Updike.

Exercise

Read the following excerpts from Chekhov's "The Kiss," especially with a view toward determining the rhetorical modes used, and working from them to the elements they hint at. Then answer the questions following each excerpt.

(All ellipses in these excerpts appear in the original.)

I. On his way back he met with a little adventure. When he had gone half-way he noticed he had taken a wrong turning. He distinctly remembered that he ought to meet three sleepy footmen on his way, but he had passed five or six rooms, and those sleepy figures seemed to have vanished into the earth. Notic-ing his mistake, he walked back a little way and turned to the right; he found himself in a little dark room which he had not seen on his way to the billiard-room. After standing there a little while, he resolutely opened the first door that met his eyes and walked into an absolutely dark room. Straight in front could be seen the crack in the doorway through which there was a gleam of vivid light; from the other side of the door came the muffled sound of a melan-choly mazurka. Here, too, as in the drawing-room, the windows were wide open and there was a smell of poplars, lilac and roses. . . .

Ryabovitch stood still in hesitation. . . . At that moment, to his sur-prise, he heard hurried footsteps and the rustling of a dress, a breathless femi-nine voice whispered "At last!" And two soft, fragrant, unmistakably feminine arms were clasped about his neck; a warm cheek was pressed to his cheek, and simultaneously there was the sound of a kiss. But at once the be-stower of the kiss uttered a faint shriek and skipped back from him, as it seemed to Ryabovitch, with aversion. He, too, almost shrieked and rushed towards the gleam of light at the door. . . .

   1. Underline all descriptive effects—the sights and sounds along the way—and decide what they contribute to the scene as a whole. What about "sleepy footmen," "melancholy mazurka," "poplars, lilac and roses"?

   2. Bracket all reflective effects—whatever could not be noticed by an ob-jective observer, but must come from Ryabovitch's "point of view." Such expressions as, "He distinctly remembered," "Noticing his mis-take," "as it seemed to Ryabovitch," will help you locate the reverie.

3. The drama in this passage is restricted to two words: "At last!" In what mode then is the remainder of the passage?

4. What element does the first sentence, with its use of the term "adventure," hint at? Is this confirmed by the rhetorical mode most extensively used, in the answer to the last question?

5. Is there anything in this "adventure" that requires Ryabovitch to be a special kind of character? It may be more appropriate, or ironic, that the adventure happened to someone shy, but couldn't it have happened to any guest returning from the billiard-room? Is anything revealed about the character of the lady, except that she kissed the wrong man? How then do you assess the role of character in this passage?

6. Is there any theme hinted at in this passage? Can Ryabovitch's experience be very easily or sensibly generalized: "When you're at a party in a strange house, frequent the dark and empty rooms"? How then do you assess the role of theme in this passage?

II. (This excerpt in the story immediately follows the first one.)

When he went back into the drawing-room his heart was beating and his hands were trembling so noticeably that he made haste to hide them behind his back. At first he was tormented by shame and dread that the whole drawing-room knew that he had just been kissed and embraced by a woman. He shrank into himself and looked uneasily about him, but as he became convinced that people were dancing and talking as calmly as ever, he gave himself up entirely to the new sensation which he had never experienced before in his life. Something strange was happening to him. . . . His neck, round which soft, fragrant arms had so lately been clasped, seemed to him to be anointed with oil; on his left cheek near his moustache where the unknown had kissed him there was a faint chilly tingling sensation as from peppermint drops, and the more he rubbed the place the more distinct was the chilly sensation; all over, from head to foot, he was full of a strange new feeling which grew stronger and stronger. . . . He wanted to dance, to talk, to run into the garden, to laugh aloud. . . . He quite forgot that he was round-shouldered and uninteresting, that he had lynx-like whiskers and an "undistinguished appearance" (that was how his appearance had been described by some ladies whose conversation he had accidentally overheard). When Von Rabbek's wife happened to pass by him, he gave her such a broad and friendly smile that she stood still and looked at him inquiringly.

"I like your house immensely!" he said, setting his spectacles straight.

1. Underline all objectively descriptive and narrative effects in the passage—those unattached to Ryabovitch's reflective "point of view." (You will not come up with much.) The drama is again restricted to one line, here the last. What then is the most extensive mode here, and how does the passage as a whole contrast with the first one?

2. Does anything remarkable happen in this passage, compared to the

first? Is it significant to any possible plot that he shrinks into his thoughts and is emboldened to address his hostess? Could she be, for instance, the lady who accidentally kissed him? What then is the role of plot in this passage?

3. Does the interest of the passage seem based on what is typical of Ryabovitch, or what is special about him? Is he the same now as he was before the adventure, or is he shown changing? Is his comment to the hostess an easy and polite formality, or a rare outburst from a very shy man, which the passage as a whole builds him up to? What then is the role of character in the passage?

4. Again, is it very easy or sensible to generalize from this passage and arrive at a theme: "Accidental kisses will make a new man of you"? What then is the role of theme in the passage?

III. (This excerpt comes near the very end of the story.)

   Now that he expected nothing, the incident of the kiss, his impatience, his vague hopes and disappointment, presented themselves in a clear light. It no longer seemed to him strange that he had not seen the General's messenger, and that he would never see the girl who had accidentally kissed him instead of someone else; on the contrary, it would have been strange if he had seen her. . . .

   The water was running, he knew not where or why, just as it did in May. In May it had flowed into the great river, from the great river into the sea; then it had risen in vapour, turned into rain and perhaps the very same water was running now before Ryabovitch's eyes again. . . . What for? Why?

   And the whole world, the whole of life, seemed to Ryabovitch an unintelligible, aimless jest. . . . And turning his eyes from the water and looking at the sky, he remembered again how fate in the person of an unknown woman had by chance caressed him, he remembered his summer dreams and fancies, and his life struck him as extraordinarily meagre, poverty-stricken, and colourless. . . .

1. There is no drama in this passage. Is there any narration—any record of events? What is the mode primarily used?

2. Is there any description in the passage? Where does it occur and what is it doing there? Does it establish a romantic setting, as the descriptive effects in the first excerpt do? Ryabovitch has returned to the scene of his kiss, as he imagines the water doing. Does the comparison with the water help Ryabovitch (and the reader) see his return in a much larger perspective—not as exciting, but as cold and objective?

3. What element is involved when you are seeing things in "a much larger perspective"? In the third paragraph, are the first sentence and the last clause true only of Ryabovitch, or are they applicable to almost any modern human being? What then is the role of theme in this passage?

4. Is character as negligible in this passage as it was in the first? Or is there a closer balance between character and theme here? Is the passage a natural, thematic result of the development of Ryabovitch's character all along?

Suggestions

First look at the overall and superficial outlines of the work, its size and shape and divisions, if any are supplied. Try to get a view of the design and development of the work as a whole, to see where it's going and how it gets there. While reading the work you were caught up in the development of it; now stop and see if you can make out its design. Keeping in mind Freytag's pyramid of rising and falling action, determine how many pyramids or "curves of emotion" there are, how many larger ones, how many smaller ones within those, and where the climaxes seem to come.

You may be helped in your formal analysis by a rhetorical analysis. The heights of its "curves of emotion" will often be in the mode of drama, plainly marked in most modern fiction by quotation marks and indentations, indicating different speakers. But if one speaker speaks for a long passage without interruption, that speech may be in the mode of narration or some other mode. Of the other modes, you will have no trouble isolating the description—the parts where the story stops and you are given a static picture. You may have more trouble isolating the reverie. In older fiction reverie often appears in quotation marks like drama, only attached to "he thought" instead of "he said." In recent fiction reverie may be in italics, or it may not be differentiated from narration at all. You will have to be on the lookout for quick shifts of tense, including the future tense, especially in the first-person passages. What is left now is the narration itself, which in stories is usually the most extensive mode. Be sure to differentiate between remote narration, with long gaps of time in a few sentences, and minute narration, which is close on-the-spot reporting, often leading to a high point of drama.

Here is where to take notice of "point of view." If, outside the dramatic passages, there are no first-person statements and you can find no third-person reverie, the "point of view" is "objective." If there is a first-person narrator, there will usually be some of her or his "subjective" reverie. But you may sometimes find yourself inside the thoughts of a third person, a character other than the narrator. If the author enters the thoughts of more than one third person, the "point of view" is "omniscient." If the author enters the thoughts of only one character, the "point of view" is "restricted" or "limited."

In approaching analysis of elements, you should be able to summarize the plot, give brief sketches of the main characters, discuss the theme, describe the setting and mood, and point out anything special about the style and sound-effects of the work. The last two elements are not very often stressed in fiction: though each of the six elements exists to some extent in every literary work, one or more elements may sometimes be negligible.

Unless the plot is unusually tricky, there's no need to discuss it, for any reader will have been able to follow it without help. When asked to analyze a story, beginning students often summarize the plot, even if told not to, because that's what they think of first. It's usually more worthwhile to discuss the characters, theme, and setting of the work, for there may be more disagreement on just what these are like, especially if they aren't emphasized in the work. When theme is emphasized, it's usually strong enough to speak for itself; if not emphasized, there may be some doubt about what it could be. But though there may be much interest in discussing an element not emphasized, the best procedure is usually to scrutinize the element or elements most emphasized in the work. Why spend a lot of time on what is of little importance?

In order to justify your interest in a particular element you may wish to demonstrate that it is emphasized; or you may wish to discuss that element even if not emphasized. When weighing plot and character, remember that narration, especially remote, is the usual agent of plot, and that drama and minute narration, as well as reverie, are the usual agents of character. Determine how long a time is supposed to pass in the story, and how many characters are chiefly involved in it. A long stretch of time and a good many characters suggest an emphasis on plot; a short stretch of time and a few characters suggest an emphasis on character. Often drama will be the agent of character, and reverie of theme, but not necessarily. A more reliable sign of theme is general or abstract statements, indicating how the particular action of the work can be extended to other people and places. These will occur as some character's speculations, whether in the modes of reverie or drama: she can keep her thoughts to herself, or tell someone about them. But the theme may be strong even if you can't find many general passages. So when weighing character and theme, determine how large a class the characters seem to represent. If there's a pretty clear indication that the characters and actions are typical of many others, look for an emphasis on theme. If the characters seem to speak only for themselves, look for an emphasis on character. Plot, character, and theme are the three main elements, and if you have got this far you might consult the sections of this book that give more detailed suggestions for determining emphasis.

Of the other elements, setting is the one most likely to prove a rival of the first three. Long passages of description and reverie—objective and subjective responses to scenes—will be the best sign of an emphasis on setting. Or there may be a great many metaphors and other figures of speech, or unusual sentence-structures, which will call some attention to diction or style. In narrative poetry, which some teachers might call "fiction," sound will be of some importance, and some narrative writing in prose will also make use of prose rhythms—though such effects are relatively rare, and always of lesser importance than the primary elements. If you're reading a work in translation, of course, the original sound is altogether lost, but the other elements usually carry over to the new language.

5

Analyzing Drama

The two dramatic passages below continue the subject of saying good-bye, the first by the Norwegian playwright Henrik Ibsen (1828–1906), the second by the American playwright Eugene O'Neill (1888–1953).

The first comes at the end of Ibsen's *A Doll's House,* first staged in 1879. Nora and Torvald Helmer have been happily married and have three children. But a problem arises when a man named Krogstad appears and tries to black-mail Nora. In the past during an illness of her husband and the terminal ill-ness of her father, she borrowed money from Krogstad so that her husband and she could go on a trip to Italy for his health—but she forged her father's counter-signature on the loan, not wishing to trouble the dying man. Krog-stad threatens to reveal her secret to her husband, unless Nora will insure his promotion at the bank Torvald manages. When she refuses, he writes a letter to Torvald revealing Nora's action of the past. Torvald has just seen the letter and has humiliated Nora over her misdemeanor, but he has relented after see-ing a second letter in which Krogstad for his own reasons has withdrawn his threat. Nora and Torvald are now free, and Torvald is delighted. But Nora has a different response, as shown in this passage.

The second dramatic passage comes from Eugene O'Neill's *Beyond the Horizon,* first staged in 1920. The two Mayo brothers both love the same girl, Ruth. Andrew, a good farmer and in line to inherit his father's farm, is ex-pected to marry Ruth, while Robert, the poet and dreamer, has decided to go aboard ship with his uncle, Captain Scott. A new development arises when Ruth reveals to Robert that she loves him, not Andrew. The conversation that takes place here occurs between Mr. and Mrs. Mayo, the two sons, and Cap-tain Scott. Mr. Mayo has been hoping that Andrew will carry on the farm. He would be pleased for Robert to remain on the farm as well. But Robert is not good at farming, and Mayo is resigned to his taking a romantic voyage with his wife's brother, Captain Scott.

You will encounter a little unusual language from Captain Scott, who speaks the dialect of a New England sailor, pronouncing the word "spoil" as "spile," "voyage" as "vige," and "starboard" as "sta'b'd," and using the term "dunnage" for personal luggage.

from *A Doll's House*

NORA. (*in everyday dress*) Yes, Torvald, I have changed my things now.

HELMER. But what for?—so late as this.

NORA. I shall not sleep to-night.

HELMER. But my dear Nora—

NORA. (*looking at her watch*) It is not so very late. Sit down here, Torvald. You and I have much to say to one another. (*She sits down at one side of the table.*)

HELMER. Nora—what is this?—this cold, set face?

NORA. Sit down. It will take some time; I have a lot to talk over with you.

HELMER. (*sits down at the opposite side of the table*) You alarm me, Nora!—and I don't understand you.

NORA. No, that is just it. You don't understand me, and I have never understood you either—before to-night. No, you mustn't interrupt me. You must simply listen to what I say. Torvald, this is a settling of accounts.

HELMER. What do you mean by that?

NORA. (*after a short silence*) Isn't there one thing that strikes you as strange in our sitting here like this?

HELMER. What is that?

NORA. We have been married now eight years. Does it not occur to you that this is the first time we two, you and I, husband and wife, have had a serious conversation?

HELMER. What do you mean by serious?

NORA. In all these eight years—longer than that—from the very beginning of our acquaintance, we have never exchanged a word on any serious subject.

HELMER. Was it likely that I would be continually and for ever telling you about worries that you could not help me to bear?

NORA. I am not speaking about business matters. I say that we have never sat down in earnest together to try and get at the bottom of anything.

HELMER. But, dearest Nora, would it have been any good to you?

NORA. That is just it; you have never understood me. I have been greatly wronged, Torvald—first by papa and then by you.

HELMER. What! By us two—by us two, who have loved you better than anyone else in the world?

NORA. (*shaking her head*) You have never loved me. You have only thought it pleasant to be in love with me.

HELMER. Nora, what do I hear you saying?

NORA. It is perfectly true, Torvald. When I was at home with papa, he told me his opinion about everything, and so I had the same opinions; and if I differed from him I concealed the fact, because he would not have liked it. He called me his doll-child, and he played with me just as I used to play with my dolls. And when I came to live with you—

HELMER. What sort of an expression is that to use about our marriage?

NORA. (*undisturbed*) I mean that I was simply transferred from papa's hands into yours. You arranged everything according to your own taste, and so I got the same tastes as you—or else I pretended to, I am really not quite sure which—I think sometimes the one and sometimes the other. When I look back on it, it seems to me as if I had been living here like a poor woman—just from hand to mouth. I have existed merely to perform tricks for you, Torvald. But you would have it so. You and papa have committed a great sin against me. It is your fault that I have made nothing of my life.

HELMER. How unreasonable and how ungrateful you are, Nora! Have you not been happy here?

NORA. No, I have never been happy. I thought I was, but it has never really been so.

HELMER. Not—not happy!

NORA. No, only merry. And you have always been so kind to me. But our home has been nothing but a playroom. I have been your doll-wife, just as at home I was papa's doll-child; and here the children have been my dolls. I thought it great fun when you played with me, just as they thought it great fun when I played with them. That is what our marriage has been, Torvald.

HELMER. There is some truth in what you say—exaggerated and strained as your view of it is. But for the future it shall be different. Playtime shall be over, and lesson-time shall begin.

NORA. Whose lessons? Mine, or the children's?

HELMER. Both yours and the children's, my darling Nora.

NORA. Alas, Torvald, you are not the man to educate me into being a proper wife for you.

HELMER. And you can say that!

NORA. And I—how am I fitted to bring up the children?

HELMER. Nora!

NORA. Didn't you say so yourself a little while ago—that you dare not trust me to bring them up?

HELMER. In a moment of anger! Why do you pay any heed to that?

NORA. Indeed, you were perfectly right. I am not fit for the task. There is another task I must undertake first. I must try and educate myself—you are not the man to help me in that. I must do that for myself. And that is why I am going to leave you now.

HELMER. (*springing up*) What do you say?

NORA. I must stand quite alone, if I am to understand myself and everything about me. It is for that reason that I cannot remain with you any longer.

HELMER. Nora! Nora!

NORA. I am going away from here now, at once. I am sure Christine will take me in for the night—

HELMER. You are out of your mind! I won't allow it! I forbid you!

NORA. It is no use forbidding me anything any longer. I will take with me what belongs to myself. I will take nothing from you, either now or later.

HELMER. What sort of madness is this!

NORA. To-morrow I shall go home—I mean, to my old home. It will be easiest for me to find something to do there.

HELMER. You blind, foolish woman!

NORA. I must try and get some sense, Torvald.

HELMER. To desert your home, your husband and your children! And you don't consider what people will say!

NORA. I cannot consider that at all. I only know that it is necessary for me.

HELMER. It's shocking. This is how you would neglect your most sacred duties.

NORA. What do you consider my most sacred duties?

HELMER. Do I need to tell you that? Are they not your duties to your husband and children?

NORA. I have other duties just as sacred.

HELMER. That you have not. What duties could those be?

NORA. Duties to myself.

HELMER. Before all else, you are a wife and a mother.

NORA. I don't believe that any longer. I believe that before all else I am a reasonable human being, just as you are—or, at all events, that I must try and become one. I know quite well, Torvald, that most people would think you right, and that views of that kind are to be found in books; but I can no longer content myself with what most people say, or with what is found in books. I must think over things for myself and get to understand them.

HELMER. Can you not understand your place in your own home? Have you not a reliable guide in such matters as that?—have you no religion?

NORA. I am afraid, Torvald, I do not exactly know what religion is.

HELMER. What are you saying?

NORA. I know nothing but what the clergyman said, when I went to be confirmed. He told us that religion was this, and that, and the other. When I am away from all this, and am alone, I will look into that matter too. I will see if what the clergyman said is true, or at all events if it is true for me.

HELMER. This is unheard of in a girl of your age! But if religion cannot lead you aright, let me try and awaken your conscience. I suppose you have some moral sense? Or—answer me—am I to think you have none?

NORA. I assure you, Torvald, that is not an easy question to answer. I really don't know. The thing perplexes me altogether. I only know that you and I look at it in quite a different light. I am learning, too, that the law is quite another thing from what I supposed; but I find it impossible to convince myself that the law is right. According to it a woman has no right to spare her old dying father, or to save her husband's life. I can't believe that.

HELMER. You talk like a child. You don't understand the conditions of the world in which you live.

NORA. No, I don't. But now I am going to try. I am going to see if I can make out who is right, the world or I.

HELMER. You are ill, Nora; you are delirious; I almost think you are out of your mind.

NORA. I have never felt my mind so clear and certain as to-night.

HELMER. And is it with a clear and certain mind that you forsake your husband and your children?

NORA. Yes, it is.

HELMER. Then there is only one possible explanation.

NORA. What is that?

HELMER. You do not love me any more.

NORA. No, that is just it.

HELMER. Nora!—and you can say that?

NORA. It gives me great pain, Torvald, for you have always been so kind to me, but I cannot help it. I do not love you any more.

HELMER. (*regaining his composure*) Is that a clear and certain conviction too?

NORA. Yes, absolutely clear and certain. That is the reason why I will not stay here any longer.

HELMER. And can you tell me what I have done to forfeit your love?

NORA. Yes, indeed I can. It was to-night, when the wonderful thing did not happen; then I saw you were not the man I had thought you.

HELMER. Explain yourself better—I don't understand you.

NORA. I have waited so patiently for eight years; for, goodness knows, I knew very well that wonderful things don't happen every day. Then this horrible misfortune came upon me; and then I felt quite certain that the wonderful thing was going to happen at last. When Krogstad's letter was lying out there, never for a moment did I imagine that you would consent to accept this man's conditions. I was so absolutely certain that you would say to him: Publish the thing to the whole world. And when that was done—

HELMER. Yes, what then?—when I had exposed my wife to shame and disgrace?

NORA. When that was done, I was so absolutely certain, you would come forward and take everything upon yourself, and say: I am the guilty one.

HELMER. Nora—!

NORA. You mean that I would never have accepted such a sacrifice on your part? No, of course not. But what would my assurances have been worth against yours? That was the wonderful thing which I hoped for and feared; and it was to prevent that, that I wanted to kill myself.

HELMER. I would gladly work night and day for you, Nora—bear sorrow and want for your sake. But no man would sacrifice his honor for the one he loves.

NORA. It is a thing hundreds of thousands of women have done.

HELMER. Oh, you think and talk like a heedless child.

NORA. Maybe. But you neither think nor talk like the man I could bind myself to. As soon as your fear was over—and it was not fear for what threatened me, but for what might happen to you—when the whole thing was past, as far as you were concerned it was exactly as if nothing at all had happened. Exactly as before, I was your little skylark, your doll, which you would in future treat with doubly gentle care, because it was so brittle and fragile. (*Getting up.*) Torvald—it was then it dawned upon me that for eight years I had been living here with a strange man, and had borne him three children—. Oh, I can't bear to think of it! I could tear myself into little bits!

HELMER. (*sadly*) I see, I see. An abyss has opened between us—there is no denying it. But, Nora, would it not be possible to fill it up?

NORA. As I am now, I am no wife for you.

HELMER. I have it in me to become a different man.

NORA. Perhaps—if your doll is taken away from you.

HELMER. But to part!—to part from you! No, no, Nora, I can't understand that idea.

NORA. (*going out to the right*) That makes it all the more certain that it must be done. (*She comes back with her cloak and hat and a small bag which she puts on a chair by the table.*)

HELMER. Nora, Nora, not now! Wait till to-morrow.

NORA. (*putting on her cloak*) I cannot spend the night in a strange man's room.

HELMER. But can't we live here like brother and sister—?

NORA. (*putting on her hat*) You know very well that would not last long. (*Puts the shawl round her.*) Good-bye, Torvald. I won't see the little ones. I know they are in better hands than mine. As I am now, I can be of no use to them.

HELMER. But some day, Nora—some day?

NORA. How can I tell? I have no idea what is going to become of me.

HELMER. But you are my wife, whatever becomes of you.

NORA. Listen, Torvald. I have heard that when a wife deserts her husband's house, as I am doing now, he is legally freed from all obligations towards her. In any case I set you free from all your obligations. You are not to feel yourself bound in the slightest way, any more than I shall. There must be perfect freedom on both sides. See, here is your ring back. Give me mine.

HELMER. That too?

NORA. That too.

HELMER. Here it is.

NORA. That's right. Now it is all over. I have put the keys here. The maids know all about everything in the house—better than I do. To-morrow, after I have left her, Christine will come here and pack up my own things that I brought with me from home. I will have them sent after me.

HELMER. All over! All over!—Nora, shall you never think of me again?

NORA. I know I shall often think of you and the children and this house.

HELMER. May I write to you, Nora?

NORA. No—never. You must not do that.

HELMER. But at least let me send you—

NORA. Nothing—nothing—

HELMER. Let me help you if you are in want.

NORA. No. I can receive nothing from a stranger.

HELMER. Nora—can I never be anything more than a stranger to you?

NORA. (*taking her bag*) Ah, Torvald, the most wonderful thing of all would have to happen.

HELMER. Tell me what that would be!

NORA. Both you and I would have to be so changed that—. Oh, Torvald, I don't believe any longer in wonderful things happening.

HELMER. But I will believe in it. Tell me? So changed that—?

NORA. That our life together would be a real wedlock. Good-bye. (*She goes out through the hall.*)

HELMER. (*sinks down on a chair at the door and buries his face in his hands*) Nora! Nora! (*Looks round, and rises.*) Empty. She is gone. (*A hope flashes across his mind.*) The most wonderful thing of all—?

(*The sound of a door shutting is heard from below.*)

from *Beyond the Horizon*

(*The door from the yard opens, and* ROBERT *enters. He is smiling happily, and humming a song to himself, but as he comes into the room an undercurrent of nervous uneasiness manifests itself in his bearing*).

MAYO. So here you be at last! (ROBERT *comes forward and sits on* ANDY's *chair.* MAYO *smile slyly at his wife*) What have you been doin' all this time—countin' the stars to see if they all come out right and proper?

ROBERT. There's only one I'll ever look for any more, Pa.

MAYO. (*reproachfully*) You might've even not wasted time lookin' for that one—your last night.

MRS. MAYO. (*as if she were speaking to a child*) You ought to have worn your coat a sharp night like this, Robbie.

SCOTT. (*disgustedly*) God A'mighty, Kate, you treat Robert as if he was one year old!

MRS. MAYO. (*notices* ROBERT'S *nervous uneasiness*) You look all worked up over something, Robbie. What is it?

ROBERT. (*swallowing hard, looks quickly from one to the other of them—then begins determinedly*) Yes, there *is* something—something I must tell you—all of you. (*As he begins to talk* ANDREW *enters quietly from the rear, closing the door behind him, and setting the lighted lantern on the floor. He remains standing by the door, his arms folded, listening to* ROBERT *with a repressed expression of pain on his face.* ROBERT *is so much taken up with what he is going to say that he does not notice* ANDREW's *presence.*) Something I discovered only this evening—very beautiful and wonderful—something I did not take into consideration previously because I hadn't dared to hope that such happiness could ever come to me. (*Appealingly*) You must all remember that fact, won't you?

MAYO. (*frowning*) Let's get to the point, son.

ROBERT. (*with a trace of defiance*) Well, the point is this, Pa: I'm not going—I mean—I can't go tomorrow with Uncle Dick—or at any future time, either.

MRS. MAYO. (*with a sharp sigh of joyful relief*) Oh, Robbie, I'm so glad!

MAYO. (*astounded*) You ain't serious, be you, Robert? (*Severely*) Seems to me it's a pretty late hour in the day for you to be upsettin' all your plans so sudden!

ROBERT. I asked you to remember that until this evening I didn't know myself. I had never dared to dream—

MAYO. (*irritably*) What is this foolishness you're talkin' of?

ROBERT. (*flushing*) Ruth told me this evening that—she loved me. It was after I'd confessed I loved her. I told her I hadn't been conscious of my love until after the trip had been arranged, and I realized it would mean—leaving her. That was the truth. I *didn't* know until then. (*As if justifying himself to the others*) I hadn't intended telling her anything but—suddenly—I felt I must. I didn't think it would matter, because I was going away. And I thought she loved—someone else. (*Slowly—his eyes shining*) And then she cried and said it was I she'd loved all the time, but I hadn't seen it.

MRS. MAYO. (*rushes over and throws her arms about him*) I knew it! I was just telling your father when you came in—and, Oh, Robbie, I'm so happy you're not going!

ROBERT. (*kissing her*) I knew you'd be glad, Ma.

MAYO. (*bewilderedly*) Well, I'll be damned! You do beat all for gettin' folks' minds all tangled up, Robert. And Ruth too! Whatever got into her of a sudden? Why, I was thinkin'—

MRS. MAYO. (*hurriedly—in a tone of warning*) Never mind what you were thinking, James. It wouldn't be any use telling us that now. (*Meaningly*) And what you were hoping for turns out just the same almost, doesn't it?

MAYO. (*thoughtfully—beginning to see this side of the argument*) Yes; I suppose you're right, Katey. (*Scratching his head in puzzlement*) But how it ever come about! It do beat anything ever I heard. (*Finally he gets up with a sheepish grin and walks over to* ROBERT) We're glad you ain't goin', your Ma and I, for we'd have missed you terrible, that's certain and sure; and we're glad you've found happiness. Ruth's a fine girl and'll make a good wife to you.

ROBERT. (*much moved*) Thank you, Pa. (*He grips his father's hand in his*).

ANDREW. (*his face tense and drawn comes forward and holds out his hand, forcing a smile*) I guess it's my turn to offer congratulations, isn't it?

ROBERT. (*with a startled cry when his brother appears before him so suddenly*) Andy! (*Confused*) Why—I—I didn't see you. Were you here when—

ANDREW. I heard everything you said; and here's wishing you every happiness, you and Ruth. You both deserve the best there is.

ROBERT. (*taking his hand*) Thanks, Andy, it's fine of you to— (*His voice dies away as he sees the pain in* ANDREW'S *eyes*).

ANDREW. (*giving his brother's hand a final grip*) Good luck to you both! (*He turns away and goes back to the rear where he bends over the lantern, fumbling with it to hide his emotion from the others*).

MRS. MAYO. (*to the* CAPTAIN, *who has been too flabbergasted by* ROBERT'S *decision to say a word*) What's the matter, Dick? Aren't you going to congratulate Robbie?

SCOTT. (*embarrassed*) Of course I be! (*He gets to his feet and shakes* ROBERT'S *hand, muttering a vague*) Luck to you, boy. (*He stands beside* ROBERT *as if he wanted to say something more but doesn't know how to go about it*).

ROBERT. Thanks, Uncle Dick.

SCOTT. So you're not acomin' on the *Sunda* with me? (*His voice indicates disbelief*).

ROBERT. I can't, Uncle—not now. I wouldn't miss it for anything else in the world under any other circumstances. (*He sighs unconsciously*) But you see I've found—a bigger dream. (*Then with joyous high spirits*) I want you all to understand one thing—I'm not going to be a loafer on your hands any longer. This means the beginning of a new life for me in every way. I'm going to settle right down and take a real interest in the farm, and do my share. I'll prove to you, Pa, that I'm as good a Mayo as you are—or Andy, when I want to be.

MAYO. (*kindly but skeptically*) That's the right spirit, Robert. Ain't none of us doubts your willin'ness, but you ain't never learned—

ROBERT. Then I'm going to start learning right away, and you'll teach me, won't you?

MAYO. (*mollifyingly*) Of course I will, boy, and be glad to, only you'd best go easy at first.

SCOTT. (*who has listened to this conversation in mingled consternation and amazement*) You don't mean to tell me you're goin' to let him stay, do you, James?

MAYO. Why, things bein' as they be, Robert's free to do as he's a mind to.

MRS. MAYO. *Let him!* The very idea!

SCOTT. (*more and more ruffled*) Then all I got to say is, you're a soft, weak-willed critter to be permittin' a boy—and women, too—to be layin' your course for you wherever they damn pleases.

MAYO. (*slyly amused*) It's just the same with me as 'twas with you, Dick. You can't order the tides on the seas to suit you, and I ain't pretendin' I can reg'late love for young folks.

SCOTT. (*scornfully*) Love! They ain't old enough to know love when they sight it! Love! I'm ashamed of you, Robert, to go lettin' a little huggin' and kissin' in the dark spile your chances to make a man out o' yourself. It ain't common sense—no siree, it ain't—not by a hell of a sight! (*He pounds the table with his fists in exasperation*).

MRS. MAYO. (*laughing provokingly at her brother*) A fine one you are to be talking about love, Dick—an old cranky bachelor like you. Goodness sakes!

SCOTT. (*exasperated by their joking*) I've never been a damn fool like most, if that's what you're steerin' at.

MRS. MAYO. (*tauntingly*) Sour grapes, aren't they, Dick? (*She laughs.* ROBERT *and his father chuckle.* SCOTT *sputters with annoyance*) Good gracious, Dick, you do act silly, flying into a temper over nothing.

SCOTT. (*indignantly*) Nothin'! You talk as if I wasn't concerned nohow in this here business. Seems to be me I've got a right to have my say. Ain't I made all arrangements with the owners and stocked up with some special grub all on Robert's account?

ROBERT. You've been fine, Uncle Dick; and I appreciate it. Truly.

MAYO. 'Course; we all does, Dick.

SCOTT. (*unplaced*) I've been countin' sure on havin' Robert for company on this vige—to sorta talk to and show things to, and teach, kinda, and I got my mind so set on havin' him I'm goin' to be double lonesome this vige. (*He pounds on the table, attempting to cover up this confession of weakness*) Darn all this silly lovin' business, anyway. (*Irritably*) But all this talk ain't tellin' me what I'm to do with that sta'b'd cabin I fixed up. It's all painted white, an' a bran new mattress on the bunk, 'n' new sheets 'n' blankets 'n' things. And Chips built in a book-case so's Robert could take his books along—with a slidin' bar fixed across't it, mind, so's they couldn't fall out no matter how she rolled. (*With excited consternation*) What d'you suppose my officers is goin' to think when there's no one comes aboard to occupy that sta'b'd cabin? And the men what did the work on it—what'll *they* think? (*He shakes his finger indignantly*) They're liable as not to suspicion it was a *woman* I'd planned to ship along, and that she gave me the go-by at the last moment! (*He wipes his perspiring brow in anguish at this thought*). Gawd A'mighty! They're only lookin' to have the laugh on me for something like that. They're liable to b'lieve anything, those fellers is!

MAYO. (*with a wink*) Then there's nothing to it but for you to get right out and hunt up a wife somewheres for that spick 'n' span cabin. She'll have to be a pretty one, too, to match it. (*He looks at his watch with exaggerated concern*) You ain't got much time to find her, Dick.

SCOTT. (*as the others smile—sulkily*) You kin go to thunder, Jim Mayo!

ANDREW. (*comes forward from where he has been standing by the door, rear, brooding. His face is set in a look of grim determination*) You needn't worry about that spare cabin, Uncle Dick, if you've a mind to take me in Robert's place.

ROBERT. (*turning to him quickly*) Andy! (*He sees at once the fixed resolve in his brother's eyes, and realizes immediately the reason for it—in consternation*) Andy, you mustn't!

ANDREW. You've made your decision, Rob, and now I've made mine. You're out of this, remember.

ROBERT. (*hurt by his brother's tone*) But Andy——

ANDREW. Don't interfere, Rob—that's all I ask. (*Turning to his uncle*) You haven't answered my question, Uncle Dick.

SCOTT. (*clearing his throat, with an uneasy side glance at* JAMES MAYO *who is staring at his elder son as if he thought he had suddenly gone mad*) O' course, I'd be glad to have you, Andy.

ANDREW. It's settled then. I can pack the little I want to take in a few minutes.

MRS. MAYO. Don't be a fool, Dick. Andy's only joking you.

SCOTT. (*disgruntedly*) It's hard to tell who's jokin' and who's not in this house.

ANDREW. (*firmly*) I'm not joking, Uncle Dick (*As* SCOTT *looks at him uncer-*

tainly) You needn't be afraid I'll go back on my word.

ROBERT. (*hurt by the insinuation he feels in* ANDREW'S *tone*) Andy! That isn't fair!

MAYO. (*frowning*) Seems to me this ain't no subject to joke over—not for Andy.

ANDREW. (*facing his father*) I agree with you, Pa, and I tell you again, once and for all, that I've made up my mind to go.

MAYO. (*dumbfounded—unable to doubt the determination in* ANDREW'S *voice—helplessly*) But why, son? Why?

ANDREW. (*evasively*) I've always wanted to go.

ROBERT. Andy!

ANDREW. (*half angrily*) You shut up, Rob! (*Turning to his father again*) I didn't ever mention it because as long as Rob was going I knew it was no use; but now Rob's staying on here, there isn't any reason for me not to go.

MAYO. (*breathing hard*) No reason! Can you stand there and say that to me, Andrew?

MRS. MAYO. (*hastily—seeing the gathering storm*) He doesn't mean a word of it, James.

MAYO. (*making a gesture to her to keep silence*) Let me talk, Katey. (*In a more kindly tone*) What's come over you so sudden, Andy? You know's well as I do that it wouldn't be fair o' you to run off at a moment's notice right now when we're up to our necks in hard work.

ANDREW. (*avoiding his eyes*) Rob'll hold his end up as soon as he learns.

MAYO. Robert was never cut out for a farmer, and you was.

ANDREW. You can easily get a man to do my work.

MAYO. (*restraining his anger with an effort*) It sounds strange to hear you, Andy, that I always thought had good sense, talkin' crazy like that. (*Scornfully*) Get a man to take your place! You ain't been workin' here for no hire, Andy, that you kin give me your notice to quit like you've done. The farm is your'n as well as mine. You've always worked on it with that understanding; and what you're sayin' you intend doin' is just skulkin' out o' your rightful responsibility.

ANDREW. (*looking at the floor—simply*) I'm sorry, Pa. (*After a slight pause*) It's no use talking any more about it.

MRS. MAYO. (*in relief*) There! I knew Andy'd come to his senses!

ANDREW. Don't get the wrong idea, Ma. I'm not backing out.

MAYO. You mean you're goin' in spite of—everythin'?

ANDREW. Yes. I'm going. I've got to. (*He looks at his father defiantly*) I feel I oughn't to miss this chance to go out into the world and see things, and—I want to go.

MAYO. (*with bitter scorn*) So—you want to go out into the world and see thin's! (*His voice raised and quivering with anger*) I never thought I'd live to see the day when a son o' mine'd look me in the face and tell a bare-faced lie! (*Bursting out*) You're a liar, Andy Mayo, and a mean one to boot!

MRS. MAYO. James!

ROBERT. Pa!

SCOTT. Steady there, Jim!

MAYO. (*waving their protests aside*) He is and he knows it.

ANDREW. (*his face flushed*) I won't argue with you, Pa. You can think as badly of me as you like.

MAYO. (*shaking his finger at* ANDY, *in a cold rage*) You know I'm speakin' truth—that's why you're afraid to argy! You lie when you say you want to go 'way—and see thin's! You ain't got no likin' in the world to go. I've watched you grow up, and I know your ways, and they're my ways. You're runnin' against your own nature, and you're goin' to be a'mighty sorry for it if you do. 'S if I didn't know your real reason for runnin' away! And runnin' away's the only words to fit it. You're runnin' away 'cause you're put out and riled 'cause your own brother's got Ruth 'stead o' you, and—

ANDREW. (*his face crimson—tensely*) Stop, Pa! I won't stand hearing that—not even from you!

MRS. MAYO. (*rushing to* ANDY *and putting her arms about him protectingly*) Don't mind him, Andy dear. He don't mean a word he's saying! (ROBERT *stands rigidly, his hands clenched, his face contracted by pain.* SCOTT *sits dumbfounded and open-mouthed.* ANDREW *soothes his mother who is on the verge of tears*).

MAYO. (*in angry triumph*) It's the truth, Andy Mayo! And you ought to be bowed in shame to think of it!

ROBERT. (*protestingly*) Pa!

MRS. MAYO. (*coming from* ANDREW *to his father; puts her hands on his shoulders as though to try and push him back in the chair from which he has risen*) Won't you be still, James? Please won't you?

MAYO. (*looking at* ANDREW *over his wife's shoulder—stubbornly*) The truth— God's truth!

MRS. MAYO. Sh-h-h! (*She tries to put a finger across his lips, but he twists his head away*).

ANDREW. (*who has regained control over himself*) You're wrong, Pa, it isn't truth. (*With defiant assertiveness*) I don't love Ruth. I never loved her, and the thought of such a thing never entered my head.

MAYO. (*with an angry snort of disbelief*) Hump! You're pilin' lie on lie!

ANDREW. (*losing his temper—bitterly*) I suppose it'd be hard for you to explain anyone's wanting to leave this blessed farm except for some outside reason like that. But I'm sick and tired of it—whether you want to believe me or not—and that's why I'm glad to get a chance to move on.

ROBERT. Andy! Don't! You're only making it worse.

ANDREW. (*sulkily*) I don't care. I've done my share of work here. I've earned my right to quit when I want to. (*Suddenly overcome with anger and grief; with rising intensity*) I'm sick and tired of the whole damn business. I hate the farm and every inch of ground in it. I'm sick of digging in the dirt and sweating in the sun like a slave without getting a word of thanks for it. (*Tears of rage starting to his eyes—hoarsely*) I'm through, through for good and all; and if Uncle Dick won't take me on his ship, I'll find another. I'll get away somewhere, somehow.

MRS. MAYO. (*in a frightened voice*) Don't you answer him, James. He doesn't know what he's saying. Don't say a word to him 'til he's in his right senses again. Please James, don't——

MAYO. (*pushes her away from him; his face is drawn and pale with the violence of his passion. He glares at* ANDREW *as if he hated him*) You dare to—you dare to speak like that to me? You talk like that 'bout this farm—the Mayo farm—where you was born—you—you—— (*He clenches his fist above his head and advances threateningly on* ANDREW) You damned whelp!

MRS. MAYO (*with a shriek*) James! (*She covers her face with her hands and sinks weakly into* MAYO'S *chair.* ANDREW *remains standing motionless, his face pale and set*).

SCOTT. (*starting to his feet and stretching his arms across the table toward* MAYO) Easy there, Jim!

ROBERT. (*throwing himself between father and brother*) Stop! Are you mad?

MAYO. (*grabs* ROBERT'S *arm and pushes him aside—then stands for a moment gasping for breath before* ANDREW. *He points to the door with a shaking finger*) Yes—go!—go!—you're no son o' mine—no son o' mine! You can go to hell if you want to! Don't let me find you here—in the mornin'—or—or—I'll *throw* you out!

ROBERT. Pa! For God's sake! (MRS. MAYO *bursts into noisy sobbing*).

MAYO. (*he gulps convulsively and glares at* ANDREW) You go—tomorrow mornin'—and by God—don't come back—don't dare come back—by God, not while I'm livin'—or I'll—I'll—— (*He shakes over his muttered threat and strides toward the door rear, right*).

MRS. MAYO. (*rising and throwing her arms around him—hysterically*) James! James! Where are you going?

MAYO. (*incoherently*) I'm goin'—to bed, Katey. It's late, Katey—it's late. (*He goes out*).

MRS. MAYO. (*following him, pleading hysterically*) James! Take back what you've said to Andy. James! (*She follows him out.* ROBERT *and the* CAPTAIN *stare after them with horrified eyes.* ANDREW *stands rigidly looking straight in front of him, his fists clenched at his sides*).

SCOTT. (*the first to find his voice—with an explosive sigh*) Well, if he ain't the devil himself when he's roused! You oughtn't to have talked to him that way, Andy 'bout the damn farm, knowin' how touchy he is about it. (*With another sigh*) Well, you won't mind what he's said in anger. He'll be sorry for it when he's calmed down a bit.

ANDREW. (*in a dead voice*) You don't know him. (*Defiantly*) What's said is said and can't be unsaid; and I've chosen.

ROBERT. (*with violent protest*) Andy! You can't go! This is all so stupid—and terrible!

ANDREW. (*coldly*) I'll talk to you in a minute, Rob. (*Crushed by his brother's attitude* ROBERT *sinks down into a chair, holding his head in his hands*).

SCOTT. (*comes and slaps* ANDREW *on the back*) I'm damned glad you're shippin' on, Andy. I like your spirit, and the way you spoke up to him. (*Lowering his voice to a cautious whisper*) The sea's the place for a young feller like you that isn't half dead 'n' alive. (*He gives* ANDY *a final approving slap*) You 'n' me 'll get along like twins, see if we don't. I'm goin' aloft to turn in. Don't forget to pack your dunnage. And git some sleep, if you kin. We'll want to sneak out extra early b'fore they're up. It'll do away with more argyments. Robert can drive us down to the town, and bring back the team. (*He goes to the door in the rear, left*) Well, good night.

ANDREW. Good night. (SCOTT *goes out. The two brothers remain silent for a moment. Then* ANDREW *comes over to his brother and puts a hand on his back. He speaks in a low voice, full of feeling*) Buck up, Rob. It ain't any use crying over spilt milk; and it'll all turn out for the best—let's hope. It couldn't be helped—what's happened.

ROBERT. (*wildly*) But it's a lie, Andy, a lie!

ANDREW. Of course it's a lie. You know it and I know it,—but that's all ought to know it.

ROBERT. Pa'll never forgive you. Oh, the whole affair is so senseless—and tragic. Why did you think you must go away?

ANDREW. You know better than to ask that. You know why. (*Fiercely*) I can wish you and Ruth all the good luck in the world, and I do, and I mean it; but you can't expect me to stay around here and watch you two together, day after day—and me alone. I couldn't stand it—not after all the plans I'd made to happen on this place thinking—— (*his voice breaks*) thinking she cared for me.

ROBERT. (*putting a hand his brother's arm*) God! It's horrible! I feel so guilty—to think that I should be the cause of your suffering, after we've been such pals all our lives. If I could have foreseen what'd happen, I swear to you I'd have never said a word to Ruth. I swear I wouldn't have, Andy!

ANDREW. I know you wouldn't; and that would've been worse, for Ruth would've suffered then. (*He pats his brother's shoulder*) It's best as it is. It had to be, and I've got to stand the gaff, that's all. Pa'll see how I felt—after a time. (*As* ROBERT *shakes his head*)—and if he don't—well, it can't be helped.

ROBERT. But think of Ma! God, Andy, you can't go! You can't!

ANDREW. (*fiercely*) I've got to go—to get away! I've got to, I tell you. I'd go crazy here, bein' reminded every second of the day what a fool I'd made of myself. I've got to get away and try and forget, if I can. And I'd hate the farm if I stayed, hate it for bringin' things back. I couldn't take interest in the work any more, work with no purpose in sight. Can't you see what a hell it'd be? You love her too, Rob. Put yourself in my place, and remember I haven't stopped loving her, and couldn't if I was to stay. Would that be fair to you or to her? Put yourself in my place. (*He shakes his brother fiercely by the shoulder*) What'd you do then? Tell me the truth! You love her. What'd you do?

ROBERT (*chokingly*) I'd—I'd go, Andy! (*He buries his face in his hands with a shuddering sob*) God!

ANDREW. (*seeming to relax suddenly all over his body—in a low, steady voice*) Then you know why I got to go; and there's nothing more to be said.

ROBERT. (*in a frenzy of rebellion*) Why did this have to happen to us? It's damnable! (*He looks about him wildly, as if his vengeance were seeking the responsible fate*).

ANDREW. (*soothingly—again putting his hands on his brother's shoulder*) It's no use fussing any more, Rob. It's done. (*Forcing a smile*) I guess Ruth's got a right to have who she likes. She made a good choice—and God bless her for it!

ROBERT. Andy! Oh, I wish I could tell you half I feel of how fine you are!

ANDREW. (*interrupting him quickly*) Shut up! Let's go to bed. I've got to be up long before sun-up. You, too, if you're going to drive us down.

ROBERT. Yes. Yes.

ANDREW. (*turning down the lamp*) And I've got to pack yet. (*He yawns with utter weariness*) I'm as tired as if I'd been plowing twenty-four hours at a stretch. (*Dully*) I feel—dead. (ROBERT *covers his face again with his hands.* ANDREW *shakes his head as if to get rid of his thoughts, and continues with a poor attempt at cheery briskness*) I'm going to douse the light. Come on. (*He slaps his brother on the back.* ROBERT *does not move.* ANDREW *bends over and blows out the lamp. His voice comes from the darkness*) Don't sit there mourning, Rob. It'll all come out in the wash. Come on and get some sleep. Everything'll turn out all right in the end. (ROBERT *can be heard stumbling to his feet, and the dark figures of the two brothers can be seen groping their way toward the doorway in the rear as*

(*The Curtain Falls*)

Commentary

Plays are traditionally divided into "acts," and sometimes into "scenes" within the acts. The passage from *A Doll's House* comes at the end of Act III— the end of the play. The passage from *Beyond the Horizon* comes at the end of Act I of three acts. Both passages appear to be continuous, single units, but the second, from O'Neill, is in several turns or segments, sometimes called "French scenes," a new one of which occurs whenever a character enters or leaves the stage. As some entrances and exits are relatively insignificant, however, it's best to look closely at the actual promptings between the characters to determine each play's inherent segments, turns, or confrontations of drama.

These segments, each with its "curve of emotion," are more easily seen in the passage from O'Neill. The first includes Robert's announcement to his mother and father and uncle (and his brother Andrew, whose presence has not been noted) that he's not going on the voyage and is going to marry Ruth instead. His parents, and later his brother, congratulate him. In the second segment, the uncle, Scott, works up his disapproval and outrage that Robert is not going with him; and Andrew surprises them all by announcing that he will go in Robert's place. In the third segment, the father, Mayo, becomes enraged at Andrew's decision to leave the farm; this passage rises to a climax at Mayo's angry, "Yes—go!" The end of this segment is clearly marked as a "French scene" by the exit of mother and father and uncle, leaving Robert and Andrew alone for the last segment, in which Andrew seeks Robert's approval for his decision to go on the voyage; and at its climax, Robert admits that if he were in Andrew's place, "I'd go."

The dialogue between Nora and Helmer has no breaks caused by entrances or exits; both characters are on stage until the very end. Still, a close inspection of the drama reveals several turns or "curves of emotion" within their conversation. The first begins with Nora's entrance (she has changed from party dress to everyday dress), rises to a climax with her announcement "And that is why I am going to leave you now," and closes with Helmer's expression of horror. In the second turn Helmer initiates a series of appeals intended to dissuade her from her decision; Nora remains firm against all of them. A new turn arises when Torvald asks, "And can you tell me what I have done to forfeit your love?" which prompts Nora to offer her explanation of what has happened between them. In the last turn, Helmer begs her once more not to leave and proposes a series of alternatives; but Nora leaves.

As for rhetorical modes, you might be tempted to say, as these are both plays, they are entirely in the mode of drama. They are indeed mostly, but not entirely, dramatic. The stage-directions—in both scripts, plainly marked by parentheses and italics—are, as stage-directions usually are, descriptive and narrative: "in everyday dress" is descriptive and "sits down at opposite side of the table" is narrative. Another type of stage-direction might be called "emotional suggestions to the actors," such as "undisturbed," "regaining his composure." These might be considered modifications of narration: "She continues speaking, undisturbed." Or they might be considered clues to the thoughts of the characters and thereby suggestive of reverie.

Apart from stage-directions, are the speeches of the characters entirely dramatic? Yes, in the sense that one character is addressing another; but occasionally the posture of direct address slips and another mode seems to occur. Nora reviews her life with her father and husband; the account is tinged with her reflections, but it is a narrative account. Later she gives her account, again a narrative account, of what has happened during the day, in answer to Helmer's asking what he has done to forfeit her love. She gives her account, and he closes it with "I see, I see." In this passage, Helmer's "dramatic" speeches are mainly interruptions of the story, or requests for her to continue. Also, when Nora speculates at the end of this passage on what might bring them back together, she is, more clearly than elsewhere, expressing her thoughts out loud, and it is almost as if she allows Helmer to hear her reverie: "Ah, Torvald, the most wonderful thing of all would have to happen. . . . our life together would be a real wedlock." In fact, whenever a dramatic speaker engages in the past tense or the future tense, especially over several sentences or speeches, she or he is slipping partly into narration or reverie. In the following speech, though Nora is still talking to Helmer, she is not addressing him so much as telling him a story of the past, and her thoughts about the future: "I know nothing but what the clergyman said, when I went to be confirmed. He told us that religion was this, and that, and the other. When I am away from all this, and am alone, I will look into that matter too. I will see if what the clergyman said is true, or at all events if it is true for me."

In the passage from O'Neill the stage-directions are much more extensive, accommodating the additional characters and their activities, and giving the passage as a whole a more narrative emphasis than the passage from Ibsen. In the speeches themselves, Scott describes the starboard cabin he has fitted up for Robert and his books. Earlier, Robert tells of his conversation with Ruth, which is narrative and "indirect drama"—indirect because he reports their spoken words without quoting them: "Ruth told me this evening that—she loved me. It was after I'd confessed that I loved her." Later, Andrew tells Robert his thoughts about what his life would be like if he stayed on the farm: "And I'd hate the farm if I stayed, hate it for bringin' things back. I couldn't take interest in the work anymore, work with no purpose in sight. Can't you see what a hell it would be? Put yourself in my place . . ." The last sentence switches from his hypothetical reverie to a direct dramatic address to Robert. The passages from both plays, then, while extensively dramatic, include hints or actual switches to other modes.

Before taking up the elements of these passages, we need to take a closer look at the drama itself, to see how it moves in and out of its various turns or segments. We will be studying what the characters say as well as why they say what they say: the text and the "subtext"—the motivations underlying the speeches of the characters.

In the passage from Ibsen, Nora enters with a new posture that surprises Helmer. She, who has been his subservient "doll," now has a new quiet assurance. She has risen superior to him and she "distances" him—as if pushing him away from her. His questions and comments are attempts at embrace, attempts to bring her back closer to him: "What sort of expression is that to use about our marriage?" "Not, not happy?" But at each of his attempts, she rises above and away from him. This "curve of emotion" rises to Nora's climax: "And that is why I am going to leave you now." At this announcement, Helmer expresses his horror in the form of exclamations and accusations: "I won't allow it!" "What sort of madness is this!" These expressions of outrage have a superficial posture of pushing her away from him, but he is denying only her desire to leave; actually he is trying to bring her back to him and his understanding of their marriage. His charge, "You blind, foolish woman!" does bring her round slightly. She gives in to him somewhat when she says, "I must try and get some sense, Torvald." She is at least willing to explain, to conciliate him as far as she can. But she continues coolly expressing her independence of him and his values: she keeps moving away from him. Helmer is trying to "bring her back to her senses," closer to him; and his petition to her rises to his sense of a climax, his strongest claim: "You do not love me any more." Such an appeal would have previously moved her to an assurance of her love, no doubt. But she meets even this charge, and admits it. He questions her certainty, trying to break it down, and then appeals for an explanation, which constitutes a further weakening of his stance against her: "And can you tell me what I have done to forfeit your love?" She meets this challenge as cool-ly as before, but she moves a little closer to him in her willingness to explain. She narrates the events of the day as she now sees them: she has risked every-thing for him and he has risked nothing for her. She was sure he would offer to take the blame; but he didn't, and even now he refuses to recognize his obliga-tions as she sees them: he says "no man would sacrifice his honor for the one he loves." Her answer may be taken as a last-minute petition to him to come closer to her sense of marital obligation: "It is a thing hundreds of thousands of women have done." He implicitly refuses and so confirms her decision. She remains victorious in her independence, her separateness from him. Helmer says, "I see, I see," and begins a new series of petitions in the form of alterna-tives to her decision. He is bending to her wishes, as he sees them, still trying to win her back, but his new posture is an even weaker one than before. He offers to become a different man, asks her to wait till the next day, or to live like brother and sister. But she denies each petition, refuses each attempt at an embrace. She insists on a symbolic return of each other's rings. He is defeated and makes a few more futile appeals, asks if she will think of him, if he may write to her. She closes with a wistful, not very hopeful, reflection on what would have to happen for her to return. And she goes. She has been on the way out throughout their conversation, and he has been trying to keep her there. She leaves, the unhappy victor in their interchange.

In the passage from O'Neill, Robert enters the family grouping of fa-ther, mother, and uncle and narrates his previous conversation with Ruth, leading to his decision of remaining on the farm. This decision brings him closer to his parents and moves him away from his agreement with or commit-ment to his uncle and the voyage. The parents are subsequently pleased and offer him in their speeches a form of renewed embrace, emotionally welcom-ing him back to their household. But Scott is suppressing his disapproval and his disappointment at having his offer rejected. When the parents invite him to congratulate Robert, he does so grudgingly with embarrassment, slowly working up to his expression of disapproval. As Robert and his father offer each other new commitments to his membership in the household—they are subtextually embracing—Scott begins to express his disappointment and an-ger. He is superficially pushing Robert away from him, but he is really trying to bring him back to the voyage and himself. He rages at both Robert and Mayo, and also at women and marriage in general, in his anger. But the moth-er and father are confidently superior to his disapproval of marriage and tease his bachelorhood, basking in the security they have in each other. When Scott tells at length of his preparations for Robert and his discomfiture with the men on the ship, Mayo teases him with the possibility he might find a woman to take Robert's place. The tease is a taunt, an implied rejection of Scott and his way of life; and Scott responds angrily, "You kin go to thunder, Jim Mayo!"—a comparable rejection of his brother-in-law.

Now Andrew comes forward with a new claim on their attention and announces that he will go in place of Robert. This decision is an acceptance of Scott and a rejection of his parents and their farm—from him, the son who seemed cut out to be a farmer. As the conversation continues, we expect and find that Scott embraces his decision and that his parents question it until they see he is firm. His father now responds angrily with a hurt sense of Andrew's rejection of him. Mayo insults him and charges that Andrew is simply a disappointed lover and running away from the proposed marriage of Robert and Ruth. As it turns out, his charge is true, but Andrew lies and denies the charge. Father and son rise to a pitch of angry countercharges and denials of each other. As Andrew insists he's sick of the farm and hates it, his father—horrified, angry, and hurt—denies him in even more emotional and permanent terms—he disowns Andrew: "Yes—go!—go!—You're no son o' mine—no son o' mine!" As Robert and Mrs. Mayo try to restrain him, to bring the father and son back together again, Mayo storms off. He leaves, but he has been the one rejected, and his anger means that he would have wanted a closer embrace and commitment from his favored son Andrew. Scott tries to soothe Andrew from the emotional blow he has had from his father, but goes on to offer Andrew a welcoming embrace into the fellowship of the voyage. He leaves, confident that his cabin will be occupied; he has had a success after his disappointment in Robert.

Now the brothers confront each other alone and more quietly review their new postures toward each other. Andrew puts a hand on Robert's back, assuring him of his unchanged friendship. Robert is baffled and is trying to understand the decision, perhaps to talk Andrew into staying home. Andrew is implicitly seeking Robert's assent to his decision and he petitions Robert to understand and approve it. He reflects on what his life would be like if he remained and closes with the dramatic climax of this segment, "Put yourself in my place .. What'd you do then?" When Robert says "I'd—I'd go, Andy!" he is reluctantly approving Andrew's decision and subtextually pushing him away, into the decision Andrew is already confident in. They close the scene with renewed expressions of their devotion to each other; neither has won in the exchange. They have attained a brotherly closeness, but they are resigned to their separation from each other.

This closer inspection of the drama itself prepares us for an analysis of the elements in each passage. In the most obvious sense the Ibsen passage, in its focus on just the two characters and their attitudes toward each other, stresses characterization, whereas the O'Neill passage, with its greater number of characters and changes toward each other, stresses the plot. Of course, plot is of some importance in the Ibsen passage too, especially in the narrative passages in which Nora gives the background, or "exposition" for her status as a housewife and "doll" and for her realization that Helmer hasn't measured up to her own ideal of self-sacrifice. But the major plot of *A Doll's House* is by now over, the complicated situation by which Nora has put herself in the power of a man who wishes to be promoted by her husband. The "event" of this passage is Nora's departure itself, which occurs at the very end and is certainly no surprise by then. This event itself is the narrative termination of the plot; the build-up to the departure, which the passage is almost exclusively devoted to, is a dramatic development of character.

Just as we must not minimize plot in the passage from Ibsen because it stresses characterization, so we must not minimize characterization in the passage from O'Neill because it stresses plot. We must see the justifiable pride in Robert when he announces to his family that Ruth loves him and that he is prepared to turn his life around as a result; and the warmth with which both parents, but especially his mother, receive him back into their household. We must see Scott's sense of betrayal when he learns that Robert has given up the prospect of his companionship, especially when the married couple treat his bachelorhood so lightly. Finally, we must not miss the disappointment but also the courage in Andrew, who abandons one previously secure future at hand for a new and very insecure one at sea.

But we also find in the passage from O'Neill a number of changes in the bearings of the characters toward each other, which we might call "events" of the plot. Robert announces his decision to remain on the farm, and abandon the voyage, and marry Ruth; as a result of which his parents are pleased and his uncle infuriated; as a result of which Andrew announces his decision to abandon the farm and go on the voyage; as a result of which his uncle is surprised but pleased, and his father infuriated; as a result of which the two brothers discuss their change of plans and agree that they have made the right decisions. For a passage of drama, then, the dialogue from O'Neill is unusually devoted to developing a chain of events, a plot. The plot of neither passage is clearly tragic or comic. Because in both the characters seem to be dominated by their situations, rather than rising above them, the plots of both would appear to be modern ironic ones; and, as both are based on separation, they are closer to tragedy than to comedy.

As for theme, we need to ask what are the themes of the passages as well as how urgently each passage insists on its themes. In general the theme of the Ibsen passage is relationships between husbands and wives and of the O'Neill passage the relationships between brothers and between sons and parents. If we try to develop or specify these themes, we find we can do so easily for the Ibsen passage but that in the O'Neill passage we can hardly go further than the general or vague subject we have already mentioned. What ideas issue from that stretch of drama about sons or parents or lovers? From the perspective of Robert, we might derive the idea that when fortune opens up a new, better prospect we hadn't previously dreamt of we should take advantage of it even if we must cancel an immediate plan. From the perspective of Andrew we derive an opposite idea: when fortune denies an immediate hope we must undertake a new attempt, even if its prospects are uncertain.

I have with some difficulty extracted these themes from the O'Neill passage, because the passage itself doesn't seem to insist on the recognition of them. The young men seem to be choosing mainly for themselves and not for others like themselves—a class of all sons or of certain sons, let us say, for whom they are the spokesmen. And the remainder of the play does not exactly endorse either son's choice—certainly shows Robert's at least to have been the wrong one for him.

In the Ibsen passage by contrast we have a discussion, not just of individual choices, but of values and principles. The passage really demands that we decide whether a wife should remain in a marriage that treats her like a doll, or escape to insecurity but independence; and the passage seems to insist that we agree with Nora and see her choice as better, as nobler than remaining in thoughtless subservience—and not just for herself but for all or most self-respecting women. How does the passage achieve this thematic victory for Nora? By endowing her character with courage and dignity and insight; Helmer in contrast is halting, ill-tempered, selfish, and, in his ideas, unthinkingly conventional. He recites the tired ideas intended to keep a husband like himself dominant and a wife like Nora subservient. Characterization and theme are working in close harmony, and the stronger Nora seems as a character the stronger her ideas appear to be; whereas Helmer's character and ideas come across as feeble. The passage seems to have been designed to bring the audience round to an approval of Nora's character and ideas. In fact, the ending of *A Doll's House* was seen at once as revolutionary in its theme; and it is still revolutionary to those who have Helmer's ideas about marriage.

Because the passage from Ibsen is translated into English, we have lost some of its style and most or all of its sound. The expressiveness of actors would probably give us dynamics of loud and soft at similar places no matter what the language of production, but the sounds of individual words (other than the names) are entirely altered in translation. Similarly, the style is necessarily somewhat altered, though we can see that Ibsen's characters talk in plain, undecorated middle-class syntax and sentences; and we would assume that the diction of the original is similar. O'Neill seems to be working for a more distinctive style reflective of rural and seagoing diction, a lower-class dialect of the United States of his day.

The O'Neill passage also seems to be raising a question of setting: whether it is better to be on a farm or a ship. And that question gives perhaps a slight attention to setting missing from the Ibsen passage. Ibsen's stage-directions for *A Doll's House* seem to suggest: picture a typical middle-class setting. The typicality of the Helmer household also points to its general significance—again, to its theme.

In comparing and contrasting these two passages of drama, we conclude that the Ibsen passage heavily stresses characterization and theme, whereas the O'Neill passage stresses plot and diction, without really overlooking characterization, the element drama usually best develops. Students who may be tempted to read all of *A Doll's House* and *Beyond the Horizon* from these brief excerpts should note that this analysis of elements is restricted to these passages. I have chosen from Ibsen a passage heavily expressive of the elements of character and theme. An earlier passage from the play might have seemed more of a storytelling passage, like the passage from O'Neill. Similarly, a later passage from the O'Neill play might have given us something more expressive of the elements of character and theme. Indeed the title, *Beyond the Horizon,* invites us to see the thematic importance of escaping from the immediate and humdrum; and so does the remainder of the play. A full analysis of the full plays would need to be based on as close an analysis of all the passages of both plays.

Exercise

Read the following excerpts from *A Doll's House,* in which the separate speeches are run together, without stage-directions. You will probably find it quite easy to separate them, to mark with diagonal slashes the breaks between speakers or the names of speakers at the beginning of speeches. This exercise will give you a close look at the rhetorical progression of drama. You will remember one of these excerpts; the other two introduce two additional male characters, Krogstad and Dr. Rank. After you have separated the speeches, answer the questions following each excerpt.

I. But you must believe me, Mr. Krogstad; it is not in my power to help you at all. Then it is because you haven't the will; but I have means to compel you. You don't mean that you will tell my husband that I owe you money? Hm!—suppose I were to tell him? It would be perfectly infamous of you. To think of his learning my secret, which has been my joy and pride, in such an ugly, clumsy way—that he should learn it from you! And it would put me in a horribly disagreeable position—Only disagreeable? Well, do it, then!—and it will be the worse for you. My husband will see for himself what a blackguard you are, and you certainly won't keep your post then. I asked you if it was only a disagreeable scene at home that you were afraid of? If my husband does get to know of it, of course he will at once pay you what is still owing, and we shall have nothing more to do with you. Listen to me, Mrs. Helmer. Either you have a very bad memory or you know very little of business. I shall be obliged to remind you of a few details.

    1. In this passage one of the speakers is putting the other on the spot, and the other is trying bravely to act as if it doesn't matter. Other than one having something to threaten the other with, does the passage reveal individual differences of character between the speakers, or are they talking mainly to clarify the issues between them?

2. Both speakers use the future tense. Are they expressing private thoughts and so revealing their characters, or are they talking of the future as a means of developing possible later repercussions? What element is based on sequential possibilities between the present and the future?

3. Is any theme being hinted at here? Do the characters speak to express ideas, or possible events? Does it matter exactly in what room or setting such a conversation occurs? What importance have theme and setting here, then?

II. And if I asked you now for a—? No! For what? For a big proof of your friendship—Yes, yes! I mean a tremendously big favor—Would you really make me so happy for once? Ah, but you don't know what it is yet. No—but tell me. I really can't, Doctor Rank. It is something out of all reason; it means advice, and help, and a favor—The bigger a thing it is the better. I can't conceive what it is you mean. Do tell me. Haven't I your confidence? More than anyone else. I know you are my truest and best friend, and so I will tell you what it is. Well, Doctor Rank, it is something you must help me to prevent. You know how devotedly, how inexpressibly deeply Torvald loves me; he would never for a moment hesitate to give his life for me. Nora—do you think he is the only one—? The only one—? The only one who would gladly give his life for your sake. Is that it? I was determined you should know it before I went away, and there will never be a better opportunity than this. Now you know it, Nora. And now you know, too, that you can trust me as you would trust no one else. Let me pass. Nora! Helen, bring in the lamp. Dear Doctor Rank, that was really horrid of you. To have loved you as much as anyone else does? Was that horrid? No, but to go and tell me so. There was really no need—What do you mean? Did you know—? Nora—Mrs. Helmer—tell me, had you any idea of this? Oh, how do I know whether I had or whether I hadn't? I really can't tell you—To think you could be so clumsy, Doctor Rank! We were getting on so nicely. Well, at all events you know now that you can command me, body and soul. So won't you speak out? After what happened? I beg you to let me know what it is. I can't tell you anything now.

1. In this passage one speaker asks the other for a favor and the other agrees to comply so extravagantly that the first speaker decides not to ask for the favor after all. Something happens, then—an event which advances the plot; but you might almost say that nothing much happens: the favor is not even specified. Consider this passage, in contrast to the first, which hints at narrative developments in the future. Does this one, or does something private develop which indicates the special relationship between the speakers and their individual attitudes toward each other? Is plot or character of most importance here?

2. Do you find any generalizations here hinting toward a possible theme? Is the nature of doing someone, anyone, a favor the topic of discussion, or is the talk a matter of this favor between these individual speakers?

3. Are the attitudes of the characters toward each other constant in this

passage, as in the first, or do their attitudes toward each other change in the course of the passage? Why does the one character decide to express his strong feelings for the other, and why does the other character decide not to ask for the favor she begins by wanting to ask? If a change in character is the main development here, what is the element mainly expressed?

III. To desert your home, your husband and your children! And you don't consider what people will say? I cannot consider that at all. I only know that it is necessary for me. It's shocking. This is how you would neglect your most sacred duties. What do you consider my most sacred duties? Do I need to tell you that? Are they not your duties to your husband and your children? I have other duties just as sacred. That you have not. What duties could those be? Duties to myself. Before all else you are a wife and a mother. I don't believe that any longer. I believe that before all else I am a reasonable human being, just as you are—or, at all events, that I must try and become one. I know quite well, Torvald, that most people would think you right, and that views of that kind are to be found in books; but I can no longer content myself with what most people say, or what is found in books. I must think over things for myself and get to understand them.

1. Consider the role of plot in this excerpt. Does any present event occur or is any future development suggested, as in the first excerpt?
2. Consider the role of character in this excerpt. The characters differ, but do their differences reveal individual and changing attitudes toward each other in the course of this passage, as in the second excerpt?
3. Consider the use of generalizations here: what people will say, duties to husband and children, and duties to oneself. Is the main achievement of the passage a sharpening of general and thematic differences between the speakers, and an attempt to convince the listener of what one rather than the other says, as if the ideas are the chief emphasis here?

Suggestions

A full-length play may be too unwieldy a subject for a short discussion. It's wise to take a section of a play, one act (or "episode" in a classical drama) or, as in the examples above, a single significant segment of a play. If you take a unit designated by the author as a whole (a whole play, or a whole act or scene), you should be able to find the form of Freytag's pyramid in it—rising action to a climax and then falling action. If you isolate a significant passage on your own you will usually find that it too is in the form of Freytag's pyramid.

Since not all passages in a play—even exclusive of stage-directions—are uniformly dramatic, you might be governed by a rhetorical analysis in determining which passage to choose for discussion. Passages of narration regularly occur throughout a play, and are called "expository" when they occur early and serve to bring the audience up to date on what it needs to know in order to follow the play. Such passages may come in the form of a long speech from a single character, or may be a mutual review by two or more characters, in which case the separate statements they make will be narrative or past-tense statements, even though they appear to be dramatic. Passages of reverie also are frequent in plays, sometimes in the form of "asides" to the audience, which other characters on the stage are not supposed to hear; or in the form of soliloquies spoken by one character when alone. Even if other characters are present, though, one may lose touch with the others and start ruminating. These traces of reverie are usually in mixed tenses, including future as well as past and present. Descriptive passages often occur in stage-directions, and sometimes in the drama itself. But unless there is some special reason to study description, narration, or reverie in a play, you'll probably choose a passage more clearly dramatic—a passage in which two or three characters immediately confront each other, revealing something special about each of their attitudes toward the others, and somehow manage to change these attitudes in the course of the passage.

The sequence of these changes some critics call the "subtext." The characters begin their conversation with certain attitudes toward each other and speak in order to express them or to change the attitudes reflected back at them by the others. Not every line will involve a change of attitude; it may take a series of lines to express an attitude, or to get one changed. The text and the stage-directions are the only guides to these attitudes, and they may be implied instead of stated. "Why do you want to visit him again?" may be the closest a character comes to expressing his jealousy. If this is what "reading between the lines" means, you will have to read between the lines.

If you succeed in analyzing the subtext you'll see what is really happening in a passage, and will be in a good position to say something of its elements. If the passage serves mainly to get an action accomplished, a murder or a marriage, a promise or a rejection, there's obviously some emphasis on plot. But even if nothing spectacular comes about in the scene, there will usually be some kind of a psychological victory or defeat. Characters usually talk back and forth in order to get the better of each other. If the passage serves mainly to get an idea expressed—or implied if it isn't exactly stated—there is obviously some emphasis on theme. Of course, there will always be some suggestion of theme, for however individualized the characters, they will share some qualities with others they might be speaking for as well as themselves.

But if the passage you have chosen is fully dramatic, it must have some revelation of character, and may very likely emphasize character above other elements. Emphasis on setting is not common in drama, but may occur when the characters present are responding more to their location than to each other. Diction is also crucial in drama, since the exact words spoken back and forth are more exposed and pregnant than in narration; and sound-effects, especially in verse plays, may also be important.

6

Analyzing Poetry

The two poems below are goodbyes of an old man and a young woman. "Ulysses," by the English poet Alfred, Lord Tennyson (1809–92) tells of the last departure of the hero of Homer's *Odyssey*, sometimes called Odysseus, and sometimes, as here, Ulysses. The second, by the American poet Sylvia Plath (1932–63), tells of her third suicide attempt.

Ulysses has now been home on his island Ithaca for some time since he returned from his long voyage following the Trojan war, in which he fought with such heroes as Achilles, and was helped by such gods as Athene. He finds his life at home has become dull; he feels his people are a savage race and he does not enjoy governing them. He loves his son Telemachus and leaves him to the daily job of governing his people. Unlike Telemachus, he wants to drink life "to the lees"—to the dregs at the bottom of the glass—as he has always, sailing by the Hyades, a constellation whose appearance usually meant rain. He addresses his mariners or fellow sailors in the moonlight and encourages them to come with him on a last adventure. They are not as strong as they used to be, but they are still able to see what else there is to see, even if they die in the attempt. If they do die, they may find the Happy Isles or Elysium, where heroes were thought to go after death. All the experience he has had seems to form an arch through which he sees the remaining experience he has not yet had. Ulysses wishes always for more and more life and adventure.

The speaker in "Lady Lazarus" is a young woman who has just revived from her third suicide attempt. She reminds herself of Lazarus in the Bible (Luke 16: 19–31), who rose from the dead. She sees the life she has had also as comparable to the experience of a Jewish victim in a Nazi concentration camp during World War II. She sees her attendants (probably at a hospital) as spectators at some peep show or at a miracle looking for some relics or remnants of her as if she has been a saint. Later she sees her spectator as a Nazi officer rummaging about her remains to find some little treasures from her Jewish corpse. Since her attempt has been unsuccessful and she still lives, she says a ghostly hello to the world as well as an implied goodbye to what it offers. The poet herself, Sylvia Plath, succeeded in committing suicide February 11, 1963. "Lady Lazarus" is a denial of the value of life, as "Ulysses" is an affirmation of its value.

Ulysses

It little profits that an idle king,
By this still hearth, among these barren crags,
Match'd with an aged wife, I mete and dole
Unequal laws unto a savage race,
That hoard, and sleep, and feed, and know not me.   5
I cannot rest from travel; I will drink
Life to the lees. All times I have enjoy'd
Greatly, have suffer'd greatly, both with those
That loved me, and alone; on shore, and when
Thro' scudding drifts the rainy Hyades   10
Vext the dim sea. I am become a name;
For always roaming with a hungry heart
Much have I seen and known,—cities of men
And manners, climates, councils, governments,
Myself not least, but honor'd of them all,—   15
And drunk delight of battle with my peers,
Far on the ringing plains of windy Troy.
I am a part of all that I have met;
Yet all experience is an arch wherethro'
Gleams that untravell'd world whose margin fades   20
For ever and for ever when I move.
How dull it is to pause, to make an end,
To rust unburnish'd, not to shine in use!
As tho' to breathe were life! Life piled on life
Were all too little, and of one to me   25
Little remains; but every hour is saved
From that eternal silence, something more,
A bringer of new things; and vile it were
For some three suns to store and hoard myself,
And this gray spirit yearning in desire   30
To follow knowledge like a sinking star
Beyond the utmost bound of human thought.
  This is my son, mine own Telemachus,
To whom I leave the sceptre and the isle,—
Well-loved of me, discerning to fulfil   35
This labor, by slow prudence to make mild
A rugged people, and thro' soft degrees
Subdue them to the useful and the good.
Most blameless is he, centred in the sphere

Of common duties, decent not to fail   40
In offices of tenderness, and pay
Meet adoration to my household gods,
When I am gone. He works his work, I mine.
   There lies the port; the vessel puffs her sail;
There gloom the dark, broad seas. My mariners,   45
Souls that have toil'd, and wrought, and thought with me,—
That ever with a frolic welcome took
The thunder and the sunshine, and opposed
Free hearts, free foreheads,—you and I are old;
Old age hath yet his honor and his toil.   50
Death closes all; but something ere the end,
Some work of noble note, may yet be done,
Not unbecoming men that strove with Gods.
The lights begin to twinkle from the rocks;
The long day wanes; the slow moon climbs; the deep   55
Moans round with many voices. Come, my friends.
'T is not too late to seek a newer world.
Push off, and sitting well in order smite
The sounding furrows; for my purpose holds
To sail beyond the sunset, and the baths   60
Of all the western stars, until I die.
It may be that the gulfs will wash us down;
It may be we shall touch the Happy Isles,
And see the great Achilles, whom we knew.
Tho' much is taken, much abides; and tho'   65
We are not now that strength which in old days
Moved earth and heaven, that which we are, we are,—
One equal temper of heroic hearts,
Made weak by time and fate, but strong in will
To strive, to seek, to find, and not to yield.   70

Lady Lazarus

I have done it again.
One year in every ten
I manage it—

A sort of walking miracle, my skin
Bright as a Nazi lampshade,   5
My right foot

A paperweight,
My face a featureless, fine
Jew linen.

Peel off the napkin   10

O my enemy.
Do I terrify?—

The nose, the eye pits, the full set of teeth?
The sour breath
Will vanish in a day.   15

Soon, soon the flesh
The grave cave ate will be
At home on me

And a smiling woman.
I am only thirty.   20
And like the cat I have nine times to die.

This is Number Three.
What a trash
To annihilate each decade.

What a million filaments.   25
The peanut-crunching crowd
Shoves in to see

Them unwrap me hand and foot—
The big strip tease.
Gentlemen, ladies   30

These are my hands
My knees.
I may be skin and bone,

Nevertheless, I am the same, identical woman.
The first time it happened I was ten.   35
It was an accident.

The second time I meant
To last it out and not come back at all.
I rocked shut

As a seashell.   40
They had to call and call
And pick the worms off me like sticky pearls.

Dying
Is an art, like everything else.
I do it exceptionally well.   45

I do it so it feels like hell.
I do it so it feels real.
I guess you could say I've a call.

It's easy enough to do it in a cell.
It's easy enough to do it and stay put.   50
It's the theatrical

Comeback in broad day
To the same place, the same face, the same brute
Amused shout:

'A miracle!'   55
That knocks me out.
There is a charge

For the eyeing of my scars, there is a charge
For the hearing of my heart—
It really goes.   60

And there is a charge, a very large charge
For a word or a touch
Or a bit of blood

Or a piece of my hair or my clothes.
So, so, Herr Doktor.   65
So, Herr Enemy.

I am your opus,
I am your valuable,
The pure gold baby

That melts to a shriek.   70
I turn and burn.
Do not think I underestimate your great concern.

Ash, ash—
You poke and stir.
Flesh, bone, there is nothing there—   75

A cake of soap,
A wedding ring,
A gold filling.

Herr God, Herr Lucifer
Beware   80
Beware.

Out of the ash
I rise with my red hair
And I eat men like air.

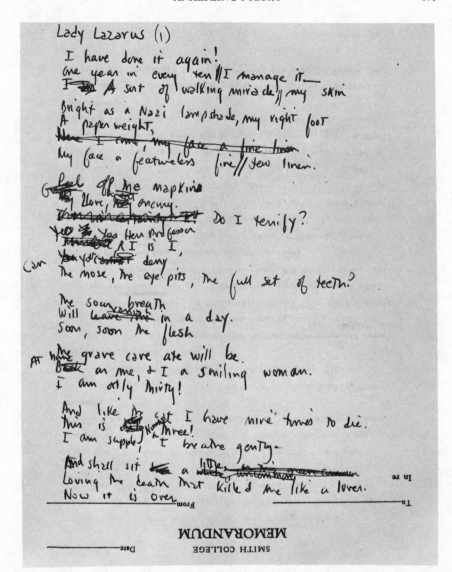

Lady Lazarus (1)

I have done it again!
one year in every ten // I manage it—
I ~~did~~ A sort of walking miracle // my skin
Bright as a Nazi lampshade, my right foot
A paperweight,
~~there I ome, my face a fine thing~~
My face a featureless, fine // Jew linen.

~~Peel off the~~ napkin
~~My~~ Love, ~~my~~ enemy.
~~there is nothing~~ Do I terrify?

~~Yes~~ Yes Herr Professor
~~????~~ AI is I,

~~Do you cannot~~ deny
The nose, the eye pits, the full set of teeth?

The sour breath
Will ~~leave~~ in a day.
Soon, soon the flesh

The ~~home~~ grave cave ate will be.
~~Back~~ on me, & I a smiling woman.
I am only thirty!

And like ~~the cat~~ I have nine times to die.
This is Number Three!
I am supple, & breathe gently—

And shall sit ~~& a little uncommon green colour~~
Loving the death that killed me like a lover.
Now it is over.

Draft versions (1) and (2) of "Lady Lazarus" by Sylvia Plath are from the Plath archives at Smith College. Copyright 1983 by Ted Hughes. Final version appears in *Ariel*, copyright 1965 by Ted Hughes. Reprinted by permission of Olwyn Hughes.

Lady Lazarus (2)

~~As~~ I am involved & still, a wax madonna.
What a mesh
. to annihilate each decade!

~~Why do they choose me!~~
What a million filaments!
~~And Each time he execution~~
~~a is different~~
The peanut-crunching crowd
Shoves in to see

Them un~~wrap~~wrap me hand and foot—
The big strip tease!
Gentlemen, ladies

These are my hands, my knees.
I may be skin & bone,
I may ~~~~ ~~be~~ be Japanese

~~Nevertheless~~
~~I live at the same address~~
Nevertheless, I am the same, identical woman.
Yes, lady, I'm like you,
I have a child or two.

Yessir, yessir
Mough they 'doctor's say it's rare
Each time I rise, I rise a ~~~~ virgin.

Commentary

"Ulysses" is in three parts known as "verse paragraphs," with indentations marking the divisions at lines 33 and 44. We cannot call the units formed by these divisions the introduction, body, and conclusion, for the middle part is the slightest—almost a digression on Ulysses' son Telemachus. The first paragraph is an assessment of his condition at home in Ithaca in relation to his previous experience. The second paragraph characterizes Telemachus, and in it Ulysses leaves the island to his governance. The third paragraph is an invitation to what lies ahead for Ulysses and his comrades. So the three sections suggest past, present, and future rather than introduction, body, and conclusion.

"Lady Lazarus" is in twenty-eight three-line stanzas, or tercets. This poem too seems to fall into three parts, though not so marked. The first includes the first eleven stanzas and sets the scene of reviving the attempted suicide. The second includes the next seven stanzas, tells of past attempts, and generalizes on dying. The third section, the last ten stanzas, returns to the present scene, and includes a dramatic address to the spectators at the scene of revival. Like "Ulysses," then, "Lady Lazarus" has a short middle section, this time on the past, whereas the first section is about the present, and the last hints at the future.

A common distinction between "dramatic" and "lyric" discourse, originated by Plato, is according to whether the speaker is the poet or someone else. In a lyric statement the poet supposedly speaks in his or her own voice, whereas in a dramatic statement the poet impersonates someone else. According to this distinction, "Ulysses" qualifies as dramatic and "Lady Lazarus" as lyric, because Tennyson was certainly not Ulysses, whereas Sylvia Plath could herself be the speaker in her poem, since she did make several attempts at suicide. But this distinction needs to be observed with care, because even when a poet seems to be speaking in person, the "speaker" of the poem may be artistically altered, qualified, or exaggerated from the actual life of the poet; and in an apparently "dramatic" address the poet may well have chosen a speaker because of an affinity between the poet and the supposed "speaker." Plato's distinction of whether the poet speaks in person or not was helpful in originally distinguishing rhetorical modes, but these modes are best differentiated by the actual features of sentences and connections between them.

Like most poems, these are mostly in the mode of reverie, but the sections dealing with the past—part one of "Ulysses" and part two of "Lady Lazarus"—suggest narration. Both poems also contain passages of description, especially in the third section of "Ulysses" and the first section of "Lady Lazarus." Ulysses describes the scene in which he addresses his fellow mariners: "There lies the port; the vessel puffs her sail; / There gloom the dark, broad seas." Also: "The lights begin to twinkle from the rocks; / The long day wanes; the slow moon climbs; the deep / Moans round with many voices." The allure of the sea, as seen in these descriptions, heightens Ulysses' sense of adventure and makes the invitation to his mariners all the more inviting. In "Lady Lazarus" the woman who has attempted suicide describes herself: "my skin / Bright as a Nazi lampshade, / My right foot / A paperweight, / My face a featureless, fine / Jew linen." She also describes "the peanut-crunching crowd" and offers some descriptive details of her revival, some of which may be more fanciful or metaphorical than actual.

The poems come closest to drama in their presumed dramatic addresses, Ulysses to his comrades, the lady to her spectators. Ulysses addresses no one until the third section and then his address remains constant: "My mariners . . . you and I are old," and "Come, my friends . . . Push off . . ." The lady addresses in the first section "Gentlemen, ladies, / These are my hands . . . ," and later changes her address to "So, so, Herr Doktor. / So, Herr Enemy," and "Herr God, Herr Lucifer / Beware / Beware." Her address changes from the immediate spectators to hypothetical Nazi officers and to God and the devil.

The reflective quality of the poems is apparent throughout but comes across most plainly in the passages suggestive of future time—sometimes, though not always, in the future tense. Ulysses says in the first section, "I will drink / Life to the lees," and in the second section hints at what will happen at home after he has gone: "by slow prudence to make mild / A rugged people, and thro' soft degrees / Subdue them to the useful and the good." And the third section of "Ulysses" is both future and hypothetical in its implications: what Ulysses means to do, where he means to go, and what may happen to him and his fellows on their voyage. "Lady Lazarus" does not refer as extensively to the future, but it closes with a forward-looking hint, a warning: "Out of the ash / I rise with my red hair / And I eat men like air."

In most poems, plot is of little importance. These poems, more than most, and especially in their narrative passages, hint at some plot. "Ulysses" suggests the story of a man who has, after many adventures, returned home for a while, but leaves the governance of his island to his son and embarks on a last adventure or series of adventures. "Lady Lazarus" suggests the story of a woman who, after several previous suicide attempts, has just revived after her third one and faces her spectators with an at least temporary return to living. But if we were to read these or most poems primarily for their plots we would probably be disappointed. We do not learn the "end" of these stories—the final voyage or the final suicide attempt—and not much of their beginnings—the events occurring prior to the actual scenes of the poems. We focus instead on a time of heightened perception in the speakers, when Ulysses realizes he can no longer remain at home, when the lady of Plath's poem faces her spectators or accusers after her most recent, perhaps her most significant, attempt—the one in which she has best realized what dying means to her. The plots of these poems, such as they are, serve primarily to point at characterization. Note that the suggested plots and settings of these poems differ considerably, for "Ulysses" suggests the romantic adventures of Odysseus in Frye's plot of romance and in Frye's third or heroic setting, whereas "Lady Lazarus" is more tragic or ironic in its plot and in setting is probably at Frye's fifth or hellish level.

The speakers in both poems seem anxious to tell us about themselves, to differentiate themselves from others. Ulysses is a man whose need for adventure is so great that, even in old age, it is greater than the young man's, his son Telemachus. The contrast between the father and the son who would be content to remain at home in everyday administration has led some readers to assume that Ulysses condemns or despises his son; but he only contrasts his son with himself: "He works his work, I mine." The speaker in "Lady Lazarus" sees herself as someone with a gift, a "call," for dying. She does not, like Ulysses, pick on another single person as a contrast, but her references to others, "The peanut-crunching crowd," and the "Herr Doktor . . . Herr Enemy," show that she too thinks of how she differs from others. If we read these poems to discover unique characters, then, we will be amply rewarded; characterization in both poems is prominent. Ulysses characterizes himself as a "gray spirit yearning in desire / To follow knowledge like a sinking star, / Beyond the utmost bound of human thought." The lady characterizes herself as one who "does" death "exceptionally well," as one who eats men "like air"—as readily as she breathes.

What ideas do these poems put forth? We will not go wrong if we begin by thinking of Tennyson's poem as an invitation to life and Plath's as an invitation to death: one celebrates the excitement of life, the other sees existence as a living hell. The lines in "Ulysses" most expressive of theme are perhaps those on experience: "all experience is an arch wherethro' / Gleams that untravell'd world whose margin fades / For ever and for ever when I move." However much we experience is nothing but an arch, an invitation, to the experience yet unexperienced. The lines in "Lady Lazarus" most expressive of theme are perhaps: "What a trash / To annihilate each decade. / What a million filaments." These difficult lines perhaps suggest that life is such trash it must be periodically annihilated or ended—its million filaments, which might be exciting to Ulysses, are to her confirmation of the need for annihilation. The poems could not be said to prove these themes as an essay might; but both poems might be seen as lively exercises in demonstration of these ideas; and theme in both poems is of almost equal importance with characterization. In the end we might feel that the themes of both poems serve primarily to help characterize the speakers; in poems that stress theme the speakers serve primarily as spokespersons for the ideas that are magnified.

An analysis of the sound-effects of these poems would begin by observing that "Ulysses" is in "blank verse" and "Lady Lazarus" in "free verse"—both close to the normal sound-effects of conversation or prose. Almost every line of "Ulysses" has exactly ten syllables. An occasional line may seem to have eleven syllables: "Yet all experience is an arch wherethro'." But even in this line, if the word "experience" is slurred to three instead of four syllables—"yence"—the syllables come out to ten. The endings of the lines do not rhyme ("blank" means having no rhyme), though we hear an occasional similarity of sound—"when" (9), "men" (13), "governments" (14), or "are" (67), "hearts" (68), or "will" (69), "yield" (70).

In "Lady Lazarus" the lines vary a great deal in length ("free" means not exactly measured), though the poet has arranged her lines in threes, inviting us to see the poem in "stanzas" like older poetry in which each stanza was identical in shape with the first. She offers us rhymes—true rhymes and partial or "slant" rhymes—such as we might expect in older, more clearly stanzaic poetry. Some of the similarly sounding endings are: "again" (1), "ten" (2), "linen" (9), "napkin" (10); "foot" (6), "paperweight" (7); "teeth" (13), "breath" (14); "be" (17), "me" (18), "thirty" (20), "Three" (22), "see" (27); "decade" (24), "crowd" (26); "tease" (29), "ladies" (30), "knees" (32); "ten" (35), "accident" (36), "meant" (37); "seashell" (40), "call" (41); "else" (44), "well" (45), "hell" (46), "real" (47), "call" (48), "cell" (49), "theatrical" (51), "miracle" (55); "brute" (53), "shout" (54), "out" (56); "charge" (57), "charge" (58), "heart" (59), "charge" (61); "goes" (60), "clothes" (64); "burn" (71), "concern" (72), "stir" (74), "there" (75), "Lucifer" (79); "ring" (77), "filling" (78); and "Beware" (80), "Beware" (81), "hair" (83), "air" (84). A few of these may be considered accidental, but added together they certainly indicate the poet's effort to fashion her poem according to certain echoes or rhymes. The sound-effects of "Lady Lazarus," then, even if its verse is "free," call more attention to themselves than do the sound-effects of "Ulysses."

Tennyson has chosen a blank-verse style suggestive to his readers of earlier English poets in blank verse—Shakespeare and Milton, for instance—and of the heroic, epic tradition of Homer and Vergil. He seems to go out of his way occasionally to choose old-fashioned diction or syntax: "It little profits," "Old age hath yet his honor, "something ere the end," "smite/ The sounding furrows." His similes and metaphors are also reminiscent of earlier heroic poetry: "I will drink/ Life to the lees"—as if life were wine; "a hungry heart"—as if hearts could be hungry; "drank delight"—as if delight were something to drink; "all experience is an arch"—as if experience could be seen as architecture; "To rust unburnish'd, not to shine in use"—as if a dull life were a rusty brass pot; "this gray spirit"—as if spirits could have different colors; "To follow knowledge like a sinking star"—as if new experience could be astronomical. As is frequent in imagery, an abstraction such as life, delight, experience, knowledge is given a concrete reference such as wine, an arch, a brass pot, a star.

Unlike Tennyson, Plath has chosen a diction starkly modern. She uses familiar modern expressions: "will be / At home," "Shoves in," "The big strip tease," "skin and bone," "it feels like hell," "stay put," "knocks me out," "There is a charge." She also refers to the familiar idea that a cat has nine lives and offers such prosaic, unmemorable expressions as "I am only thirty," "It was an accident," "like anything else," "I guess you could say," "It really goes," "Do not think I underestimate your great concern." In contrast to these familiar expressions she introduces oddly new constructions: "walking miracle," "What a trash / To annihilate each decade," "The eyeing of my scars," "the hearing of my heart," "I turn and burn." Her most odd constructions come out in the form of similes and metaphors, which, unlike Tennyson's, seem devised to suggest shocking or violent actions. Several suggest that her body, though alive again, is a corpse burned in a Nazi concentration camp, to be probed by her executioners: "my skin / Bright as a Nazi lampshade," "My face a featureless, fine / Jew linen"—references to the use of the flesh of dead Jews to make lampshades. She sees herself later as a child victim, "The pure gold baby / That melts to a shriek. / I turn and burn"—as if the executed is still partly alive, moving and shrieking. She enlarges this imagined scene, as if her executioners ("Herr Doktor . . . Herr Enemy") are probing her remains to find possible valuables:

> Ash, ash—
> You poke and stir.
> Flesh, bone, there is nothing there—
>
> A cake of soap,
> A wedding ring,
> A gold filling.

In the middle part of the poem she imagines the crowd around her as present at the exhumation of a saint's grave: "to see / Them unwrap me hand and foot," "These are my hands / My knees," "For the eyeing of my scars, there is a charge," "For a word or a touch / Or a bit of blood / Or a piece of my hair or my clothes." In these imagined or metaphorical scenes she sees herself as a victim or a martyr.

She also sees the scenes of her revival metaphorically as if she has gone to a cave to die. "Soon, soon the flesh / The grave cave ate will be / At home on me." In her narrative account of her second suicide attempt, she may also refer to a cave, perhaps a seaside cave or scene. "I rocked shut / As a seashell / They had to call and call / And pick the worms off me like sticky pearls." Comparing and contrasting the styles of the two poems, we must conclude that as Plath's style is more daring and calls more attention to itself, it counts for more in the disposition of elements than does Tennyson's style.

The treatment of setting in the two poems differs considerably. Tennyson gives us a strong sense—but without elaborate description—of Ulysses' island and his life there, as well as of the excitement lying "beyond the sunset." These constitute the actual locations of the actions of the poem. Plath does not tell us much directly of where the action of her poem takes place, but she gives us a number of metaphorical, presumably imaginary settings, in a "grave cave," a place where a "peanut-crunching crowd" watches a "big strip tease"—perhaps a circus or carnival setting; another location, the setting of her second attempt, presumably near the sea for she compares herself to a seashell and says they picked worms off her like sticky pearls; another setting of the exhumation of a saint; and another of Nazi officers stealing mementoes from a Jewish victim. As Tennyson's settings are consistent and actual, they seem to weigh more heavily in his poem than do the varied but apparently metaphorical settings of Plath's poem.

Both poems, then, seem to stress characterization over theme and plot, and the poem by Plath seems to give us a secondary stress on style and sound, whereas the poem by Tennyson gives us a secondary stress on setting.

Exercise

Read the three Frost poems below, in which the lines are run together as in prose. Mark the soft and loud syllables and determine the metrical pattern and rhyme scheme, if any; mark the ends of lines with diagonal slashes, and the ends of stanzas with double slashes. This exercise will give you an idea of the contribution made by sound-effects to the poems, and how these sound-effects regulate their designs. Then answer the questions following each poem.

I. *"The Investment"*

Over back where they speak of life as staying ("You couldn't call it living, for it ain't"), there was an old, old house renewed with paint, and in it a piano loudly playing. Out in the ploughed ground in the cold a digger, among unearthed potatoes standing still, was counting winter dinners, one a hill, with half an ear to the piano's vigor. All that piano and new paint back there, was it some money suddenly come into? or some extravagance young love had been to? Or old love on an impulse not to care—not to sink under being man and wife, but get some color and music out of life?

1. How many lines do you count? What familiar lyric form does the number of lines suggest? Is the poem in one of the two basic rhyme-schemes or designs of this lyric form?
2. This poem does not use the first person. Does it have then as strong a reflective flavor as you expect from lyrics? There's someone observing of course (the poet), but his attention seems focused on two third persons (the farmer and his wife). What rhetorical mode is suggested by the use of the third person? But does the poem tell a story—suggestive of plot—or merely hint at it?
3. The poet is the kind of character who would notice what he notices. Is there anything else special about him? Are either of the other characters especially memorable? Are they even very closely observed? What is their age? How strong is character as an element in the poem, then?
4. What is the mood of the poem? Consider the contrast of poverty and extravagance. What does mood contribute to the poem as a whole?
5. Consider especially the first two and the last two lines. Are they applicable only to the two people observed in the poem, or to a broad range of

similar people? What then is the role of theme in the poem? Which is stronger, plot or theme—or are they equally strong?

II. *"Acquainted with the Night"*

I have been one acquainted with the night. I have walked out in rain—and back in rain. I have outwalked the furthest city light. I have looked down the saddest city lane. I have passed by the watchman on his beat and dropped my eyes, unwilling to explain. I have stood still and stopped the sound of feet when far away an interrupted cry came over houses from another street, but not to call me back or say good-by; and further still at an unearthly height, one luminary clock against the sky proclaimed the time was neither wrong nor right. I have been one acquainted with the night.

1. How many lines do you count; and what is the metrical pattern and rhyme-scheme? Is this poem in the same lyric form as the first? It closes, like the first, with two rhymed lines—a couplet—but does the rest of the poem falls into four-line stanzas—quatrains—or three-line stanzas—tercets? The poem is actually written, except for the couplet, in the Italian form *terza rima*. See if you can figure out how it works.

2. The poem has a kind of narrative development, as in the first poem, but does it record the events of one special night, or of many similar nights? What then is the role of plot?

3. Add up the descriptive effects, and decide what they contribute to the mood of the poem. What then does mood or setting as a whole contribute to the poem?

4. Is theme stronger or weaker in this poem than in the first? Consider especially the contribution, and meaning, of the second to last line, and the repeated last line. Does it amount to as strong a theme as in the first poem?

5. Does the poem serve to reveal the individuality of the first-person speaker reflecting on his life and experience? Are the actions he reports and the observations he makes familiar to many, or rather special to himself? What then is the role of character in the poem?

III. *"Desert Places"*

Snow falling and night falling fast, oh, fast in a field I looked into going past, and the ground almost covered smooth in snow, but a few weeds and stubble showing last. The woods around it have it—it is theirs. All animals are smothered in their lairs. I am too absent-spirited to count; the loneliness includes me unawares. And lonely as it is that loneliness will be more lonely ere it will be less—a blanker whiteness of benighted snow with no expression, nothing to express. They cannot scare me with their empty spaces between stars—on stars where no human race is. I have it in me so much nearer home to scare myself with my own desert places.

1. How many lines in this poem; and what is the metrical pattern and

rhyme scheme? Is it a fixed form or one apparently devised for the present poem?

2. Does the poem make more or less use of description than the other two poems? What then is the importance of setting in the poem?
3. Again there seems something special about the poet's observations; but does he seem to concentrate on his inner feelings, or on what they reveal about the world outside himself? What is the importance of character in the poem?
4. Consider especially the last quatrain. Does it offer an observation uniquely appropriate to the poet, or does he seem to be urging others to adopt his general attitude? What then is the role of theme in the poem?
5. Do the distinctiveness in the setting, and in the poet's character, emerge from the poem for their own sakes, or to justify the general observation with which the poem closes? What then seems to be the governing element in the poem?

Suggestions

Analyzing the sound-effects of a poem gives an immediate sign of its formal design. Meter, length of lines, rhymes and other decorative effects, and size and shape of stanzas, are all devices of sound and make up the regularity of a poem's design, when it is regular. Sound is usually less important than sense or meaning (the other elements put together), but in poetry it provides a good entrance to the subject of formal design. Formal development needn't exactly follow design. The sentences may be a better guide to development and they needn't, though they often do, exactly square with the metrical design of lines and stanzas.

Diction and style, which in fiction at least are not usually of foremost significance, may also provide a useful entrance to a poem. Images and metaphors, and structure of sentences, have important bearings on the meaning, and are rewarding and revealing in their own right. Explication, or careful explanation of the text, generally begins with sound and style and makes them give up their full quota of meaning. So the usually minor elements, sound and diction, may provide the easiest approach to analyzing a poem; and they may lead into a full explication of form and meaning. But rhetorical analysis and analysis of the other elements will also show what given poems are like and how they work.

There is such a thing as narrative poetry, which may sometimes be considered fiction, sometimes poetry. There is also purely descriptive poetry. And there is the dramatic monologue, not to mention dialogues which are not quite plays. But these are borderline cases, and most poems or "lyrics" are primarily in the mode of reverie. Even when in a given poem other modes seem more extensive, they can be best put together and understood as issuing from the thoughts of the "I" in the poem, however closely that speaker represents the author. Reverie is the most inclusive of the modes and can accommodate any of the others to itself; it is also the most dominant and when it occurs even briefly will tend to put the others under its control. Some poems begin in the mode of narration, but by the end the narrative appears to be significant mainly for its effect on the poet. Some poems begin dramatically, but by the end the drama appears to be addressed to somebody dead, or otherwise not there, and so the drama must have been in the poet's thoughts.

A close rhetorical analysis is in any case very helpful in analyzing poetry, and often more interesting and useful than in analyzing fiction or drama. A whole poem is usually so short that all its traces of mode come and go quickly, and you are sometimes hard pressed to decide just which modes have occurred. The signs of a mode may not be in a whole series of sentences, as in fiction or drama, but in single sentences of even parts of them. Individual sentences may mix tenses and persons so that there is some doubt of just which mode predominates. So you must be more careful and subtle in assigning modes to poetry than to fiction or drama.

The rhetorical analysis is the best approach to the analysis of elements in a poem. The plot, unless there is a fair amount of narration, may be very slight, apparently nonexistent. Some critics claim a lyric poem has no plot, in fact, but I prefer to observe whatever traces there are of one. Usually there is both a "story," an implied background to the situation, and also a sequence of events or effects in the development. But character and theme are usually stronger in a poem. The speaker's thoughts will always be revealing of his character and sometimes of other characters he is thinking of; and his thoughts will always have stated or implied general meanings. Again, the question is whether the poet seems to speak mainly for herself alone, stressing character, or for others of her kind, stressing theme. The poem may also state generalizations, philosophic speculations, directly, and these are of course thematic. Mood-poems are also common, usually composed of description of a scene and the poet's response to it.

Since poems are often harder to understand than stories or plays, they are more in need of explication, which may be assisted by discussion of sound and diction and their relative emphasis in the work. But even in poems, the other elements are more likely to be emphasized, and separate discussions of a poem's characters or themes or settings will be very helpful and significant. Or, as in the discussion of fiction and drama, two elements may be shown to be in close competion in a poem. Since poetry is the most carefully constructed and compressed discourse, it deserves the most careful analysis.

Last

Many students and some critics would like to assign ranks and ratings to works of art, as if Shakespeare would get an A plus and others would be ranked below him. But just as there might be differences of opinion in one class about one poem, so there often arise differences of opinion between one critic and another, or between one historical period and another, in judging a work of art. So the best advice is to keep an open mind and constantly try to enlarge your perspective of the possibilities of literature and the other arts. I hope that in the course of reading this book, you have read and come to enjoy some of the works that were new to you. And I hope that this process will continue for a long long time.

Some think of literature and the other arts as frills if not frivolities and consider only such solid subjects as science and business suitable for the modern world—as if the arts could somehow be evaded, as if one could exclude them from life. But the arts are everywhere and inescapable. Even citizens who do not often go to concerts or visit art galleries, who do not go to see movies or read books and magazines and newspapers, hear almost a constant buzz of radio or watch a constant flicker of television. Advertisers compete in their exploitation of the arts to capture the attention of the consumer. Popular tunes offer a form of music and poetry. Stories are told around the table at lunch or dinner. So the question is not whether or not to indulge in the arts, but whether or not to accept passively what is offered you or to learn to respond more actively and intelligently to the arts. The study of literature and the other arts, present and past, gives you an expanded vision of the human imagination and liberates you from the limited styles and tricks of immediate and short-term claims on your ears and eyes and intelligence. You're no longer restricted to thinking of architecture and poetry along the lines of what somebody has managed to put up today for your inspection. In this book I've tried to consider literature in itself, apart from everything else it may be connected to, and apart from any evaluation of it. Now I will mention some of these connections and show how they lead to questions of value.

If you push literature in one direction, toward the actual or factual, it becomes history, as in the "fictionalized" biography or the historical novel; if you push it in the other direction, toward the ideal or hypothetical, it becomes philoosophy, as in the philosophic dialogue or the theater of ideas. Apparently literature is most comfortable between the two, with only incidental bearings on either. If you try to write a novel or a play with a start in history or philosophy you may end up with mere journalism or propaganda. For literature, like painting and music, has a constantly exciting connection with real life, but also an existence in itself. Music here provides a clearer example than literature or painting: What sounds outside itself can music be thought to "imitate"? The "special effects" of musicians imitating the wind and waterfalls and birdcalls have been limited and occasional at most. So writers and painters, though they may have some "experience" they are thinking of, are really trying to develop the internal necessities of literature or painting in themselves. Music and painting are the assortments of sounds and sights, not that people have necessarily heard or seen, but that they could imagine; so literature is a collection of the events and emotions imagined by people, whether they have ever experienced them or not.

Human behavior and the reasons for it form the content of both psychology and literature; an alliance between these two is then at least as important as any of those mentioned so far. But psychology is interested in types, and in individuals only as they reveal types. Literature is interested directly and abidingly in individuals, though some works of literature may be and have been treated by psychologists as generalized "case-histories." Criticism, or the study of literature, is, according to Northrop Frye, a social science, devoted, like the other social sciences, to the products of human actions; literature from this point of view is what people write down about what they have been able to imagine about their own private affairs. Frye, in a parallel between criticism and mathematics, points out that criticism has the same central, hypothetical relationship to the other social sciences that mathematics has to the natural sciences (*Anatomy of Criticism,* pp. 350–54).

If all the possible works of literature could ever be written and you could ever read them, you would know all imaginable human events and emotions. Short of this, you can read widely in literature and get a fair idea of what the possibilities are. The more you read, the more you have an idea not only of what human behavior is like, but of what it might or should be like; and this brings you into the area of ethics, which may seem the strongest tie with literature mentioned so far, and the one most clearly leading to value. A historical or psychological bias, such as Marxism or Freudianism, will lead to judgments which will seem distorted to anyone, often even to the person making them. But there is no doubt that literature presents particular human behavior, and mediates and discriminates between the better and the worse of it. Criticism is liberal because it liberates you from the restrictions of your own imagination: writers invite you to observe different events, and to feel differently about them, than you have done before. All the while they are goading you to lead a different—maybe a better—life.

But the relationship between writer and reader is reciprocal, for while the book changes your values, you, as a reader and potential critic, can change its value. Usually your judgment of a book is a reflection of your literary education, of what you have read and what you've been urged to read, as much as it is of what experiences you've had; so it's advisable that you read widely before you assert that a book is good or bad. Judgments about literary works are fascinating because they can never be final and are always subject to new slants; but that's not to say they are entirely subjective and unreliable.

Often students take courses in literature, or in criticism, so that they will be able to tell for sure which literary works are good and which bad. That's like asking that botany tell you which flowers to like; the botanist may be willing to tell which she prefers, but she would probably think you should first of all learn a little about the actual differences between flowers. The teacher of literature, like any other, must tell what his subject is like, before he tells how he likes it. Many questions of liking and disliking will be set aside or altogether dropped in the process of finding out more and more about literature itself. Furthermore, there is never any absolutely true and verifiable judgment of works of art. Even the superiority of Beethoven to the Beatles is not quite beyond the possibility of reconsideration; and it may be very productive to find out what the classic and the pop have in common.

The following is one of Frost's best-known poems; it's the last one in this book.

The Road Not Taken

Two roads diverged in a yellow wood,
And sorry I could not travel both
And be one traveler, long I stood
And looked down one as far as I could
To where it went in the undergrowth;   5

Then took the other, as just as fair,
And having perhaps the better claim,
Because it was grassy and wanted wear;
Though as for that the passing there
Had worn them really about the same,   10

And both that morning equally lay
In leaves no step had trodden black.
Oh, I kept the first for another day!
Yet knowing how way leads on to way,
I doubted if I should ever come back.   15

I shall be telling this with a sigh
Somewhere ages and ages hence:

Two roads diverged in a wood, and I—
I took the one less traveled by,
And that has made all the difference.   20

Why is this a good poem? It has all the technical competence, the smooth and easy manipulation of words, you expect from any poem worth printing. Beyond that it has certain qualities special to Frost, which you probably value if you value Frost at all. Like Wordsworth before him, he chose a language many poets would have thought too flat for poetry, and made of it the discourse of high art. This poem, this simple narrative-reflective account of a walk down a road, is a comment on the choices we all must make in life. It has also been read, I believe, as a comment on Frost's choice of poetry as a craft, and on the kind of poetry he chose to write. The road he takes is a little grassier than the other—but not markedly so. Lines 9–12, and the poem as a whole, have a thematic emphasis: You can neither take comfort in following a crowd nor congratulate yourself on your revolutionary martyrdom; when the time comes for a choice you find yourself alone, the first one up that morning, and must be guided by distant predecessors, or none. Other people, and other poets, including Wordsworth, see on the one hand a highway, which they heroically disdain, and on the other the path through the wilderness which they must clear away themselves and recommend for travel. Frost, in his poem and in his poetry, beckons to no followers. The scene, like almost any scene you turn to in Frost, immediately reminds you of his strength and truth. There is a wistful suggestion, but it turns out to be more self-satire than sentimentality: "Oh, I kept the first for another day!" The choices are getting less clear-cut, he says, and you are likely to want to take both, if either; still you can't freeze and wish for what might have been—some glamorous or certified route. You choose unguided, and your choice makes all the difference. This poem provides a good example of the "concrete universal," a concrete story with a universal implication: it ranges from sheer experience to sheer ethics. It confronts a major, maybe the major, problem of modern life and gives an unsentimental and vigorous answer to it. This poem seems to me, and I think to other modern readers, so good it's bound to last as long as anything in modern literature. But if you have a different slant on it, bring it up and we may have to reconsider.

If you can't arrive at a judgment absolutely right, are all judgments hopelessly relative, personal, and impermanent? That also seems unlikely, equally unlikely, and you may have to end up with a theory of evaluation like the "Perspectivism" of René Wellek and Austin Warren, which tries to achieve a balance between works and readers of them, between past and present and future judgments.

We must beware of both false relativism and false absolutism. Values grow out of the historical process of valuation, which they in turn help us to understand. The answer to historical relativism is not a doctrinaire absolutism which appeals to "unchanging human nature" or the "universality of art." We must adopt a view for which the term "Perspectivism" seems suitable. We must be able to refer a work of art to the values of its own time and of all the periods subsequent to its own. A work of art is both "eternal" (i.e. preserves a certain identity) and "historical" (i.e. passes through a process of traceable development). Relativism reduces the history of literature to a series of discrete and hence discontinuous fragments, while most absolutisms serve either only a passing present-day situation or are based (like the standards of the New Humanists, the Marxists, and the Neo-Thomists) on some abstract non-literary ideal unjust to the historical variety of literature. "Perspectivism" means that we recognize that there is one poetry, one literature, comparable in all ages, developing, changing, full of possibilities.

(*Theory of Literature*, 3rd ed., p. 43)

When students disagree in their judgment of a poem or play, it's possible that a more accurate explication or analysis of the work will bring them into closer agreement. But disagreements may also occur between two highly trained readers. Here, too, it's possible that further explication and analysis as backing for their judgments will bring them into closer agreement, will produce at least partial agreement. But some disagreements will always remain and neither judgment can be pronounced absolute. If critical opinion at present sides with one or another of the critics, it may reverse itself after their lifetimes. Trying to talk each other into their points of view may in fact fascinate them; eventually they will uncover each other's standards or rules or criteria of judgment, and if those too appear mutually unacceptable they may at least better understand why they disagree. In fact, it's a good rule for writers of criticism to try to express their standards, and for readers of criticism to try to discover them even if they are only suggested.

Critics of literature, including professionals as well as beginners, had better know when they are analyzing and when judging a work of art, and they had better be sure their analysis of it comes first and is as thorough as possible—to insure they know as much about it as possible beforehand. But nobody can stop them from judging and valuing it, for that was why they opened the book in the first place. Teachers can make assignments for only a semester or two; after that you never have to take a book off the shelf or go to a play except in the hope that it may gratify the dreams you didn't even know you had had.

Glossary

This glossary is obviously selective. It defines the basic terms of this book, often more briefly than in the text, and sometimes mediates between the use of terms here and elsewhere.

ABSTRACT removed or elevated from the concrete or particular; general or universal.

ALLEGORY 1. an extended or narrative comparison; an epic simile; 2. a literary work of fiction in which every event has both a concrete and an abstract significance.

ALLITERATION a likeness of sound in beginnings; an identity between two words, including only the consonant sound before the first vowel.

ANALOGY a comparison between two pairs of terms.

ANAPESTIC a kind of meter; in English composed of two soft syllables followed by a loud one.

ANATOMY a longer narrative genre, more satiric and thematic than a novel.

ANTITHESIS a negative comparison; a denial and an assertion.

ASSONANCE a likeness of loud vowel sounds.

ATTITUDE the psychological stance of one character toward another, especially in drama.

BLANK VERSE the minimal and commonest verse of English; iambic pentameter, called blank because unrhymed.

CACOPHONY unpleasant sound; like euphony, a trait found in writers interested in sound itself.

CHARACTER the element of *ethos* (also translated "nature"); the psychological inclinations of all the characters, best found in choices or conflicts; any of the four types boasting, ironic, rash, cowardly.

CHORUS a dance, or song and dance, used as an interlude or modulation between the scenes of a classical play; a commentator or narrator in a modern play.

CLOSET DRAMA drama never to be performed in the theater, but to be read in the study, or closet.

COMEDY, COMIC 1. a dramatic genre, in which an ordinary young man rises to marriage and prosperity; 2. in plot, one of the four basic plots of literature, the happy, opposed to the tragic.

CONCEIT a comparison between two things surprisingly distant.

CONCORDANCE a complete list of words in a book or an author's work.

CONCRETE the actual or special or particular; exemplification of the abstract.

CONFESSION a longer narrative genre in prose, more personal, autobiographical, and thematic than the novel.

CONFRONTATION a passage of drama, often a scene, in which two or three characters develop significant attitudes toward each other.

CONSONANCE a likeness of consonant sounds other than between just beginning ones, or alliteration.

COUPLET a pair of lines of verse, equal in length, and rhymed.

CRITICISM the study of literature or of all the arts.

CURSUS a run or cadence; a meter of prose found at the ends of sentences, or other terminations, composed of two dactyls or a dactyl and one or two trochees.

DACTYLIC a kind of meter; in English composed of a loud followed by two soft syllables.

DEFINITION the abstract form of description; a rhetorical mode mainly in inanimate third person plural and present tense, with additive connections.

DESCRIPTION a rhetorical mode mainly in inanimate third person singular and indefinite present tense, with additive connections.

DIALOGUE 1. the shorter form of the anatomy; 2. the abstract form of drama; a rhetorical mode in mixed persons, especially second, and mainly present tense, with contrary or contradictory connections.

DICTION the element of *lexis* (also translated "style"); the expression of the meaning in words.

DISCOURSE anything spoken or written, having meaning.

DITHYRAMB a classical lyric genre, wild, irregular, and enthusiastic.

DRAMA, DRAMATIC 1. a rhetorical mode in mixed persons, especially second, and mainly present tense, with contrary or contradictory connections; 2. any literature predominantly in the mode of drama; 3. exciting or effective.

DRAMATIC MONOLOGUE a poem in mixed drama and reverie, spoken by one character to another, who does not answer.

ELEMENT a basic constituent of a work; in literature, any of the six elements plot, character, theme, sound, diction, and setting.

EPIC a longer narrative genre in verse, of a great national hero; including an invocation to a muse, a beginning in the midst of action, an elevated style, and gods.

EPIPHANY a significant manifestation, of or to a character, comparable to Aristotle's *recognition;* in modern short stories often climactic, in the mode of reverie.

EPISTOLARY NOVEL a novel told in letters, written by the characters to each other, including more second-person (or dramatic) statements than is usual.

ESSAY 1. the shorter form of the confession; 2. a literary work, mainly in the mode of persuasion, in which theme overwhelms any possible plots or characters.

EUPHONY pleasant sound; used for "musical" writers, or writers interested in sound itself.

EXPLICATION a detailed interpretation of a literary work.

EXPOSITION the opening of a play, usually narrative, which serves to explain the background of the dramatic situation.

FARCE a simplified, sensational form of comedy.

FICTION 1. anything "made up" or artistically perfected from reality or imagination; 2. any literature in prose predominantly in the mode of narration.

FLASHBACK 1. a transition from earlier time; 2. a passage of narration or drama whose beginning time is earlier than the time of the previous passage.

FOOT a unit of verse larger than a syllable and smaller than a line, including one loud syllable and one or more soft ones.

FORM the pattern or structure of a work in space (design) or time (development); opposed to content.

FREE VERSE discourse largely unmetrical, but printed in broken lines; often considered more rhythmic than prose.

GENRE a class of literary works, similar in form or content or both, and specified in one or more of its elements, or in its effect on readers.

GIMMICK a trick or device needed to solve a problem of plot.

GOTHIC a quality in fiction, composed of ghosts and supernaturalism, medievalism, and horror.

HALF-RHYME also called slant-rhyme; various approximations of rhyme, made up of some consonance or assonance.

IAMBIC a kind of meter; in English composed of a soft followed by a loud syllable.

IMAGE 1. a brief picture in words, the smallest unit of literature; 2. a comparison, or just the pictorial half of one.

IMAGERY the system of images in a literary work.

IRONY, IRONIC 1. one of the four basic plots of literature, the realistic, opposite of romantic; 2. one of the four basic characters of literature, the unassuming or self-deprecating or mock-modest, opposite of the boaster or braggart; 3. in diction, a contrast, usually opposite, between what is said and what is meant.

LINE 1. in verse, one line of print; 2. in drama, one speech, or what one actor says before another speaks.

LITERATURE 1. the body of discourses preserved and repeated in their original form; 2. of the former, discourses predominantly in the concrete modes, and excluding science, philosophy, and other nonfiction; 3. discourse on what people have been able to imagine about their own private affairs; 4. discourses fictional, beautiful, or valuable.

LYRIC 1. (adj.) musical or poetical; 2. (n.) any poem; any brief, personal, emotional expression; any poem predominantly in the mode of reverie.

MELODRAMA a simplified, sensational form of tragedy.

METAPHOR a literary equation; a transference, a replacing of one word or phrase with another from a different area, including metonomy and synecdoche, a swapping of names or of part and whole.

METER any ideal measurement of sound which language may approximate; counted by number of feet per line as di-(2), tri-(3), tetra-(4), penta-(5), or hexa-(6) meter.

MODE a typical procedure or sequence for discourse or music; in literature, the concrete modes description, narration, drama, and reverie, and sometimes the abstract modes definition, process, dialogue, and persuasion.

MYTH 1. a story or plot; 2. a story about a god.

NARRATION a rhetorical mode mainly in third person and past tense, with temporal connections.

NARRATIVE GENRES joke and anecdote: very short works told for the relish of the story itself; fable and parable: short works told so as to point up a moral or theme; myth, legend, and chronicle: stories of any length about a god, a saint, or a king, respectively.

NOVEL a longer narrative genre in prose, more realistic and everyday than the romance.

NOVELETTE a narrative form of middle length, otherwise sharing qualities with the novel and short story.

OCTAVE an eight-line unit of verse, the beginning of a sonnet.

ONOMATOPOEIA a likeness of sound between a word and the thing it designates.

PARADOX a contrast between expectation and actuality, in which the actual is the unexpected: an apparent, but resolved contradiction.

PARODY a humorous imitation of a literary style.

PERSUASION the abstract form of reverie; a rhetorical mode mainly in first person plural and mixed tenses, with syllogistic connections.

PLAY the broadest dramatic genre, including any work designed for the theater, rarely lasting more than three hours.

PLOT the element of *mythos* (also translated "fable" or "myth"); the arrangement of incidents, the underlying progression of action; any of the four types comic, tragic, romantic, ironic.

POEM 1. the broadest genre of reverie usually in verse, including any work of any length designed for oral or written discourse; in modern times usually a shorter work.

POETRY 1. any literature in verse; 2. any literature, whether in prose or verse, highly compressed, noble, or elevated.

POINT OF VIEW the way the reader is led to see the action; including objective and subjective, and first or third person.

PROCESS the abstract form of narration; a rhetorical mode mainly in third person plural and present tense, with temporal connections.

PROSE discourse largely unmetrical; in printing, continuous discourse which may be broken anywhere, and hence usually printed with an even right margin.

PUN a special form of antithesis between two words similar or identical in sound, one used and the other suggested.

PURPLE PATCH a passage, usually descriptive or reflective, artfully or over-artfully obtrusive.

QUATRAIN a four-line stanza.

RECOGNITION a change of plot in which one character learns something new and significant about another.

REVERIE a rhetorical mode mainly in first person singular and mixed tenses, including future, with mock-syllogistic connections.

REVERSAL a change in plot, different or opposite from what was expected.

RHETORIC the art of persuasion or decoration in language.

RHYME a likeness of sound in endings; an identity between two words or phrases, including the last loud vowel and whatever follows it.

RHYTHM the actual sound of language with its various qualities of sound; in verse, and sometimes in prose, approximates certain meters.

ROMANCE, ROMANTIC 1. a longer narrative genre, more imaginary and mysterious than the novel; 2. in plot, one of the four basic plots of literature, the ideal, opposite of ironic.

SAGA a narrative work of middle length, in prose, but otherwise sharing many qualities with the epic.

SCANSION an analysis of the rhythm of a passage or work to determine its possible meter or rhyme-scheme.

SCHEME 1. any pattern or structure; 2. a class of figures of speech; an arrangement or rearrangement of words, including repetition and omission.

SESTET a six-line unit of verse, the ending of a sonnet.

SETTING the element of *opsis* (also translated "costuming" or "spectacle"); the sum of all visual or sensuous suggestions in a literary work, from the most objective (place or location) to the most subjective (mood or atmosphere).

SHORT STORY a shorter narrative form in prose, a compressed novel, usually emphasizing character more than plot.

SIMILE a metaphor explained, usually with "like" or "as."

SOLILOQUY a passage of reverie in a play, in which the actor speaks his thoughts aloud as if talking to himself.

SONNET a lyric genre in 14 lines, composed of an octave and a sestet, or three quatrains and a couplet, and often on the subject of love; including the Italian, rhyming *abba abba,* with various schemes in the sestet; and the English, usually rhyming *abab cdcd efef gg.*

SOUND the element of *melos* (also translated "song" or "melody"); in literature, everything the ear hears, apart from what the mind understands; what someone gets from a recitation in a language he doesn't know.

STANZA a recurring unit of verse, patterned by number and length of lines, and sometimes by rhyme.

STICHOMYTHIA a dramatic sequence between two characters in which each line of drama takes only one line of verse.

STOCK CHARACTER a type of character often recurring in works of the same or similar genres.

STORY 1. the broadest narrative genre, including any work of any length designed for oral or written telling; 2. the implied narrative background of the actual plot.

STREAM OF CONSCIOUSNESS the psychological process recorded by the rhetorical mode of reverie.

STROPHE-ANTISTROPHE the turn and counter-turn of the chorus or dancers in the classical theater.

STYLE a way of writing, in an author, a school, or a period; a composite of traits in sound, diction, and often setting and the primary elements as well; vertically, any of the three overall styles, high, middle, and low; and horizontally, any of the three styles, expansive (Ciceronian or baroque), "even" (rococo), and sparse (Senecan or mannerist).

SUBTEXT the underlying psychological development of a play or passage of drama, composed of turns and counter-turns, as characters change their attitudes toward each other.

SYLLOGISM the basic structure of argument or persuasion, composed of a major premise, a minor premise, and a conclusion; parodied in the mode of reverie with statements in past, present, and future tenses.

SYMBOL an image or object with a consistent if complicated signficance throughout a work.

SYNTAX in grammar, the arrangement of words.

TALE a shorter narrative form, a compressed romance, emphasizing plot and setting more than character.

THEME the element of *dianoia* (also translated "thought"); the sum of all abstract or general implications in a literary work; the argument or thesis of a work.

THESIS a position or case to be argued; the theme of a work whose plot and character are negligible.

TONE the tone of the speaker's voice, whether solemn or sneering, friendly or unfriendly, etc.—as if the literary work is spoken dramatically to an audience; tone may be related to the elements of character, theme, or diction.

TRAGEDY, TRAGIC 1. a dramatic genre, in which there is a change from happiness to unhappiness in the fall of a significant man; 2. in plot, one of the four basic plots of literature, the unhappy, opposed to the comic.

TRAGICOMEDY a dramatic genre, in which a tragedy is threatened but averted by a comic rise.

TRIPLET three lines of verse, rhymed and often equal in length.

TROCHAIC a kind of meter; in English composed of a loud followed by a soft syllable.

TROPE a figure of speech; a turn or twist of expression; a positive or negative comparison.

TURN a unit of drama larger than a line, smaller than a confrontation or scene, which develops sightly new attitudes between the characters.

VERSE discourse usually metrical; in printing, broken discourse always pirnted with the same uneven right margin.